Six
Literary
Lives

D0208324

Six Literary Lives

The Shared Impiety
of Adams, London,
Sinclair, Williams,
Dos Passos, and Tate

Reed Whittemore

University of Missouri Press
COLUMBIA AND LONDON

PS
129
W45
1993

Copyright © 1993 by
The Curators of the University of Missouri
University of Missouri Press, Columbia, Missouri 65201
Printed and bound in the United States of America
All rights reserved

5 4 3 2 1   97 96 95 94 93

Library of Congress Cataloging-in-Publication Data

Whittemore, Reed, 1919–
    Six literary lives : the shared impiety of Adams, London,
Sinclair, Williams, Dos Passos, and Tate / Reed Whittemore.
        p.   cm.
    Includes index.
    ISBN 0-8262-0874-6 (alk. paper)
    1. Authors, American—20th century—Biography. 2. American
literature—History and criticism. 3. Authors, American—19th
century—Biography. I. Title.
PS129.W45   1992
810.9′0052—dc20
    [B]   92–27912
                                                              CIP

∞™ This paper meets the requirements of the
American National Standard for Permanence of Paper
for Printed Library Materials, Z39.48, 1984.

Designer: Elizabeth Fett
Typesetter: Connell-Zeko Type & Graphics
Printer and Binder: Thomson-Shore, Inc.
Typeface: Sabon

    Poems of William Carlos Williams are reprinted with permission. *William Carlos Williams: Collected Poems 1909–1939.* Vol. 1. Copyright 1938. New Directions Publishing Corporation. Reprinted with permission of New Directions.
    I am grateful to the Graduate School of the University of Maryland for travel funds, a while back, which allowed me to study Upton Sinclair in the friendly depths of the Lilly Library in Bloomington. I am also grateful to the University of the South for excellent secretarial help with the whole manuscript and, of course, to Sara Fefer, my thoughtful editor at the University of Missouri Press.

FLORIDA STATE
UNIVERSITY LIBRARIES

SEP 9 1993

TALLAHASSEE, FLORIDA

To Helen

Contents

Six
Literary
Lives

Introduction

Here are six American writers of our century, though not one of them was born in our century. They are all roughly of the period in which "modernism" became an overused word (and then lapsed), but they do not share a party line (political, social, or literary). What they do share is a nineteenth-century mode of thought underlying modernism, a revisionist mode now quaint but not yet quaint enough to be summed up—except perhaps in *Cliff's Notes*—in a sentence or two.

It is a mode of thought that I was brought up to share, though I was born in 1919. I mention me because this is not just a book of biographies but also a book about biography. A subject lurking everywhere in it is that of the relationship between biographers and their subjects, something I have already written about in two books of historical essays, *Pure Lives* and *Whole Lives*.

I chose these six authors haphazardly over a period of a decade, after writing a full-length biography of one of them, William Carlos Williams. My relationship with each was a part of each study, though I personally knew well only one, Allen Tate. Also a part of each study was the problem of fitting each author to my amorphous group. I know a good bit more about biography than I did before I began, and one of the things I know is that the biographer's thinking has much to do with the thinking he assigns his biographees.

Each biographer should have a sign to that effect over his typewriter.

The sign applies to all biographers, but most obviously to those who attempt groups. To move beyond the number one is to invite, even insist on, comparison, and acts of comparison are a part of biography in which biographees do not participate.

One of the nineteenth-century authorities on biography, Edmund Gosse, must have had this show-stopper in mind when he became prescriptive—writing up "Biography" for the eleventh edition of the *Encyclopedia Britannica*—and said that biographers should simply never be identified with groups, nor with the "broad views" that trafficking in groups encourages. The art of the biographical set was thus demoted in 1910, and it is still looked down on by scholars as well as publishers, though practiced conscientiously in a number of good encyclopedias.

Yet the "climate of opinion" in which a biographer has his being—that climate being the thinking of his contemporaries—cannot reasonably be neglected even in psychobiography, and in a book like this one the climate is basic. It was basic in the old days of biography too, but the old biographers had a simpler view of climate than the social sciences now allow us. They also had a simpler view of what makes a manageable set. At the turn of the century the short biographies by Elbert Hubbard—and a bit earlier those by James Parton—were "little journeys" among Americans (mostly) who had fulfilled nineteenth-century dreams of worldly success. That tradition, now immeasurably cheapened by *People* magazine's lifebites, was also the main tradition in Europe until modern times, a tradition in which the selection of sets was mechanical: *Lives of the Poets, Lives of the Artists, Chronicles of the Rulers of England, Scotland and Ireland, Lives of the Saints,* and so on. For convenience let me say that Plutarch, with his *Lives of the Noble Grecians and Romans,* started the ball rolling, and when he did so he was as little troubled by climatic problems as Hubbard or Parton. He simply picked out about fifty prominent leaders of the two cultures that his birth and upbringing had given him (he was born in Greece, but he was a Greco-Roman citizen), and went at them. But Plutarch, blessed with two cultures, then added something that most of his successors have not. He paired his subjects: Greek against Roman, one against one.

In doing so he had to specify and describe the qualities of the beings he was comparing, qualities of character drawn from his own A.D. 90 Greek upper-class, Athenian-educated, full-of-Aristotle, landowning Greek head. In doing so he therefore brought the thoughts of a class society in which it was normal (and ethical) to assume that upper-class males were born to governance, and were, for that public, social reason, potential subjects for biography *at* birth. For Hubbard and Parton later it was normal to assume that individuals—sometimes even females (Parton produced a collection of "daughters of genius")—*rose* to biography. But whether in aristocracies or "commonwealths," success or failure in governance became the base for judgement in biography, until strange characters such as saints, artists and poets moved in.

And the governance base—still prevalent in the genre—is also often still described as a moral base, though Machiavelli introduced static on that point. It is a base by which the subject's performance for his society is the material out of which the biographer creates a picture of his character, to the exclusion or neglect of the individual's private doings. Machiavelli came along to treat the exclusion ironically and to point out that upright public performance—that of being "merciful, faithful, humane, sincere [and] religious"—could be plain dangerous, it sometimes being necessary "to act against faith, against charity, against humanity and against religion . . . to maintain the state." But in many ways Plutarch was a Machiavellian before his time—both of them had sophisticated views of public morality, and both were clearly convinced that "maintain[ing] the state" took precedence over maintaining the self. These pieties underlay the works of Parton and Hubbard as well, and remain with us today lumpily, about once a month. But on the other days now there are steady biographical diversions into private lives, lives lived, as it were, outside of history.

Plutarch began his life of Alexander the Great by asserting that he was writing biography, *not* history. What he seems to have meant, however, had nothing to do with his writing an account of Alexander in history, making history. It meant that he was essentially a great man historian and not in competition with historians like Thucydides, who traced the affairs of armies and peoples. Certainly any reader of his life of Alexander gets the impression that Alexander's army was merely an appendage to the man himself as he personally conquered the world on his horse, Bucephalus. And some modern historians— who are not my subject here—have been sufficiently offended by Plutarch's focus to change it, eliminating as much of the judgment-of-character side to his "lives" as they can without rewriting his work completely. This is a mistake I think—a character and his history go together—but I mention the historians' trick with Plutarch merely to apologize for my own omissions here. Literary biography is different from governance biography in that a reader can, and probably should, go to reading Adams and the others straightaway—their works *are* their history—but the obligation to study the character behind the "history" remains, and it can't be well met by just studying the characters' expressed ideas. So my apologies. I have tried to stir life in gently while proceeding. Luckily my subjects' ideas and writings do touch on, reach out for, their lives of governance, or at least engagement. These are not inward-looking writers (at least in their writings!), and I like them for that.

I do wish, however, that I had thrown in a genuine official of some sort—a weakness of mine. One of my early projects in learning about biography (in the fifties) was to study comparatively the writings of recent American presidents. For some reason I started with Hoover, who began his autobiography with a description of a childhood winter day of sliding, tummy down, on a sled. Good, I said to myself, a simple straightforward chap. Then I hopped over to Roosevelt (FDR), and oh, I hadn't been with him for half an hour in the library before I realized (after all, I had been brought up with my father's hatred of the man) that FDR had speechwriters, fancy ones, and I was on a wild-goose chase. I therefore pass on the news here that Hoover was our last serious presidential writer (possible exception: Truman!). Writing is for writers in our time. Leaders no longer have time for writing except, for the moment, the one in Czechoslovakia.

But what is it that literary writers who are not leaders can do to maintain the state? I look around me and see a literary culture firmly fixed in its privacy, looking over a high fence at journalists and their kind who still attempt social maintenance. And I remember growing to consciousness in the thirties when the fence was not up. Climate change? Of course. And the Moscow Trials, Hitler, and World War II did much to effect it. But of what did the change consist? Perhaps this study is a stab at finding out. None of my six was an Alexander or even a Hoover—though Adams suffered all his life from not being an Adams in the White House, and Upton Sinclair came close to the governorship of California. If the six of them could have lived in the same neighborhood at the same time, they would have discovered, perhaps out on the golf course, that three in their group were politically conservative and three vaguely radical. They also would have discovered—but not until they were old and out together talking rather than playing on the golf course—that they all had put themselves out on a *limb* with their society at some time or another; further, they had written (and written, and written) about being out on the limb. Except for these connections they would not, I think, have been a friendly sixsome.

True, there were a few minor personal connections: Adams was Tate's favorite ideological enemy; London and Sinclair actually worked together in a socialist organization; Williams and Dos Passos both wrote short biographical sketches of American leaders. Would these have served for eighteen holes? No, it is I, the biographer, who have put them together, and casually, somehow sharing their climate of thought as writers standing apart from their culture, yet serving it too, unlike their literary successors today. Especially, I have shared their contradictory feelings about the culture and what writers should do in it.

The source of such feelings in my own case goes oddly back to Yale, an unlikely place for such conditioning now, but less so in the late thirties. That sad decade had us reading of hungry proletarians and fat capitalists (they should be doing the same at Yale now, but are they?); it had us thinking of literature as full of Freudians and imagists, but also of those who are now called ideologues, writers declaring that the study of mankind included the study of man's mind as well as his id; it didn't *tell* us that ideology was dead. The age was hardly pre-professional, but compared to our own it was professionally naive. Its intellectual resources were primarily those of the nineteenth century, when the sciences were still having trouble telling each other apart, and the humanities, when they were not stored under the Acropolis, had a way of seeming like sciences too. (See the appendix here, "Three Nineteenth-Century Naturalists.") In such a climate we were apt to read literature for what it said, and some of our important literary reference points were not owned by the English department. In such a climate *dialectic* was not a dirty word, Freshman English was called "rhetoric," opposites lived in comfortable combat, "consensus" had not, as I recall, been invented, and we saw no harm in talking "issues" and *The Waste Land* in the same seminar. In a sense this book began in that climate. The point is important because we have no such climate now.

A way of pointing up the change is to mention Shaw and Ibsen, two giants of the earlier climate now quite out of fashion. They were important back then, because they were (a) always chattering about social matters, and (b) always having a fine time shocking audiences, not with nudity and sex but by taking irreverent *mental* positions. Irreverent? For some time I've been looking for the right adjective for my set, but *irreverent* doesn't seem quite it. (Too cute). Dissident? (Insufficient). Revolutionary? (Too heavy). Revisionary? (Too light). Impious?—*Impious* does seem close, not only because the social complaints of writers like Ibsen and Shaw were affronts to conventional religious and cultural pieties, but also because the word has a classical base. The rich complexities of Socrates's trial and conviction are still with us, and they all converged upon what, in the translations I know, was called impietism. To his accusers he had been conspiring with enemies of the state (that was impietism) and leading youth to be scornful of the state's gods (that was impietism too). Among many modern interpreters impietism has been thought merely dissent from the cultus. Merely? *Merely* will not do. The crucial Socratic impiety was procedural, and that was not a "merely" matter but an impious way of thinking, teaching, and knowing. And in the climate before World War II it was still crucial.

Since 399 B.C. we have had many phrases for the procedure, but the most useful here is *skeptical inquiry,* now an endangered species.[1] It is with us in the words of commencement speakers and declared there to be the sine qua non of true learning, and it is with us in comic strips and government probes. But in tough professional places it has been demoted. The complexities of learning are such that skepticism now is conventionally channeled and restricted. We have specialized inquiry; only experts within given fields are thought to know enough

---

1. At its best skeptical inquiry is logically rigorous, but the mythical man from Missouri and the Connecticut Yankee who takes no wooden nickels are not known for their rigor. For them skeptical inquiry is a way of life, a stance rather than a discipline.

For Socrates it was both, the stance being his know-nothing approach to pedagogy, the rigor being his arguments against the knowers. For my six subjects it was heavily stance, lightly argument, though their capacities for rigorous argument varied greatly. They were not philosophers by profession or inclination (no, sometimes Jack London had great expectations here); still, the phrase *skeptical inquiry* seems spacious enough to apply to their mental climate.

I'm provoked to this footnote by reading an excellent recent study of Shelley's political prose by Terence Alan Hoagwood, *Skepticism and Ideology* (Iowa City: University of Iowa Press, 1983), which pointed steadily to the rigor of the tradition of skeptical inquiry. Professor Hoagwood's account also suggested to me the curious illogic of our drift to narrow professional inquiry.

to be knowledgeably skeptical. Also we must live every day at the edge of the great gap between the humanities of academe—where, after all, Socrates resided—and our bottom liners. A precarious life. If any new Socrates should appear he might well jump over to the social sciences. A terrible thought? Yes, but detachment such as that which the humanities are now practicing was no part of his skepticism. He was piously impious, that is, active in his impiety. He was also anti-rhetorically rhetorical in public. To top off his contradictions he was, in private, a conspicuously public lover and drinker—or so Plato tells us.

My six subjects contained roughly similar contradictions. Adams was an anti-Washington Washingtonian, an anti-capitalist capitalist and an anti-historian historian. Capitalist-socialist London was a romantic Darwinian. Political logician Sinclair made wild forays into the psychic world and had a mystique about his stomach. Anarchist Dos Passos moved from communism to *The National Review*. Williams shuttled daily, for fifty years, between doctoring and poetry. And polemical southerner Tate, finding little to choose between Russian communism and northern capitalism, spoke steadily against both but lived half of his life up North.

I ridicule all these "positions," but I hope kindly. Much strength, energy, and talent were released by the climate of impiety of the time, a climate fostering contradictions.

Our climate is now much altered, and I am one of those who thinks that science has done this for us. Though no Catholic I like the way Jacques Maritain saddled the Cartesians, in a fine phrase, with "the decay of speculative understanding." (From *The Dream of Descartes*.)

The decay was less evident before World War II. Or, to put it the way some scientists might, the ignorance was more evident. Daniel Bell is one of the scientists, and in his book *The End of Ideology*, he puts the change later, twenty years after the war. So be it. Whichever date is right, the fact of a change remains. As a way of combating Bell's charge—that ideological thought was a primitive mental proceeding that we humans have now left behind—I must point to the complexities of such inquiry long before the "end." Two English literary figures and their idealizing may be more telling here than my American subjects. I mean Winston Churchill and W. H. Auden.

They may not seem a credible pair (I can't imagine the two of them talking to each other), but Churchill was literary enough to win the Nobel Prize for Literature—for his war histories—in 1953, five years after Eliot won it. I remember writing an impious essay about him at the time, saying that yes he was literary but not *good* literary ("Churchill and the Limitations of Myth"), and I wasn't alone. Almost everything Churchill stood for at war's end was something for my literary set to be impious about. Eliot himself—the often-thought head of that set—had jibed about Churchill's heavy rhetoric back in the thirties, even before Churchill became prime minister. (Discussing public oratory Eliot said, "If we proceed from bad to worse we arrive at length at the prose style of Mr. Winston Churchill," *Criterion,* 8:32) And the young Auden—born 1907—had also been issuing impieties about inspirational verbiage at that time, though without mentioning Churchill.

Auden in the thirties was not Socratic procedurally. Especially in his prose he enjoyed making vast and unqualified assertions. He was a strong Freudian and wrote a brilliant piece in which he sided with Freud in disapproving of ideological generalizations (both of them were, of course, full of such broadbrush matter). He also generalized in fields other than psychology—in religion, education, art, government, and 'isms—and did so as if he were competing for a prize in dogmatism. Yet he managed not to sound dogmatic. He managed to communicate that he was just testing, trying out his own positions by putting them down firmly, sometimes in a manner reminiscent of Oscar Wilde. In other words, his approach was speculative even as he pontificated.

And one of the subjects of his speculative pontification was, naturally, pontification: "Poetry is not concerned with telling people what to do, but with extending our knowledge of good and evil." "The task of psychology, or art for that matter, is not to tell people how to behave, but to render them better able to choose." "Democracy assumes, I think correctly, the right of every individual to revolt against his government by voting against it." (From *The English Auden,* ed. Edward Mendelson, New York: Random House, 1972.)

This was not literary modernist talk but, let us say, thirties Ibsenism. Then in 1939, Auden—having performed as a reporter in Spain, where he sided with the Communists—wrote two of his now most-anthologized poems, his elegy to Yeats (who had died that year) and his "September 1, 1939." In both of these he buttressed his impiety with editorial adjectives—"low, dishonest decade," for instance—and stern pronouncements, the most famous being, "Poetry makes nothing happen." In neither was he concentrating on the European enemies of England in its new war, but on the culture at home where he kept hearing "the windiest militant trash"—such as Churchill's?—that "Important Persons shout." Yet at the end of both poems, having gloomed for dozens of lines, he suddenly decided to be hopeful. In winding up the Yeats elegy, he found hope in "the farming" of good Yeatsian verse from which "the healing fountain" might spring forth. And he closed "September 1, 1939" with a kind of prayer in which, "beleaguered by . . . negation and despair," he begged his own muse to "show an affirming flame."

I mention these surely ideological resolutions as preface to saying that twenty years later I heard Auden tell an audience of admirers in Minneapolis how much he disliked the endings of both poems. Both were faked, he said—dishonest. They were bursts of stagy eloquence. They were just another reflection of the sociopolitical hypocrisy of the late thirties period.

Auden had as sensitive an ear for windy trash as anyone of his generation, but most of us present in Minneapolis—including Allen Tate, who gave the party—felt that he was overreacting, picking unfairly on his own very moving affirmations. Were they not quite unlike Churchill crying out, for example, that the English should "arise again and take our stand for freedom as in the olden times"? Perhaps. At any rate there was Auden in his slippers—he had gout—wishing he could remove both poems from the anthologies. In his own unpredictable way he had moved over to the later Bell position.

And now, another few decades later, the collapse of the U.S.S.R. has produced a flood of anti-ideological writers so firm in their new faith that we probably need a new label for them. Here is a sample of their energies, from the *Nation* in mid–1992, written by Clancy Sigal, who describes himself as a former socialist with now "dogma weary shoulders." He declares that "most of us are guilty," and he tells us we must somehow liberate ourselves from "shining, self-serving, martyred, declamatory, Prussian-descending narrow rhetoric." How? We must start to think "for ourselves, afresh, out of our own unique, unassailable (except by ourselves) personal experience."

All of my biographees were too old to move to the Bell position, much less to that of the new, should we call them uniquists? The late nineteenth century was their home ground intellectually, an age full of spaciously skeptical inquirers, even literary ones. So it is that age, and my subjects' attentiveness to the climate of thought of that age, which is my focus here.

ONE

Henry Adams and the Super Forces

Does the Adams industry need another biography of Henry Adams, even a short one? The justification for *this* one is that much of the recent compiling, editing and writing has been directed at his private life, with the result that the books for which he is still best known have been demoted, they being works that deal with his private life only indirectly. My intent here is simply to put them back where they used to be and especially to put back the large social themes he expressed in them.[1]

For many reasons Henry Adams did not follow his father, grand-

1. The works of central thematic interest are these: his two novels, *Democracy* and *Esther; Mont-Saint-Michel and Chartres; The Education of Henry Adams;* and a small essay volume with an "Introduction" by his brother Brooks published following Henry's death, *The Degradation of the Democratic Dogma* (New York: Macmillan, 1919), which includes "A Letter to the Teachers of History" (1910). I can't limit myself to what an excellent recent biographer, Patricia O'Toole, calls, a bit ironically, "the riches of his intellect," but those riches will be my focus. Then there are the riches of brother Brooks himself in his *Law of Civilization and Decay* (1896). Brooks's cyclical theories influenced Henry's thinking greatly, as is shown by historian Charles Beard in a fifty-page "Introduction" to a 1939 edition (New York: Knopf) of the book. Finally, there are now available six volumes of *The Letters of Henry Adams,* compiled by editors J. C. Levenson, Ernest Samuels, Charles Vandersee, and Viola Hopkins Winner (Cambridge: Harvard-Belknap, 1988). These volumes prove, among much else, that Adams was one of the most industrious correspondents in history. For his remarks to friends I have quoted directly from the letters in these volumes where possible, but have otherwise had recourse to the three-volume biography by Ernest Samuels, *Henry Adams* (Cambridge: Harvard, 1964); and three other peripheral biographies: *Clover* by Otto Friedrich (New York: Simon and Schuster, 1979); *The Five of Hearts* by Patricia O'Toole (New York: Clarkson Potter, 1990), which deals with Adams's relations with Clover, John and Clara Hay, and Clarence King; and *Henry Adams and Friends* by Harold Dean Cater (Boston: Houghton Mifflin, 1947).

father, and great-grandfather up to the public service heights of Washington, though he came to know those heights well. He wasn't detached from the government there—far from it—but he wasn't in it either. Some of the social gloom of his big books may well be blamed on simple bystander disappointment.

Furthermore, he may well have deserved to be a bystander, an old and rich bystander with a liking for the old and rich. Certainly he had no physical qualities that seemed to signal leadership, especially in a democracy. As described by his biographer Ernest Samuels, he was very short, and as a Harvard student he was "handsome and earnest" but soon became "prematurely gray and bald." As a young traveler to Europe he tended toward plumpness, cultivated a small beard, and smoked cigars, but by thirty he had a liver ailment, suffered from "chronic dyspepsia," and had thinned out. His eyes gave him trouble when he read too much, and though he became a great world traveler, he could be depended on, on any voyage, to become seasick and to joke about it. By thirty-five he had achieved snobbery, and "in the intimacy of his seminars" as an assistant professor of history at Harvard, "he smoked his cigar and sipped his vintage sherry serenely aware that such privileges were not for students." He spoke "a nasal and anglicized drawl," and though he was witty and could be most friendly, he exuded an excess, for plainer folk, of good breeding and of high-brow attentiveness to abstractions.

Not that he could help the loftiness, being an Adams. As a child he sometimes lived in the Quincy House of his grandfather, John Quincy Adams, and he was even once led by the hand—when he didn't want to go—to school by that grandfather. Then as a boy and young man he was introduced to the inside of Washington and the White House—and then to the great in England—by his Congressman and ambassador and vice-presidential candidate father. On the Brooks side of his family he had money (and his wife had money), and so he could be aloof from money (though not economics) while partaking of the power of money. He could also be aloof from class distinctions, being himself distinct. He could even be aloof from learning because he was learned, and thus he steadily professed, like Socrates, to ignorance. No admirer of the common man, except as a democratic abstraction, he favored instead patrician Mount Vernon, where his father also took him, and had trouble reconciling his antislavery stance with his affection for Mount Vernon's furniture. He began and ended as a member of the few.

Yet he managed to escape, mostly, the genteel literary tradition around him, despite his two polite novels and a few fastidiously elevated Victorian poems. The novels were genteel, but they were thoughtful too, thoughtful in a way of which gentility and English departments have tended to disapprove. As for his other major writing ventures, they were historical-political-biographical-sociological, that is, not readily classifiable as literary, in fact not readily classifiable at all, though they were uniformly lucid and well shaped. Both *The Education of Henry Adams*—autobiography?—and *Mont-Saint-Michel and Chartres*—history?—were sweeping studies of human cultures in the large, and of the powers controlling cultures in the large, yet those qualities didn't make them anthropological either.

So his basic genre was obscure, but the source of it was not: Washington. Washington was one of the world's best places to study power, an essence intrinsic to most genres. Very early in life—before he learned that he was to be a bystander—he discovered there that he *wanted* to study it. He was barely of age when his father, newly elected to Congress, made preparations for his Washington move, and Henry wrote him that the "opening" was magnificent: "I don't see why you can't make your drawing room as necessary and famous as you please and hatch all the presidents for twenty years there." And when the father was removed to London instead, taking Henry with him as his private secretary for the duration of the Civil War, Henry still dreamed of the opening. After the war he, therefore, set out to make his own Washington drawing room a hatching place.

First he moved there as a bachelor and was quickly disabused, by the Grant Administration, of hopes for an appointment for himself. Then he retreated to Harvard, where he taught the Middle Ages, sipped his sherry, and edited the *North American Review*—but still dreamed of Washington. Then he married a brilliant and ambitious woman, Clover Hooper, who also dreamed of Washington (partly because she wished to be distant from the Adams clan in Massachusetts). So in 1877, Henry and Clover moved their dreams to Lafayette Square.

They lived there in a succession of three houses, where they could look out the windows of each and actually see the White House. Henry found irony in the presence of a statue of the enemy, Andrew

Jackson, impeding his White House view, but he found no irony in setting up a hatchery, or more politely a salon of culture, there. Washington, despite Jackson, was his culture. Or so he thought then, turning forty.

Washington had grown during the Civil War. It was no longer "a rude colony camped in the forest"—his own description of prewar Washington—but a town of 150,000 clerks, politicians, and diplomats. Henry was not interested in the clerks but in the others, the lofty ones, and for communing with the lofty ones Lafayette Square was central. He and Clover held open house daily at teatime (on Sundays sometimes at late breakfast) for the lofty, including a secretary and an assistant secretary of state, a secretary of the interior, the director of the Smithsonian, a select circle of Senators, and an occasional literary visitor, like Henry James. No lobbyists or common journalists were normally admitted, though both Henry and his close friend John Hay played at being journalists often (and Hay served as editor of the *New York Tribune* for a period), but high wits were welcome, especially if they could be witty at the expense of the White House incumbent. Rutherford Hayes was a good target, being in Henry's opinion a nonentity (and Henry, in Hayes's opinion, being a "dull owl"), but there were many other fools abounding to be witty about, including a local judge who, reported witty Clover to her father, must have been self-made because "it would be blasphemy to attribute him to any other creator." The banter and elegance at the teas were Jamesian, but there was more than banter and elegance. There was also, and occurring regularly, a heavy emphasis on ideological chatter, chatter about God and Reality and Truth and the Future. Abstract forces kept floating through the cigar smoke.

In the seventies and eighties the abstract forces in Henry's own head were still in their infancy. They would take more mature shape in the nineties, after the great financial panic and after Henry had had long talks with his younger brother, Brooks, about Brooks's amazing book, *The Law of Civilization and Decay* (which had much to do with the themes of both *Mont-Saint-Michel* and Henry's *The Education*), but in the early Washington years the forces were not central to his writing. He did, however, find plenty of them near Lafayette Square.

Evolutionary forces, for instance. He had brought evolution home with him from his London war years, having been close there to a "geological champion of Darwin," Sir Charles Lyell. And when he put evolution together with the great social changes he saw taking place in Washington, he became hipped on change itself and the need to keep up with it. Before the turn of the century he came to feel that he lived on the edge of a brand-new human age, in which the old forces of society were simply to be erased by the new. By then he understood, perhaps too well, that he was one of the old forces, understood that the Adams clan had lost its shine. But he was not content with passive regret. He had a thing about keeping up, being intellectually au courant, and so began in late middle age to study the forces of change with all the resources in his good, though bald, head. Eventually he was able to work the forces out systematically and to present the old forces of society by the Virgin at the time of the building of Chartres Cathedral, and the new forces of society by the Dynamo as he saw it shining—and heard it mystically humming—at the St. Louis Exposition of 1900. He would stand before that Dynamo and feel it "as a moral force, much as the early Christians felt the Cross," and would think of it as like the earlier symbol in being equally inexplicable, equally a manifestation of mysterious energy in the universe.

But in Washington in the seventies and eighties he was still feeling his way with his new energy. He talked about it in his parlor, especially with his geologist friend Clarence King, and wrote about it in two novels.

In a novel by the other Henry, Henry James, the characters are not usually allowed to settle down to a learned discussion of forces. What was primal for James was not idea but manner, not conceivings but sensings. But for Adams a novel was largely an idea vehicle, and it was so even if it had a Jamesian parlor at its center. His novels were *about* forces: moral, social, political, physical, and (in an abstract way) sexual. The characters were agents of the forces.

The first of his novels, *Democracy*, appeared in 1880 and was the least successful of the two, though it was the only one to achieve general circulation. Its ideas were strong and unrelenting and led to its failings elsewhere: a loose and rambling plot, and characters who had human origins but emerged as only talking forces. For Henry was careful not to investigate his characters' motives other than their traditional ones like greed and pride, careful not to go too far in. Here the genteel tradition was indeed at work in him, as also in his decision to publish the work anonymously. He was a decorous New Englander, and novels were not the place for serious thinking by decorous, male, Adamsian New Englanders.

As a result, *Democracy* was a boring affair psychologically, and the boring element was largely Henry. He lectured his readers as if he were still teaching at Harvard. He couldn't bring himself to probe his characters, and at the same time he couldn't stop talking about his grand syntheses.

But the talk itself had merit. It revealed a mind behind it that knew something of the forces it talked about, knew something about Washington's, and America's, primal sociopolitical energies. Such knowledge was conspicuous throughout, and though there are indications that Henry could be patronizing about Clover's intelligence, to his credit he endowed his novel's heroine, a female much like Clover, with that knowledge.

She was a rich New York widow, Mrs. Lightfoot Lee, who had enough time and freedom to go searching after education like Henry and Clover, and who chose, as they had, to move to Washington and have a salon. Why Washington? Well, Mrs. Lee had lived before in a society where "she knew, more or less intimately, a dozen men whose fortunes ranged between one million and forty million," and "whose fortunes kept accumulating without changing or improving the quality of their owners." So she was attracted to a city where, as she thought, the inhabitants were more receptive than they to change and growth. As Henry put it for her, she had "the feeling of a passenger on an ocean steamer whose mind will not give him rest until he has been in the engine room and talked to the engineer." Washington was the nation's engine room. It was where she could "see with her own eyes the action of primary forces" and "touch with her own hand the massive machinery of society." She had Henry's feelings.

Henry James had also sensed a difference about Washington when he visited it, a difference he reported in the *American Scene*. He felt it was dramatically separate from the "colossal greed of New York," and, therefore, a place where the American female could come into her own and assert her female graces as she could not in New York. But of the cruder, engine-room forces, he had little to say. For James the engine rooms, even for his American figures, were not in New York *or* Washington, but abroad. And Washington was for him a pleasant, pastoral place where he could bask in "a rare light, half green, half golden." He did not go there to hatch presidents.

One could of course ask of Mrs. Lee, in *Democracy,* how she could look at the American rich of New York and not see that *their* lives were an engine room too, not see that the possession of money was more than the result of simple accumulation, and did more to the mind than render it stagnant. Washington was only the second-best place in America to look for its primary social forces, namely the money forces, the forces of James's colossal greed; but Mrs. Lee was like Henry in having money, old money, and therefore in being less sensitive to it as a force than someone less well fixed. If Henry had created her fifteen years later, after the panic of 1893, he might have made her more conscious of Wall Street and State Street greed, but in 1880 he made her sensitive about everything *except* money greed. She was an intense student of primary forces and cared little for Washington's green and golden light. She set up her salon in Lafayette Square and quickly made it an engine room.

And in that room, just as in Henry's and Clover's parlor, the engine-room forces were a mixture of the moral and the political. The lucky tea-taker there could learn that American democracy was government of the people, by the people, and for the benefit of the senators. Or he could learn that it was the hope of the world. Mrs. Lee, an idealist among force scholars, hoped it was the hope of the world, but having fallen for a senator in whom she thought that hope happily resided, she found that no, democracy was for his benefit after all, he having rigged an election to gain his office. What should she do? What had her education in primary forces led her to?

An abyss, obviously. It frightened her. She retreated abruptly into her high morality and rejected the senator. *Democracy* could have ended there, but did not. On the last page Henry left Mrs. Lee wondering if she hadn't been *too* good, given the town and the country and the age. In a postscript he let her last words stand as, presumably, also his own, like a moral at the end of a fable. "The bitterest part of this horrid story is that nine out of ten of our countrymen would say I had made a mistake [in rejecting the senator]."

So there she was in her solitude, with an unacceptable ethic. At least Henry was in the solitude with her.

For Mrs. Lee's dilemma was also Henry's even then (this was 1880). He too was old money (which didn't seem like money somehow) and old power; he too was morally indignant about new money and new power, as represented by Mrs. Lee's senator. Henry was full of righteousness in those years, but it was always mixed with cynicism. He and his friends constantly chattered about Washington scandals, piecing out the latest ones over tea. They were uniformly persuaded that the Jackson crowd, and then the Grant crowd, had not an enlightened, selfless thought in its collective head. At the same time Henry could be depended on to find himself naive in denying the new forces, and to tell himself to put aside his Adamsian notions of order, accommodate to modernity. So *Democracy* ended with the high struggle for which it had originally been aimed. As a novel about a man and a woman it had little of what Freud would have called "real content."

Yet at the time of its publication Henry's brother Charles Francis, Jr., who did not know that Henry had written it, reviewed it and didn't even mention the grand forces or the thinness of the humanity. No, he said it was a bad novel because it was *too* human, that is, vulgar. His words for it—as reported by Samuels—were that it had "a coarse, half educated touch." Charles, Jr., must have been persuaded that ideas were themselves vulgar, but at any rate he announced that the book had probably been written by the author of another anonymous novel of the period, *The Breadwinners*. In fact *The Breadwinners* had been written by Henry's neighbor John Hay, making the attribution a source of great ironic merriment. Henry said, "I want to roll on the floor, to howl, kick and sneeze. . . . Never, since Cain wrote his last newspaper letter to Abel, was there anything so droll." But he surely must have wondered about his brother's notions of the coarse and half-educated, Henry whose literary sensibilities were so delicate that he had trouble describing his novel characters physically—unlike Hay who liked to insert heavy innuendos about the wonders of the female form. *The Breadwinners* was not at all like *Democracy*. John Hay was an important editor and became an important secretary of state, but he was a bad poet and a worse novelist. And *The Breadwinners* was a debacle. It started as a love story, and became an antilabor story, and then it didn't know what it was. Certainly it never had an illuminating word to say about primary forces. Henry's brother would have been on sounder ground if he had said that *Democracy* had been written by the author of *Daisy Miller*.

Yet it had a solid though bowdlerized base in Henry's own marital life, as is not the case with any James novel. And, particularly, it had a base in the character of Clover. (The same is true of his second novel, *Esther.*) There is some disagreement among biographers about Clover's relationship with Henry and about her intellectual interests, but there is none about her intelligence and wit, none about her psychic instability, and none about her large role in persuading Henry that women were a better human bargain than men. Ernest Samuels, who is perhaps still foremost among modern Adams scholars, studied her at length and decided that she had a mind with interests like Henry's, and maybe a better mind at that. He reported, for instance, that Henry James was so impressed with Clover's intellectual dominance in the household that he said, after Clover's suicide, "We never knew how delightful Henry was till he lost her; he was so proud of her that he let her shine as he sat back and enjoyed listening to what she said and what others let her say." Further, of Clover's letters home to her father, Samuels declared that they had an unusually "masculine energy," an energy that made evident her capacity to supply that "domination at the hands of women which he [Henry] craved." But new caches of letters—reported by Otto Friedrich—have weakened the Samuels thesis about her intellectual dominance. It is true that Henry wrote, in a letter to a friend just before his marriage, "She rules me as only American women rule men, and I cower before her," but in the same letter he said—for the letter was a momentary bit of male braggadocio—"She is very open to instruction. We shall improve her." And a number of recent psychobiographic accounts do undermine the image of a Clover looked up to, a Clover not patronized.

The difference is striking. For example, in an introduction to an old (1947) collection of letters, Harold Dean Cater said, "Theirs was a happy marriage, and together they entered upon a social and intellectual life such as few marriages know." Yet later analysts, busily probing for "real content," have worried about their sexual relationship (who was responsible for their childlessness?), and what it must have been like for Clover to sail up the Nile on her honeymoon with a husband who carted along a trunkload of books about medieval legal institutions. (Patricia O'Toole writes that they had leased a sailable, rowable, poleable, towable dahabeah with a crew of eleven, and visited with other rich Americans en route.) At this point Friedrich draws heavily on Clover's weekly letters to her father, and he suggests, convincingly, that Clover could be bored to tears with Henry's intellectual life.

That she was remarkably quick and perceptive seems agreed upon and is confirmed in her reported comments. Of an admirer, "Harry" James, she said that it would be good for him "to go to Wyoming and run a hog ranch." Of Herbert Spencer she reported that he looked "like a complacent crimson cow." Such a mind was not to be "improved" readily. Unfortunately there was also the "sickness."

The braver diagnosticians have simply called her a manic-depressive in a family with a manic history. She had her first seizure—or first at least within the confines of their marriage—on their Egyptian honeymoon when Henry was reading his German law books and she (according to Friedrich) was reading George Eliot's *Middlemarch* and soaking up a bit of feminism. The seizure was brief, the honeymoon improved, and Henry reported in a veiled manner to his father-in-law that she was in "better condition" than he had ever known her to be (this—from Samuels—presumably indicating that he and the father had already somehow discussed the condition). Thereafter for more than a decade the marriage seemed strong (except that Clover did not find Henry's parents at all receptive to her), and her health, though frail, did not cause alarm. Their Washington salon became a marital triumph; they had common friends, common concerns. On the surface there appeared to be nothing between them to render suspect the perfection that Henry piously insisted on after her death (when he could mention her at all): "For twelve years I had everything I most wanted on earth." What was he hiding from himself or his friends when he said that? Even the psychobiographers I have read do not pretend to know, though everyone points to her excessive dependence on her father. In the Adams texts there is just one confirming clue to the father's role. This is in *Esther,* when Esther's father says he has hated Esther's suitor ever since he has known him. It is not enough. In real life the father is not known to have said any such thing. And in real life there was enough marital compatibility, most evidence suggests, to override such feelings, if the father had them.

There remains the *Esther* note of trouble, and though *Esther* is more gracefully, elegantly abstract than *Democracy,* its connections with Henry and Clover are closer. It was written in 1883 and published in 1884. Not only was Clover the model for Esther, but Clover's father was the model for Esther's father, and Henry described at length, one year before his father-in-law's death, the death of Esther's father. With this novel, as with *Democracy,* Henry concealed his authorship, but this time he adopted a female pseudonym, Francis Snow Compton, and enforced secrecy upon his publisher, Henry Holt. Even friend John Hay seems not to have known about it. Did Clover herself? Presumably she did (though I have only seen her knowledge denied[2]), and anyway, *Esther* is such a strong and admirable character that no reader, thinking only of the book and ignorant of Clover's suicide, could understand why Henry should have been guilt-ridden. But of course he was. Clover died, a year after the book's appearance, by taking a chemical used in photography to which he had introduced her.[3]

The primary forces in *Democracy* were politics and ethics, but in *Esther,* Henry focused on religion, science, and aesthetics. And he shifted the novel's scene from Washington to New York, finding there another set of characters who were rich and ideological. A malicious reviewer could sum it all up as a heroine discussing religion and aesthetics with miscellaneous talking heads for three hundred pages.

There was also in the novel, it is true, a love affair. The heroine's suitor was a minister in a fashionable Episcopalian church, who was a full-blown primary-force man in his own pulpit. For his primary wooing assignment he decided to win Esther over from scientific agnosticism, and delivered a sermon (in church) to do so that was summarized for three pages at the beginning of the novel, so that Esther and the other talking heads could express opinions about it (after church) for many pages more. Esther was not herself a practicing, card-carrying scientist but, like Clover, the loyal daughter of one, and she had as a good friend a scientist modeled after Henry's geologist friend Clarence King. Eventually the scientist put his conflict with the minister, named Hazard, this way:

> Hazard and I have had it out fifty times, and discussed the whole subject till night reeled, but we never got within shouting distance of each other. He might as well have stood on the earth, and I on the nearest planet, and bawled across.

2. Robert Spiller, "Introduction," *Esther* (New York: Scholars' Facsimiles and Reprints, 1939).

3. The latest account of the suicide I have seen, O'Toole's, is also the fullest. Aside from the act itself the background was her father's final illness (1884), which she spent with him in Boston. (Henry visited regularly.) Upon her father's death she returned to Washington and became depressed to a degree noticed by all her friends, and Henry wrote to a friend saying she was "a good deal off her feed" (Samuels). On the morning of the act she professed to be "somewhat better," then went upstairs and took the chemical.

Then Esther in her turn told Hazard, upon rejecting him,

> You will be angry with me for saying it, but I never saw you conduct a service without feeling as though you were a Priest in a Pagan temple, centuries apart from me. At any moment I half expected to see you bring out a goat or a ram and sacrifice it on the high altar. How could I, with such ideas, join you at communion. What I have said proves that I am not fit to be your wife. Let me go in peace.

The ingredients of fitness as a wife need not all be love and warmth and duty, but need they all be right ideas either? Without great success the novel tried not to say so, tried to fish up a bit of passion. It had Esther reject Hazard excitedly, and then turn around and also reject the scientist who rushed in to catch her on the rebound. Her last words were to the scientist, and they complicated the novel's message in much the way that Mrs. Lee's last words in *Democracy* had. Esther said, "But George. I don't love you. I love him." This stunner seems to have led O'Toole in *The Five of Hearts* to declare that the love element is indeed what the novel is all about. She avers, "Many critics and biographers [O'Toole could well have had me in mind] have seen Esther as the author's investigation of the paradox of faith in an age made skeptical by science, but the novel reveals less of the author's concern for the relation of man and God than his lifelong perplexity over the relation of man and woman."

In our deconstructed age each reader is of course allowed his own interpretation, but O'Toole's not only centers on the novel's weakest thread, the "love interest," but takes the thread away from Adams and supplies her own. The novel does have merit elsewhere, and it has it where Adams's characters chatter in the way a malicious reviewer would deride. The chatter is intelligent discussion of the split between religion and culture in Adams's time. Essentially the book is like a play by Ibsen and Shaw, and though not as good, it needs to be judged on those terms—that is, ideologically—and not psychoanalyzed.

So much for the two novels. They were a gesture in mid-life toward a smaller literary form than the grand one his mind was trying to fit itself to. Henry was a born writer, an elegant writer, a precise and yet spacious writer who believed everything in his mental range capable of being put down. So, trying to achieve competence in all the available genres, he settled on the novel briefly, as a diversion adequate for describing drawing-room life as lived by an Adams on Lafayette Square. And two other genres he entered upon, poetry and letter writing, were diversionary too.

He seems to have written poetry rarely—usually when he was traveling in far-off places—yet he was a proficient if old-fashioned prosodist. Poetry was a good island-diversion for him, and so were letters; he was at ease with both, on vacation really. Yet his ancestry kept telling him that the major form for an Adams was neither those nor the novel, but history, history, history.

But was history one genre or many? He tried several models, starting with biography, and they all seemed to fit, all except biographies of other Adamses than himself. The other Adamses were history, but they were awkward subjects for him psychologically. So his first and only major effort at biography was a study of a public servant in the world of Adamses, Albert Gallatin.

Gallatin was a member of the House of Representatives when John Adams was president, and minister to Great Britain when John Quincy Adams was president. He was also a Jeffersonian, and he served as secretary of the treasury under both Jefferson and Madison. The Gallatin biography was Henry's way into his major history, that of the Jefferson and Madison administrations.

Among the ranks of Washington leaders Gallatin was a model intellectual: "His laborious mind had studied America with infinite care, and he retained so much knowledge of European affairs as to fit him equally for the State Department or the Treasury." (He had been born in Switzerland, moving to America at 19.) He "was also one of the best talkers in America, and perhaps the best informed man in the country." Most important, he was always ready "to grapple with the ideas and methods of the coming generation." The grappling was what interested Henry, and it made the biography a tribute to the mixture of intellect and stamina represented by Gallatin.[4] At this stage in Henry's career (he was just over forty) he still seemed to believe, with Thomas Carlyle, that leadership mattered.

As a young man Henry admired Carlyle, and he could be impressed with Carlyle's assertion, on the very first page of *On Heroes, Hero-worship and the Heroic in History,* that "Universal History, the

---

4. Gallatin became president at eighty (long after retirement from government service) of the New York Historical Society, and at eighty-two he founded the American Ethnological Society.

history of what man has accomplished in this world, is at bottom the History of Great Men who have worked here." But when Carlyle raged against America in the sixties, Henry (who was in London hearing it all) gave him up[5] and moved slowly away, in his own thinking, from Carlyle's "great man" approach to history. By the time of his *History of the United States during the Administrations of Jefferson and Madison* he had completely changed his tune, at least in dealing with Jefferson. In the first volume about the man, he delayed introducing Jefferson at all, for 185 pages. For those pages he took up, instead, "controlling influences."

He began with the physical America of 1800, then moved to the conservative "habits of life and thought" that made 1800 a stagnant moment in American history, and then produced three sectionally focused chapters on the nation's collective intellect in 1800. The accounts were wittily ironic, Henry in his element, casting balanced Johnsonian aspersions upon representative figures in each region,[6] but they were certainly accounts of influences rather than leaders. Henry was practicing an abstract sociological procedure that was moving in on academia even as he wrote and that would dominate his later writings. When he finally came to Jefferson himself he was attentive to, and sympathetic with, Jefferson's individual character, but was inclined to present him as a good man unable to stem the influences. He had come to power as a champion of state's rights but "had driven States to the verge of armed resistance." He had begun by practicing economy but had spent more than his predecessor. He had preached peace but had brought the country to the "necessity" of war with the world's two greatest powers. And "he who longed like a child for sympathy and love left office as strongly and almost as gen-

5. In *The Education* he said that Carlyle's outbursts had made it seem as if a "general darkness" had fallen on human faith.

6. Aaron Burr's New York gave him unusually malicious energy and enabled him to be malicious about Jefferson's Virginia at the same time: "The intellectual and moral character of New York left much to be desired. . . . New York cared little for the metaphysical subtleties of Massachusetts and Virginia, which convulsed the nation with spasms almost as violent as those that, fourteen centuries before, had distracted the Eastern Empire in an effort to establish the double or single nature of Christ. . . . The Virginians aimed at maintaining a society so simple that purity would suffer no danger and corruption gain no foothold. . . . No more curious speculation could have been suggested to the politicians of 1800 than the question whether New York would corrupt Virginia, or Virginia would check the prosperity of New York."

erally disliked as the least popular president who preceded[7] or followed him." Henry was not whipping Jefferson but the "controlling influences." A leader could be impious about them—and Jefferson was, and John Adams was—but the influences seemed to be in charge anyway.

In the Madison volumes (there were four volumes for each president) this theme surfaced little, largely because the volumes were concerned with the complicated war years during which the influences were, as it were, a given. Here Henry turned his attention to political and diplomatic studies of individual Machiavels sparring with each other. It was as if he had moved from sociology to political science, and the switch made dull reading. The pages were crammed with interminable tricky squabbles of a kind for which our capital is famous. That Madison survived the War of 1812, and came out on the other side as president of a country in which major squabbles had died down, was probably not Madison's fault. Henry was able to send him into retirement ironically uttering sweet words about peace on earth and goodwill to men and return to sociology—that is, science rather than "great men." By his new gospel it was democracy that was doing this to the profession of history. America was a new social phenomenon "without kings, nobles or armies; without church, traditions and prejudices" and therefore "a subject for the man of science rather than for dramatists and poets." In other words, it was a country in which the processes of evolution were indeed in charge. As he put it there were "laws of human progress," and "they were matter not for dogmatic faith, but for study." Henry thus ended his uneven history of two administrations with words promoting history—if it were to survive—as a science, and this was the theme he would put forth ten years later (1894) when he became president in absentia of the newly founded American Historical Association. Writing from Guadalajara he told that organization that history was in the process of becoming a science whether they liked it or not.

His preoccupation with evolution as part of the historian's genre had been evident in the discussions in *Esther* in which, for example, the heroine told her Episcopalian minister suitor she didn't think she

7. The unpopular predecessor was of course John Adams. Henry quoted a friend of Gallatin's saying, "I verily believe one year more of writing, speaking and appointing would render Pr. Jefferson a more odious President, even to democrats, than John Adams."

could worship any *person* at all. By middle age Henry seems to have persuaded himself that the great forces of science had a future that great men of traditional history and biography did not.

And the death of Clover, the shock of his life, must have contributed to the shift, weakening his earlier intellectual commitments, just as it weakened his ties to Washington and country and made him, for years, a wanderer on the earth. Soon after the death a friend mentioned Clover to him, and he held up his hand, saying, "I cannot bear it"; he was also heard to mutter that he had died with her. As far as history was concerned he did not, however, die; he simply transferred his allegiance to the kind of history we see in the *Mont-Saint-Michel* volume and in *The Education,* a history of social essences, the essences of whole cultures, races, human masses. Switching to masses was not a happy fate for an Adams, but he was obviously convinced of the verities of force to be found there, and he lectured his colleagues in history about it, telling them they should join him. In *Mont-Saint-Michel* he had a point; individuals seemed irrelevant to his abstract theme. But in *The Education* he was dealing, after all, with an Adams—himself. The combining of force and personality was tricky there. He had to be inclusive, going beyond the self, but he had to be exclusive too. At least he chose to be. He chose to exclude, from this, his own biography, twenty years, the years with Clover and immediately after her death.

Of course he had always been a strong man for excisions. As editor of the *North American Review* he had steadily practiced what Samuels calls "wholesome surgery" on articles submitted to him. But the omission of twenty years was not wholesome, and it was not to be explained by his insistence that the deleted years were not relevant to his educational essence. In one way the surgery could be called a positive act, a gesture to Clover comparable to his commissioning of the sorrowing figure by Augustus Saint John that rests, untitled, over her grave in Washington.[8] But otherwise it was, surely, an unhealthy psychological display of what his education had not taught him to

8. Friedrich suggests that the most conspicuous gesture to Clover was the writing of the *Mont-Saint-Michel* volume itself, in which Henry "restated his belief that 'Nature rewards the female as the essential, the male as the superfluity of her world.'" Essentially, says Friedrich, "it is a book about women," and the woman to whom he addressed his words—Clover. That is all very well psychoanalytically, but I note that he had to assert this theme via the thirteenth century.

cope with *except* by omission. His troubles with the flesh had surfaced in the novels; now they were surfacing for real. Luckily they were rewarding troubles. The *Mont-Saint-Michel* volume and *The Education* are his greatest works.

For his own long-sentence reasons Henry's friend Henry James was feeling his way among great forces too in the 1880s, but his great forces were not dynamos and evolution. They were the familiar social forces of class against class, with Americans representing the modern forms of class sensibility and Europeans representing the old. The players in James's fictions had little to say about saurians and thermodynamics. They did not inquire into the respective roles of science and religion in the world, and they did not think it decorous even to mention great forces in the parlor. They could lead lives that subjected them to great forces, but they could not explicate great forces. James did not clutter his parlor dramas with theory.

His early heroine Daisy Miller can be cited here, though she was less intellectual than Jamesian heroines to come, and she could not have told a dynamo from a proletarian. She was like his later heroines in her mental processes, which were undialectical. She was not primitive, but she could be depended on to be instinctive. Her decision to go forth alone on the Roman streets with an unknown male—though somehow proper by her own standards—was not a decision reached by any describable rationale. She just couldn't see why she couldn't do what she wanted to do, and so she headed out the door. Isabel Archer of *Portrait of a Lady* was instinctive too but more vocal about it. She arrived at her rejections of a number of suitors by steadily asserting her God-given or America-given right to run her own life and thought. "We see our lives," she explained like a good teacher, "from our point of view; that is the privilege of the weakest and humblest of us."

Of course Daisy and Isabel were both private, unpolitical persons, not committed to hatching presidents or charting the future of religion and science: but even the public figures in James's novels were usually mum about their public lives. The English lord in *Portrait of a Lady,* by name of Warburton, was described as one of the most powerful men in England, and a vocal radical too, yet he said not a word of politics in the novel, being too well bred to bring up "issues" except in the House of Lords. James never took his readers to the House of Lords.

The one James novel in which the big forces were allowed to surface importantly was *The Princess Cassamassima,* a daring ideological venture for him, and a failure. He began it in his first year in London, and he said later that the germ of the book came to him while walking London's streets. His hero "sprung up . . . out of the London pavement," and though he was named, prettily, Hyacinth, this Hyacinth plunged like a warrior into the class struggle and was quickly converted, along with his princess-friend, to socialism. Then the princess and he strolled intellectually through their pages asking highbrow rhetorical questions about revolution:

> Is everything that is gathering force, underground, in the dark in the night, in the little hidden rooms, out of sight of governments and policemen and idiotic "statesmen"—heaven save them!—is all this going to burst forth some fine morning and set the world on fire? Or is it to sputter out and spend itself in vain conspiracies, be dissipated in sterile heroisms and abortive isolated movements?

Some critics, notably Lionel Trilling, were quite taken by such talk, and they announced that the novel showed the depths of James's social consciousness. Others, notably Maxwell Geismar, found the talk ludicrous, showing instead James's "own abiding prejudices, social ignorance and infantile obsessions." Both sides were partly right. James was thoroughly attentive to social forces in the novel and often gave a glimpse of the range of his talent beyond that for which he is now known. He showed also that he had a better eye than Henry Adams for seeing the people around him. (He saw the servants, for instance, as well as the gentlefolk; he knew what a worker was, and he could describe the workplace, unlike Adams.) But later, in the New York edition of his works, he said he was unhappy with the novel, having decided—I'd say correctly—that he had forced the characters to fit the forces, making them "too interpretative of the muddle of fate, or in other words too divinely, too priggishly clever."

Still, if James had carried on with the experiment in *The Princess Cassamassima,* he might now have a quite different reputation.

What is a writer anyway? An organization now exists in New York called Poets and Writers that carries our cultural confusion in its title. The organization is kind and benevolent, it prints a directory of poets and writers, and perhaps it will soon expand to include poets and writers and thinkers. Then it would have a trinity. On the left side of the trinity the poets would sit without a thought in their heads but full of deep feelings. On the right would sit the thinkers, busy at their syllogisms, their studies, their probings of "real content," but feelingless. And in the middle the writers, partaking a tiny bit of both poetry and thought, would recline sullenly into their mediocrity, engaging to be good at neither poetry nor thought, but writing on and on and on.

For centuries poets have been told to be thoughtless, though they have not always been obedient. But as for writers, were they not allowed to be thoughtful until our century? It would seem so. And since our century is also the age of Freud and of the social scientists, starting with Herbert Spencer and working up to Noam Chomsky, those of us who have cultivated negative feelings about the empire building in their professions may now draw conclusions. Poets and writers, we may note, seem to have been left out of the thinking process. They are expected to perform only Daisy Miller functions.

If ever there was a thinker who was a writer, it was Henry Adams. He not only wrote daily, but he was compulsive about it, unable to put his pen aside when seasick in mid-ocean, or watching sunsets in Samoa (see the Appendix for more sunsets). Writing and thinking were one in him; he thought by writing. After Clover's death he protested that his life had ended, yet he took to writing as if it *were* life. Travel enforced the writing, history and science enforced the writing. He came to live a lonely existence in many countries[9] during which he wrote letters, poems, and, most urgently, satisfying reams of prose about his great forces. Then one particular historical moment stirred him and his brother Brooks to new urgencies about the forces. That was the Panic of 1893.

There is comedy in how the brothers managed to make an archetypal pattern out of the prospective loss of their private family fortunes, but both of them had minds capable of this. They were Adamses, and the world's fate and their own were always tied together, as in a Shakespearean history play. Luckily, neither of them turned to the stage.

9. Newly published letters, together with other material uncovered by O'Toole, bring forth Henry's long-term intimacy with "Lizzie" Cameron. But in modern terms it was a most decorous affair. She seems to have declined his advances; also he seems to have relegated much of the relationship to letter-writing. For some years he wrote her, while traveling, about once a week.

Their collaboration began when Brooks, sitting at home in Quincy, cabled Henry in Switzerland (in the nineties Henry could be found anywhere except at home) that all the Adamses were about to be penniless. Henry returned immediately to share—as he put it to Elizabeth Cameron—the family's "blue fit of terror." The Adamses had enough money to have a blue fit about it, but their money interests were divided. They had State Street money and connections, but they also had non-State Street property and connections. In 1893 it was at State Street that they directed their fit. The conflict between the old and the new wealth within them became the germ of Brooks's remarkable treatise on force, *The Law of Civilization and Decay.*

Their non-State Street capital was in western lands. Brother Charles Adams, Jr., had been an apparently solid money president of the Union Pacific Railroad (removed from that office not by State Street but by Wall Street in the form of Jay Gould), but the rest of the family had landholdings, with mortgages on them, in the state of Washington. During the Panic the State Street bankers put the squeeze on western land investors (London bankers were putting the squeeze on State Street bankers), and everything would have been forfeit, according to Henry's account in *The Education,* if the bankers had not found themselves squeezing themselves and been "forced to let the mice escape with the rats." (Does this not sound like a modern financial soap?) When the Adamses came out safe, Henry, announcing that they had successfully "defied all Hell and State Street," was free to go back to his roaming, but he was now suddenly dazzled by his brother Brooks's economic precocity. Also, he had himself shown unexpectedly "expert knowledge" of stocks and bonds. He and Brooks began to work together, as they had not before.[10]

Brooks's treatise was, in its spread, far above the Panic that had motivated it. It started with Rome and explained Rome's fall in thirty pages. It dashed through the Gothic cathedrals and usury (or absence thereof) of the Middle Ages in seventy pages, thus arriving at the Reformation, where it announced modern times. Brooks's chief thesis was that money, big capitalist money like State Street money, had al-

10. From this distance Charles Francis Adams, Jr., seems the main cause of the family crisis, and his many derogatory remarks about Henry in letters suggest that the children of Charles Francis, Sr., were thoroughly divided before the Panic. CF, Jr., not only reviewed *Democracy* unfavorably but also, anonymously, Henry's *Life of Gallatin,* saying that its "ponderosity was little short of an outrage."

ways been the destroyer of civilization. Rome had gone down because a monied class took over from "the valiant and the eloquent." Byzantium became occupied by an "ostentatious, sordid, cowardly and stagnant race" because it developed as a world trade center. The Reformation reduced church power drastically, with the result that a new aristocracy installed itself, and then went busily about destroying itself. As for nineteenth-century industrialism, that phenomenon induced a crisis between the commodity people and the bankers. The bankers won, with the Bank Act of 1844, after which coin rather than commodity became the clear measure of value. The world was lost to State Street.

There were also remarks about Marx who, as the most prominent antimoney man in the late nineteenth century, earned mixed praise and annoyance from both Brooks and Henry. They could be wildly anti-capitalistic—and also anti-Semitic when they found Jews on top of the capitalist heap—but they did not favor socialist solutions either. Wrote Henry, with snobbish contempt (in a letter to Brooks, 1899), "I can now formulate Marx's theory of history as 'the survival of the cheapest, until it becomes too cheap to survive.' We are pretty cheap already, but the Trades Union is cheaper." They both managed to speak as old landed leaders of society, distressed equally by modern usury and the industrial proletariat, though more polemical about the former. As Henry put it in *The Education*, giving money only an ironical victory, nature had been busy sifting "the economic minds themselves, culling a favored aristocracy of the craftiest and subtlest types; choosing, for example, the Armenian in Byzantium, the Marwari in India, and the Jew in London."

These were words bred out of the Panic of 1893, during which Brooks and Henry had discovered in earnest that when money ran the culture, the culture went into decay. Forty years later Ezra Pound, much influenced by Brooks, would also become obsessed about usury, would write such lines as "with usura hath no man a house of good stone" (Canto 45), and would manage to have himself declared a traitor by Congress for preaching, on Rome Radio at the outset of World War II, against the monied interests behind U.S. participation in the war. But in the 1890s Brooks's book was received with more respect. For example, Theodore Roosevelt—who will appear again in my Upton Sinclair essay—was so impressed that he wrote a twenty-two-page review of it! Historian Charles Beard—in his introduction to the

1939 edition of the book—quotes extensively from the review, which described it as "replete with vivid writing" and "profound research," containing in (its theory) "a very ugly element of truth," but also cutting a "devious furrow": "Mr. Adams does not believe that any individual or group of individuals can influence the destiny of the race for good or evil . . . but we [!] do not think it is impossible . . . his theory of history breaks down at a number of points and is in need of numerous modifications and corrections." Beard's conclusion, which seems just, is that though Roosevelt didn't like the book it "had a positive influence"—in reaction, presumably, against Brooks's negativism—"on Mr. Roosevelt's thinking about the future of the United States."

As for Henry, he read Brooks's book in various drafts, and saw it for what it was, a grand theory of history and also a grand political blast. He wrote Brooks, "The gold bugs will never forgive you." He asked Brooks not to expect him to back the book publicly because he was president of the American Historical Association and felt he should not be caught selling a partisan document. Yet the book's effect on him, says Samuels, was "electric, bringing to an end the period of torpor and irresolution" in him that had begun with Clover's death. Samuels makes clear that Henry shared with Brooks all the book's urgencies. With Brooks he became an apostle of silver (though he was no fan of populist William Jennings Bryan), and with Brooks he also emerged as one of those eccentric social radicals we now call, politely, elitist.

Their radicalism began with the immediacies of 1893—"the commercial East against the agricultural South and West . . . small business against big business . . . debtors against creditors . . . producers and manufacturers against finance capitalists"—but it ended with a super chart of historical cycles that harnessed Darwin, among others, to show that the wrong people turned out to be the fittest. Samuels quotes Henry in one of his most impious moments

> I am myself more than ever at odds with my time. I detest it and everything that belongs to it, and live only in the wish to see the end of it, with all its infernal Jewry. I want to put every money lender to death, and to sink Lombard Street and Wall Street under the ocean. Then, perhaps, men of our time might have some chance of being honorably killed in battle and eaten by their enemies. I want to go to India, and be a Brahmin, and worship a monkey.

He would offer up no such violence in his semiprivate *The Education,* but the strength of his feeling there is evident. At the time of his reading Brooks's drafts his immediate response was to write a chapter for Brooks's book himself—on Art. (It was later merged—at Henry's insistence—with Brooks's text, so that Henry's name would not appear.) Samuels says of the chapter that Henry first proposed it to Brooks following his seminal tour of Normandy, during which he became convinced that "the ultimate and costliest disaster" to befall the Western world at the hands of the monied class "was aesthetic, the decline of the arts through the impoverishment of the imagination." Brooks then incorporated the theme elsewhere, putting both of them in the curious social role—curious for Puritan New Englanders—of praising medieval monks. The monks (Henry had written) had not been kept from using all the powers of the human imagination. "Their livelihood was assured; their bread and their robe were safe; they pandered to no market, for they cared for no patron." Hence their art was "not a chattel to be bought, but an inspired language in which they communed with God . . . and they expressed a poetry in the stones they carved which far transcended words." Later, on the other hand, the artist became "the creature of a commercial market, even as the Greek was sold as a slave to the plutocrat of Rome," with the result that architecture came to be ruled by money rather than miracle, painting gravitated to portraiture, poetry slacked off into prose, and a vast conclusion was attained (the book's penultimate paragraph):

> No poetry can bloom in the arid modern soil, the drama has died, and the patrons of art are no longer even conscious of shame at profaning the most sacred of ideals. The ecstatic dream, which some 12th century monk cut into the stones of the sanctuary hallowed by the presence of his God, is reproduced to bedizen a warehouse; or the plan of an abbey, which Saint Hugh may have consecrated, is adapted to a railway station.

Henry would now write *Mont-Saint-Michel and Chartres,* with the same theme lurking in it, though with the money side played down. With one part of his mind he would present an impressive theory of force for medieval society, with another part he prepared to take on modernity.

He did so just at the turn of the century, holed up in Paris like a monk himself, elaborating on the chapter and what he had encouraged Brooks himself to say, meanwhile setting the stage for a comparison, in *The Education,* between thirteenth-century unity and twentieth-century multiplicity.

But first, back to *Mont-Saint-Michel and Chartres.* It has a deceptive, guidebook aura about it that is strengthened by Adams's pretense that he is writing it for his beloved niece, as if she were a young tourist in France and he, though a tourist himself, acting as an aged cicerone. It is not, however, *intended* as a guidebook. Its detail is steadily marshaled away from the miscellaneousness that tourism encourages to its social and spiritual meaning. For with *Mont-Saint-Michel and Chartres,* Adams puts his past behind him as a dutiful facts-historian. He even ridicules "the irritating demand for literal exactness and perfectly straight lines which lights up every truly American eye," though he himself meets the demand with thoroughness (providing, for example, in a paragraph, a complete anthropological history of the Virgin Mary's rise to power). The experience of working with Brooks on historical cycles has given him new wings for the lofty, even as he piles up scholarly detail, leaving out no flèche or cathedral window in all France. Thematically his volume proposes that the masculinity of old Normandy, as seen at Mont-Saint-Michel, was replaced by the triumphant feminism of Mary, as seen in the Chartres Cathedral. It translates the progress of two architectural styles into an inclusive historical *motif*—from stone to the spiritual progress of an age.

Clover biographer Friedrich has suggested that the volume is psychologically based in Adams's relations with Clover. He has Clover playing the role for Adams that the Virgin Mary played for thirteenth-century France. He may well be right, but my sense of the book is that its private psychological content is a subordinate content at best and that Adams's own conscious intent is what deserves our respect. If it is a psychological study it is primarily a study of a people, not a person; the personal connections have only peripheral relevance, particularly since the world being described is not Adams's own, as in the later *The Education.* But in any event, as a monograph reaching for the spirit of a whole people, it is a great experiment in locating simple meaning amidst the chaos of fact. For 350 pages he builds a case for approximately a century and a half of female dominance that left life for the French male permanently "a little flat." We see the male forces of reason and justice made "ridiculous." The male becomes "docile"; he becomes her man. She owns him "as though he were her child."[11]

Clearly *Mont-Saint-Michel and Chartres* became the base upon which *The Education* was built, for in *The Education* the energy of the Virgin's ancient world is set against that of the world of the Dynamo. In the latter world, however, Henry is speaking of his own world and of his relation to it. *The Education* is personal as the earlier volume was not, even though it is in the third person and omits the Clover years. It is also, as *Mont-Saint-Michel and Chartres* was not, the big interdisciplinary pronouncement that his whole past had persistently asked of him. In it he undertook to bring science, history, philosophy, and art (and money) together—and to put his third-person self in the midst of it all. He was one of the last good minds in America to try so much. The result—though it took another Adams (Charles Truslow) to say so—was "the most important autobiography that has yet been written in America."

The Education of Henry Adams was first privately printed in 1907, an edition of one hundred copies for distribution among friends, and the heavy irony pervading it may have come partly from his awareness that he was speaking to persons who shared his fatalist patrician impieties about our democracy. It is what we might now call unliterary in its main drift, being ostensibly the chronicling of a mind rather than a sensibility, yet the sensibility is present on every page. For all its high-mindedness it is a most personal, Adams book, with four generations of the White House and Lafayette Square and Harvard and half the American embassies in Europe behind it. It is scientific, but it is also petulant and snide, witty and (occasionally) warm. It is worldly and knowing—about politics, geology, money, and human greed—but it *was* also escapist, the work of one who *had* in some sense died when Clover died. It is a work that in its abstractness can be as devoid of what Allen Tate called "civilized values" as an Adams opponent might expect, yet it is also a sort of capstone to civilization. Beyond it lies the social disintegration of which brother Brooks wrote,

11. Friedrich describes Adams's own "passion for exoneration, for absolution" and sees Clover as the person to whom he really prayed: "the woman of whom he was asking (absolution) could hardly have been other than the woman he had found lying before the fireplace—Clover, dead these fifteen years." A much less persuasive psychobiographical account has Henry's grandmother on the Adams side as the crucial female. (Edward Chalfant, *Both Sides of the Ocean.*)

yet in it the disintegrating society is steadily honored. Its pieties are for a lost past but also, erratically, for an unfolding future. Its final greatness lies perhaps in its considerate confusion.

But brother Brooks could not see the greatness. His reservations about *The Education* were those of a mind that wanted answers, wanted solutions. Brooks thought his brother was selling himself cheap as a thinker in it, Henry being in his eyes the master historian of the age and so he said later that he preferred, to *The Education,* Henry's last essays, assembled (by Brooks himself) under the title *The Degradation of Democratic Dogma,* in which Henry displayed less irony and levity and was not so clearly a defeated ego. For *The Education* is indeed the record of the end of a line.

But as such it is immense. It is a great early model for the literary negations of upcoming moderns, works like *The Waste Land* and *A Farewell to Arms,* but it is intellectually more spacious than any of its successors. It is the story of an education in failure, told by one who knew most of the varieties of failure except poverty, starting with the failures of John and then John Quincy Adams[12] in the White House, and working up to the multiple failures of Henry himself, as public servant, as private soul and, chiefly, as thinker. For he insisted that his greatest failure was the last. *The Education* is his own sad story here, and by extension the sad story of the failure of minds *like* his, confronting the twentieth century.

He had discovered, first, the incapacity of a mind—even a middling good mind—to keep up with what it had to know in the world of 1900, and second, the helplessness of any mind, good or bad, to confront successfully all the *mindless* forces—the controlling influences—around it. Particularly he had discovered that *his* kind of mind, a mind of the Enlightenment, was a cooked goose.

He belabored these deficiencies on nearly every page (and thus annoyed Brooks), saying that he had no brains for mathematics, though the new sciences demanded mathematics of him, saying that he had no common touch, yet the age demanded more and more Andrew Jacksons, saying in effect that he was incapacitated *because* he was an Adams.

In one of the most moving, but also snobbish and racist, passages

12. John Adams, as noted earlier, became celebrated for his unpopularity. John Quincy dreamed futilely of bringing science to the service of a new national order.

in the book he compared himself unfavorably with some "furtive Yacoob or Ysaac" fresh from the Polish ghetto, who entered this country "snarling a weird Yiddish to the officers of the customs," but who
had "a keener instinct, an intenser energy, and a freer hand than he,"
he who was "an American of Americans, with Heaven knows how
many Puritans and Patriots behind him." He found little consolation
in observing that he was probably less ill-fitted than his own father
had been, an ornament from another age who "could scarcely have
earned five dollars a day in any modern industry."[13] The new Americans like "Yacoob" were stronger, though they "had no time for thought"
and did not like men "who took their ideas and methods from abstract
theories of history, philosophy or theology." They were the stronger
for their "deficiencies," knowing enough to know that "their world
was one of energies quite new." Henry knew of those energies only
vicariously, across an immense cultural gap.

Then, aside from his many private deficiencies, there were the
deficiencies of his profession, history. The historians, he announced,
were a hundred years behind the scientists, with the result that history
had become "less instructive than Walter Scott and Alexander Dumas."
The scientists, like Henry, liked to inspect the world's engine rooms.
They were students of force; therefore, Henry was a student of theirs.
He had started his science studies with evolution, particularly geology, choosing it because he felt himself "hardly trained to follow Darwin's evidences" in the more difficult sciences. Geology had "wrecked

---

13. For psychobiographers, Henry's comments on his father can readily be taken
as indicative of hidden conflict between the two men. The father is presented as an
educator, not a parent, and described as a mind, not a person. Within these limits,
however, Henry is a reasonably thorough analyst of their relationship. He could be
thoroughly derogatory of him, as in this passage: "His memory was hardly above the
average; his mind was not bold like his grandfather's or restless like his father's, or
imaginative and oratorical—still less mathematical; but it worked in singular perfection, admirable self-restraint, and instinctive mastery of form. Within its range it was
a model."

Henry did not, however, fault his father any more than himself, and of their adult
relationship when he was performing a difficult filial service in wartime as his father's
secretary, he could say objectively that the situation made it necessary for him to
"imitate his father and hold his tongue," adding that he carried the imitation to the
point of believing in it, when he should have been able to imagine that the father
"might make a mistake." In other words Henry was at least capable, psychoanalytically, of bringing forth, after the fact, some of his complicated ambivalence about
Charles Francis, Sr.

the Garden of Eden" for him and sent him on to make friends of a number of American geologists, notably Clarence King and John Wesley Powell, and to make geology an extension of history for him. (It was also a constant source of metaphor for him in his failures, he being an American species that he saw becoming extinct.) Yet even after his "conversion" he retained his humanist suspicions about scientists, and though he could feel, as Lord Snow would feel later, that his colleagues in the humanities were ignoramuses in comparison with physicists, he was not sold on the physicists either, not at least until his final phase (in *The Degradation of Democratic Dogma*). In his most human moments he kept discovering what it seems always necessary for intellectual specialists to discover, that those in other fields upon whom he had come to rely were imperfect too.

The career of his friend Clarence King was the greatest of his disappointments among scientists (and is well summed up in O'Toole's *Five of Hearts*). King swam into Henry's life in the sixties, a warm, energetic atheist who was given a grant by Congress to explore, geologically, a large section of the Rockies, and whose career Henry followed closely—also going on expeditions with him—for thirty years. King was not only a good geologist, but he was literary too, wrote an eloquent prose (excerpts from his writings about the West still appear in Freshman Composition texts), and was at the time thought by some to have been the author of Henry's novel *Democracy*. In *The Education* Henry said of King that in his combining of practical skills with old-fashioned wisdom he seemed the ideal American, one of the very few born into the modern world to see truly. Then King showed how truly he could see by living a troubled secret married life in Brooklyn with a black woman, becoming extraordinarily improvident and going (temporarily) insane. By such events was Henry educated, learning, he said, that the most orderly scientific education was no guard against the disorder of an America run by blind money.

Events like the King tragedy drove Henry into the refuge of irony as he continued to perform his intellectual chores in the only way that he, an old man of the Enlightenment, knew how. Half of *The Education* is devoted to bitter commentary on the simple incapacity of most persons to *be* educated, and the other half is devoted to an equally bitter pill: when an education came, it was an education in darkness, the darkness of blind force. "Nihilism had no bottom." Here, surely, is the final impiety.

As a scientist with high ideals, John Quincy Adams had been perhaps the first, among Adamses, to suffer from the discovery that reason and light were not to lead the nation. Before he made this discovery he had faith that "a volume of energy lay stored within the union" and that a good administrator could develop that energy and direct it toward the public good. Then he found that the energy was always out of control, that order was always subordinated to self-interest, and that the subordination always created new catastrophes. Henry, following grandfather's lead, went down the years discovering that influences rather than leaders ran the country; a good man could not be kept in office, and as John Quincy Adams had put it, the best thing to do with a congressman was to treat him like a hog and hit him on the nose with a stick.

Henry even went a bit further than his grandfather. He found that the world *beyond* the nation was running without leaders too. In educating himself to chaos he shuttled between international relations and science, everywhere discovering that "chaos was the law of nature; order was the dream of man." In international relations he found rough beasts slouching everywhere but particularly in Russia, the great new "mass" that even before the revolution simply refused to fit into the old order of nations. He could be patriotic, even imperialistic about his own country when it achieved "mass," as it did in the Spanish-American War, but he saw the general drift of international affairs as downward into democracy (or socialism) and militarism. And while he was radical enough to know a rough beast when he saw one, he could not dredge up any sympathy for one. Particularly he could not sympathize with Marx, though Marx had said, he thought, good things about money. Of Marxism he said (these were his kindest words) that "some narrow trait of the New England nature seemed to blight" it for him. If he had investigated his feelings further on the subject he might have noticed that his "narrow trait" was a deep respect for property and men of property. Against all his best pessimism he kept expecting that a fine social order would somehow proceed (scientifically) out of men of property. Thus, despite early high hopes for a science of evaluating democratic humanity, he was not able to develop a faith in consensus, in the divine average, in the common man. Samuels reports that Henry even agreed with John Hay that unions were vicious, and he believed with the most popular capitalist-Darwinian of the day, sociologist Charles Sumner of Yale, that "a drunkard in the gutter is exactly where he ought to be." But when among the country's leaders he found not one effectual statesman of order, but instead dozens of rich bankers of disorder, he was still not attracted to a Marxist alternative. Instead he was persuaded of an absence of alternatives. For what he thought he had learned from studying geology, and then trying to improve his mathematics and physics, was oddly political. It was that rough beasts were destined, by universal laws of force, to take leadership away from the patricians. That shift was not, for his orderly mind, a shift of leaders but a shift from leadership to anarchy.

It was also a shift, he noted, to hard science, as a result of discoveries—like the computer!—the human mind wasn't ready for. When in the early nineties his friend Samuel Langley escorted him through a hall full of dynamos and he heard the strange hum, "he began to feel the forty-foot dynamos as a moral force, much as the early Christians felt the Cross," but after contemplating the force in the marketplace, in Washington, and in his own lagging scientific mind for a few years, he seems to have decided that it was the wrong moral. Certainly it was anti-Adams since it put purposelessness—the Adams's eternal enemy—at the heart of society and the universe.

What to do? He had to spend the rest of his life trying to discover the orderly, unified *process* of purposelessness.

First it was with his brother Brooks's grand economic cycles that he did his charting, trying to do all history in terms of vectors of economic forces. Then, meditating further on the hum of the dynamo, he decided that force could not be so restricted, and began to look elsewhere for chaos, writing Brooks: "Your economical law of History is, or ought to be, an Energetic Law of History. . . . Please give up that profoundly unscientific jabber of the newspapers about MONEY in capital letters. What I see is POWER in capitals also. You may abolish money and all its machinery, the Power will still be there."[14]

Soon he was working out a law of acceleration for human affairs, in which human knowledge obeyed pulls and pushes like an object in space, sometimes achieving status and sometimes moving to imbal-

14. Similarly Ezra Pound, after decades blaming usury for the world's ills, decided in old age that his complaints had been misdirected. The real trouble was simply human greed.

ance with all the troubled speed that Henry's own mind—faced with a novelty like the discovery of radiation—moved. He then suggested that from such mental motion human history received its prime motive power. As he put it in *The Education,* "The image needed here is that of a new center, or preponderating mass, artificially introduced on earth in the midst of a system of attractive forces that previously made their own equilibrium, and constantly induced to accelerate its motion till it shall establish a new equilibrium." The new mass he was talking about was not Russia or the dynamo, but simply knowledge itself, new knowledge suddenly being acquired for which human minds were not ready. With a little mathematical fiddling at the end of *The Education* he was able to announce, momentarily, that nineteenth-century minds *might* be ready by the year 1938—that is, one hundred years after his own birth—since by then they *might* have come to comprehend the dynamo's hum, radiation, all the rest. That would be nice, wouldn't it? Then he and his friends King and Hay would be able to revisit from the grave "a world that sensitive and timid creatures could regard without a shudder."

But on a different occasion Samuels reports that he had said, "If I could live to the end of my century—1938—I am sure I should see the silly bubble explode." And the pessimism was more native to him than the idyll. He was not good at being a utopian, and he was becoming convinced that "the scientific lawgivers of unity," whom he had hoped to emulate, were off the mark too. Soon he would indulge a more complicated arithmetic and declare 1938 too far down the road for the bubble's explosion.

Perhaps it was partly the unreal happy ending to *The Education* that Brooks took to be undesirable levity, but the book was full of levity elsewhere also, as was Henry himself in his years writing it. By then he was a wit on a grand scale, a joker at the expense of the universe. His specialty was black humor about the day of judgement, and though he grieved in an ordinary human way about private death he became an ideological fan of total extinction. Perhaps it was not so much levity as decadence, it being a world-weariness like his ancient melancholic humor, a weariness best indulged by the well-to-do.

And he was decadently world-weary in other ways also, most especially in his wanderings. His excuse for wandering was nearly always education, but education could hardly have been more extravagantly served. To do his stocktaking of vanished civilizations (while

Brooks was stimulating him with his *Law of Civilization and Decay*) he was driven to visit Cairo, Thebes, Baalbek, Damascus, Smyrna, and Ephesus. And to keep up with American affairs he had to be thousands of miles away from them, so that when the *Maine* was sunk at Havana he could write eloquent letters home about it from the upper Nile, and when McKinley was assassinated he could be shocked—not by the death, but by the accession of Roosevelt—from amidst the Scandinavian fjords. The word "decadent" does not seem too strong. After just one drab winter in Washington amid his endless travels he wrote, "I want to go-go-go-anywhere-to the devil-Sicily-Russia-Siberia-China-only keep going."

What kept him from becoming the keeper of a post-Clover salon in exotic places was, it would seem, his writing. To that he was a slave, for that he retained his puritan work ethic, and with that he was steadily saved. Yet after *The Education* there were no more large-scale writing projects on his agenda. There remained correspondence with relatives and a good handful of intellectual friends, and there remained also the writing of a short book about a poet, Bay Lodge, who had died young; but beyond these was left to him only the obligation to put down his last and gloomiest thoughts. The thoughts would occupy only a couple of essays, but the essays were ones that drove his aged mind into the depths of the disciplines with which he had always had trouble, physics and mathematics, and that made him convincingly and forever a "degradationist." The first essay was his "Rule of Phase Applied to History"; the second (not to be confused with his earlier letter to the AMA) his "Letter to American Teachers of History."

In writing these essays he did what he had done with *The Education;* he addressed them to friends and colleagues, that is, to his own chosen elite. He had always been particular about maintaining his high isolation from low thoughts, not wanting his name to be identified with novels, and favoring private printings of his more serious work. When the private edition of *The Education* appeared, a commercial editor got hold of a copy and urged a public edition on him. He said no and added, in his reply to the editor, words that Pound might have written a decade or so later, "I am in hopes a kind of esoteric literary art may survive, the freer and happier for the sense of privacy and abandon." Yet oddly—and the oddness came to reside in Pound too—he did not write down his esoterica in a private journal.

He remained a world-saver even as he prophesied the world's end. He clearly *hoped* that he and his readers would have enough force and mass to help save humans, though he told himself and them that he and they had none. Both the final essays show the undying missionary in him.

In the "phases" he enlarged upon his cyclic theories. What he did chiefly was draw an elaborate analogy between laws of force in the physical universe and laws of force in human society. As a degradationist he was now opposed to happy Darwinians like Herbert Spencer and other Victorian apostles of progress, and he placed his faith in the Second Law of Thermodynamics, the one that purported to show how "all nature's energies were slowly converting themselves into heat and vanishing into space." He believed that "vital energy obeys the law of thermal energy," and to back himself up he borrowed notions from a Yale physicist, Willard Gibbs, proposing the presence of a series of stages in the degradation process. He applied the stages to thought itself: "In this long and—for our purposes—infinite stretch of time, the substance called Thought has—like the substance called water or gas—passed through a variety of phases, or changes, or states of equilibrium."

It was positivist Auguste Comte who had suggested the analogy to him, saying that humanity's thought movement had been, historically, from the theological to the metaphysical to the positivist. Now Henry was working on his own version of Comte, and trying to do so with the mathematics of Gibbs at his elbow. He discovered, or thought he had, that the religious phase had lasted enormously long—right up to 1600—and that the following phase (which he called not metaphysical but mechanical) had lasted only three centuries. By computing the ratio between the first two phases he came up with the bad news that the third phase—which he called the electric phase—would last only $17\frac{1}{2}$ years, and would be followed by a fourth phase—which he called the ethereal phase—that would last just 4 years. He was talking, remember, about phases of thought: that is, he was trying to measure the possible intake of the human mind, what it was capable of coping with in the different phases, and his computations revealed to him that thought would be brought "to the limit of its possibilities by 1921." He added, "It may well be!" but then became generous and allowed that he might have cut phase two a bit short. If so, human thought had openings up to 2025.

Wild? Yes, but the computations were wilder than the general scheme. In effect, he was trying to formulate a law to explain the decay of his own mind, the mind that was an Adams mind and an historian's mind—and of course also a literary mind. He was trying to explain why, in 1910, his kind of mind had to defer to the mind of the physicist. In his "phase" essay he observed, "The future of Thought, and therefore of History, lies in the hands of the physicists, and that the future historian must seek his education in the world of mathematical physics." He added, "Nothing can be expected from further study on the old lines," and having made this discovery he was now ready to pass it on to his fellow historians.

In his "Letter to American Teachers of History" he did. He told them that they were in danger of becoming extinct if they did not listen to the physicists, but he went so far beyond that with his pessimism that most of them must have noted that they were in danger of extinction anyway. It was not enough for him to note that as a degradationist he was a lonely figure in history. He had to go on to say that he was opposed as well by "the energies of government, of society, of socialism, of nearly all literature and art, as well as hope, and whatever was left of instinct—all striving to illustrate not the Descent but the Ascent of Man," but that all this opposition did little to disturb what he called the lugubrious facts. These facts as he presented them consisted of quotations from learned scientists and social scientists purporting to demonstrate that the Second Law of Thermodynamics was hard at work. The sun, which had once had the diameter of Mercury's orbit, was condensing rapidly. Glaciers were moving out from the poles, and would push mankind steadily toward the equator. And human society was losing its heat energy too; it was doing what de Toqueville had prophesied for it, leveling off. It was not only heading for the age of the common man but it was, especially in its cities, exhibiting "a constantly diminishing vitality." Similarly, man as an organism was diminishing in vitality. He was following all the extinct species into oblivion by overspecialization. And here again he provided the magic date: 1921. Specialization, then, plus diminishing energy, plus increasing uniformity of conditions and of mind—all these led into the dark.

Remarkably, after such seductive gloom, he ended his "letter" modestly on an interdisciplinarian's messianic note:

> The department of history needs to concert with the departments of biology, sociology and psychology some common formula or figure to

serve their students as a working model for their study of the vital energies; and this figure must be brought into accord with the figures or formulas used by the department of physics and mechanics to serve their students as models for the working of physico-chemical and mechanical energies.

That conclusion would have been comparable to proposing the formation of an academic Committee for Dealing with Judgement Day if, in his last sentence, he had not rushed, characteristically, into irony. He said that "a complete solution" seemed "to call for the aid of another Newton."

After the history letter Henry lived another eight years. In that time he did not write anything of consequence, but he remained witty and fastidiously sour until near the end. One of his late remarks was his famous grumble to George Santayana: "So you are trying to teach philosophy at Harvard. I once tried to teach history there but it can't be done. It isn't really possible to teach anything." He also summed up his "phases" essay for a former student by telling him that it was "a scientific demonstration that Socialism, Collectivism, Humanitarianism, Universalism, Philanthropism and every other ism has come, and is the End, and there is nothing possible beyond, and they can all go play, and, on the whole, baseball is best." (Could this have been where Daniel Bell, reading, was stricken with illumination and decided to write his book, *The End of Ideology*?) Finally, he reported in a letter that he had talked with a fly in Rock Creek Park, saying to the fly, "Fly! do you want to tell me the truth about yourself?" And the fly had replied, eighty-seven times, "You be damned." He died among nieces, and his last words, according to Samuels, were to niece Elizabeth Adams and were benevolent: "Good night, my dear."

To look at this strange intellect now is to wonder how so many contradictions of modern thought could be contracted within it. It was simultaneously a traditional literary mind, a modern scientific mind, and an eighteenth-century political mind. With a slight twist of some characterological dial Henry could have been the physicist, or sociologist, or political scientist he wanted his fellow historians to be and have moved across campus to a high window where he could glower down on the humanities. Yet with another twist he could have been a modern poet.

Ezra Pound and T. S. Eliot were of course attracted to him, and

to brother Brooks, as thinkers, not poets, and it was Adamsian thinking that lay behind the most characteristic and distinctive property of
their poetry, its movement back and forth between old cultures and
new. As students of the Adamses' brand of Toryism they learned how
to take stock of vanished generations, and that learning led their poetry to the strange juxtapositions that marked, particularly, the *Cantos* and *The Waste Land*. Pound and Eliot ended their careers with the
ambiguous label of modernists for such synthesizing, while Henry
ended as an ambiguous but entrenched degradationist, struggling
with Willard Gibbs's phase law.

Why such different destinies? One reason that comes to mind is
that the Adamses missed out on some of the currents of modernity
that Pound and Eliot, coming slightly later and living among artists
rather than historians and scientists, found themselves influenced by,
the currents for instance of symbolism and *vers libre*. Yet that reason
is unconvincing. As Samuels notes, Henry's use of the Virgin and Dynamo as key symbols may be attributed in part to his rather restricted
interest in the French symbolist movement—for he seems to have
been au courant with most of the art of the time. Samuels makes the
further point that when Saint Gaudens completed the memorial to
Clover in Rock Creek Cemetery that Henry had commissioned, Henry
was full of contempt for those who, finding it wordless and unexpli-
cated at its base, wished to label it "Despair" or "Grief." He would
not, says Samuels, "affix a label to it but insisted that it should pose its
enigma directly to every beholder"—a sound symbolist position.
Given such sentiments he could readily, it would seem, have become
far more impressionist and subjective in his writings than he did become. What could have held him back?

Put the hypothetical question aside and consider for a moment
how far he *was* held back, in an actual poem, his "Buddha and Brahma,"
written in 1895 in the islands but not published until 1915 (in the *Yale
Review*). He composed it, he wrote to John Hay, to while away "a
tedious day or two," adding, "Perhaps I was a little bored by the calm
of the tropical sea, or perhaps it was the greater calm of the Buddha
that bored me." Whatever the cause, the resultant poem was an eight-
page philosophical parable in loose but competent iambic, in which
an oriental idealist and an oriental pragmatic materialist were set
against each other in dialectical combat, and the victory given to the
materialist. The resolution is of no consequence here, though it sug-

gests that even out in the islands, with the universe spread around and above him, Henry was more impressed by Force than by Mind. It is his *handling* of the poem that is, at this distance, striking. The poem is a straightforward narrative with continuous attention to clarity and coherence. It is a model of the kind of prose statement in verse that all the modernists, beginning with the symbolists, came to be in revolt against. In other words it is, except for its almost inadvertent cast of orientals, a poem of the Enlightenment, a pious poem of reason, a poem displaying formal faith in a universal order extending from gods down to verse.

What made him insist upon such strenuous prose order even as he was writing of the dominance of blind force? The answer can only be what all the answers to all the major questions about Henry come down to: he was an Adams. An Adams could *only* be a man of reason, a man of order. He could *only* keep the faith and do so against the evidence presented him by his own thoughts.

Obviously Pound and Eliot had no such imperative (though each had a good bit of New England in him). They could be intellectually but not spiritually with Henry since Henry's spirit was, after all, busy standing against his intellect. Henry could be in the vanguard of modern thought and profess to believe with the modernists that he was "a weak phenomenon in the universal order" (as Laforgue wrote), but he could not write poems as if he were a weak phenomenon. No, he had to write poems as if he were in charge. If there is any message in the insistent fragmentation of Eliot and Pound it is a message about the limits of order, a message about *poetic* limits, a message announcing that the poet is conditioned by forces beyond him. Henry also asserted that he was so conditioned, but the orderliness of his writings betrayed him.

And that is why he appears, now, as so eccentric a force himself. Despite his late-life degradationism he maintained to the end the Adams respect for order, social and intellectual, that he inherited. I can only conclude that he did indeed believe in Mind, as the following curious paragraph about himself (early in *The Education*) keeps insisting. No psychobiographer is apt to think that the passage shows an awareness of his own character's "real content"—it never seeps down *below* mind—but I believe it does. The italics are mine.

> He finished school, not very brilliantly, but without finding fault with the *sum* of his knowledge. Probably he *knew* more than his father, or his

grandfather, or his great grandfather had *known* at sixteen years old. Only on looking back, fifty years later, at his own figure in 1854, and *pondering* on the needs of the twentieth century, he *wondered* whether, on the whole, the boy stood nearer to the *thought* of 1904, or to that of the year 1. He *found himself* unable to give a clear answer. The *calculation* was clouded by the undetermined values of twentieth century *thought,* but the story (in *The Education* itself) will show his *reasons* for *thinking* that, in essentials like religion, ethics, philosophy, in history, literature, art; in the *concepts* of all science except perhaps mathematics, the American boy of 1854 stood nearer the year 1 than the year 1900.

TWO

Jack London's Best-Seller Impieties

Most of Jack London's heroes have a way of looking like Jack himself, or one of him. He was a mirror writer, though the mirror could be like the wiggly mirrors in fun houses. The hero of his novel *Martin Eden* (1909), written in mid-career, may be his best-known and least-wiggly *human* fiction, so he is a useful figure with whom to begin here the now-familiar search for the real Jack. At the beginning of the novel Martin is admitted by a servant to the front hall of a stately mansion where he does not know what to do with his hat. He starts to stuff it in his pocket, but the servant catches him and takes it from him, making Martin think, "He understands. He'll see me through the night." From the hat down Martin is no Adams.[1]

Martin is not only ignorant about what to do with hats in stately mansions, but he is also physically awkward in such places, with a tendency to knock over delicate objects and to walk "uncouthly." In

1. There have been several biographies, including one by his daughter Joan, *London and His Times,* 1939, reprint (Seattle: University of Washington Press, 1968). Perhaps the earliest is Irving Stone's *Sailor on Horseback* (Boston: Houghton Mifflin, 1938); followed by Philip S. Foner's *Jack London: American Rebel* (New York: Citadel Press, 1947); Richard O'Connor's *Jack London: A Biography* (Boston: Little Brown, 1964); and, most recently in my readings, Andrew Sinclair's *Jack* (New York: Harper & Row, 1977), which contains a reasonably complete biography, including a list of three presumably *complete* bibliographies. There has even been, and perhaps still is, a journal for admirers, the *Jack London Newsletter.* Many of his novels are close to autobiography, and the late novel *The Valley of the Moon* is a good source for episodes in his early life. The two directly autobiographical works are *The Road* and *John Barleycorn,* both of which are to be found in *The Bodley Head Jack London,* ed. Arthur Galder-Marshall (London: Bodley Head Press, 1963). Also available now is a four-volume edition of *The Letters of Jack London,* ed. Earle Labor, Robert C. Leitz III, and I. Milo Shephard (Stanford, Calif.: Stanford University Press, 1988). In the first volume of the latter are his letters to a poet friend, Cloudsley Johns, which I found most useful.

the mansion he feels ill at ease, since he has been working for a living since age eleven (he is now twenty) and been bred up in "forecastles and stokeholes, camps and beaches, jails and boozing dens, fever hospitals and slum streets." At the same time he is, in his untutored way, a lover of beauty, and as he wanders about in the mansion, he observes its landscape paintings with delight, fingers admiringly the leather covers of the books on the tables, and even picks up one of the books and peruses it. It is Swinburne. He reads a few lines and proposes to himself that he procure a copy of the Swinburne person's book at the free library.

The beauty of Swinburne—whose name Martin pronounces "Swineburn" until corrected—is soon supplemented in the mansion's parlor by a beautiful girl. She is not only beautiful but cultured, being knowledgeable about Swinburne and much else. Martin likes her tremendously, though he is embarrassed by his inelegance in her presence, and she likes Martin tremendously too, likes him because he is very masculine and serious. Soon they are talking about Swinburne, who turns out to be not quite beautiful *enough* for the girl's tastes. Together they dwell upon the beauty of poetry in general until Martin, feeling most humble, says, "I guess the real facts is that I don't know nothin' much about such things. It ain't in my class." The girl surveys his muscles and agrees with him: "I think you could make it in—in your class. You are very strong."

In Jack London's real life—according to Jack—he started to work for a living at eleven, put in time in forecastles, stokeholes, and the rest, learned much of what he knew at the Oakland Free Library (where he discovered "all the great world beyond the skyline"), had his grammar and manners polished by a cultivated woman three years his senior, appeared to many who knew him in his youth as a rough beast, yet combined the roughness with intelligence and sensitivity.

In real life he also professed great admiration for poetic beauty, and aside from writing a few well-made little poems (a truncated villanelle is included here later), he even lectured the real "Swinburne girl"'s brother one summer—Jack was twenty-three—on the intricacies of prosody.

Most important, in real life he must have had an ego equal to Martin's and must have dreamed of being a Martin, or he would not have described his fictional mate so grandly. Like most of Jack's mirror-males Martin Eden was an amazing physical specimen (Jack was

5 feet 7 inches and 165 pounds), and he was a mental powerhouse too—and full of soul. He had the "lips of a fighter and lover," lips that "could taste the sweetness of life with relish, and could put the sweetness aside and command life." He had eyes that flashed, rough hands that reached for delicacy. And even before he came to command the language he could express himself with such power that those who listened to him "saw with his eyes what he had seen." Yes, he was a natural, with the "leap and pulse of life" in him behind the "ill-fitting clothes" and "sun-burned face." There was no stopping him. Or Jack. Yet Martin, like Jack, often thought of his humble origins, and Jack certainly doubted, like Martin, that he was born to rise to culture and light: "You belong to the legions of toil, with all that is low and vulgar, and unbeautiful. You belong with the oxen and drudges, in dirty surroundings among smells and stenches. There are the potatoes now. Those potatoes are rotting. Smell them, damn you, smell them."

By the time of *Martin Eden,* thirty-year-old Jack had written some of his best-known stories and had become a repetitive mythologist about his own heights and depths. He had published twenty books in less than ten years, and he would write nearly as many more in the next seven. In all of them he drew on his own experience, enlarging and displacing the "real life" at will, but doing little damage to the self core. Fantasizing about that core had become, as it were, his profession. Thus did he exploit his life, yet also escape it.

A rich life it was, to exploit. Childhood poverty helped make him a breadwinner, a traveler, and a rebel earlier in life than any other American writer I can think of. By the time of *Martin Eden,* Jack had been a wage slave (he liked that phrase), a sailor, a boxer, a hobo, a gold rush prospector, a socialist political candidate, a big-time reporter, and much else, including an alcoholic—and he was about to become an environmentalist. Even as a writer and drinker he was always in motion. There was nothing sedentary about him, and his activism slopped over into his mental life with strenuous mental results. Most of his heroes were great rationalists who could sway large audiences and argue Socrates into a corner. Dialectic was like big-league sports for them, and though they professed, like Jack, to be great readers too, a modern mind reading *about* them is apt to wonder how they had time to sit quietly someplace with a book.

Or with themselves, for introspection—the non-Walter Mitty kind—had little place in Jack's early works. I find its first conspicuous presence early in *The Sea Wolf* (1905). It is characteristic that Jack said of his early radicalism that he had been made into a Socialist, "albeit an unscientific one," not by reading Marx but by being put in the Erie County jail.

His mother was the black-sheep daughter of an Ohio engineer with money (she had run away at sixteen). His stepfather was "a market gardener, a sturdy independent, relying on his green fingers until he was reduced to wage slavery." And the editor of *The Bodley Head Jack London,* Arthur Calder-Marshall, characterized Jack's supposed real father as "no horny-handed member of the toiling classes" but an "Irish vagabond and hokum peddler" who had written a book on astrology. Biographers have disagreed about the talents of the latter, whose name was Chaney; most of them are inclined to think of him as a fraud, but Irving Stone describes him as honorable and erudite, with "a clear, forceful and pleasing style." At least all of them seem to have agreed—and so, publicly, did the mother—that he was Jack's father. Only Jack, and possibly his father, questioned the Chaney paternity.

What is sure is that the mother was not happy about the pregnancy and tried to commit suicide just before Jack's birth. After the birth, on January 12, 1876, she was obliged to turn the nursing of the child over to a Negro woman, Mammy Jenny, and thereafter she was a mother for whom the son had respect but little love. She was a short, domineering neurotic who had been balded and stunted by a childhood disease, wore a wig and child-sized shoes, attended seances, had mystic fits, was a good cook and an accomplished spender of money, usually on lottery tickets. In the year of Jack's birth she met and married one John London.

Soon the new family—now with three children, for John London brought to the marriage two motherless daughters—set out to make a go of life by leaving the city. They leased sixty acres of land to raise potatoes and then twenty acres more for corn and other vegetables, and then they tried starting a chicken ranch, and that didn't work either. In his writings Jack said little of those early years—though he did mention the rotten potatoes—but the memories he passed on were of penury and constant motion. He was in a cluttered room, somebody outside was beating a carpet, and he put his hands to his ears and cried. Or he was trying to feed a small dog, and suddenly, a St. Bernard entered left front, gobbled up the small dog's meal, and departed. Or he was in a schoolroom, famished, stealing a meal from a girl's lunch basket. What he put down always had meaning, always led somewhere—he was an orderly narrator—but between the lines was aimlessness. Between the lines was a flickering image of parents living in darkness while the hero grew to manhood. The stepfather aged rapidly. Soon they were obliged to leave their leased acres and move back to Oakland, where their money problems became still worse. (These problems are described in the opening pages of his late-life autobiographical novel, *The Valley of the Moon.*) In Oakland the mother tried to run a boarding house, and when she failed at that, she settled into mysticism, lotteries, and occasional music teaching, while the stepfather took jobs as a night watchman. At eleven Jack suddenly found that he was the chief family supporter, with a paper route and a job in a bowling alley. At fifteen he worked in a canning factory—never, he insisted, for less than ten hours a day. He thus became a member of the toiling masses early, and hated it. In his accounts his hatred was always clear, decisive, positive. He kept walking out of the sweatshops, out of Oakland, out of family duties. He gloried in departures.

He wanted to go to sea. He had learned to sail a little skiff in San Francisco Bay, and now he became a capitalist boatman, buying for three hundred dollars an oysterboat called the *Razzle Dazzle*. He had not made the money but borrowed it from Mammy Jenny, who had been most happy to oblige. "Would she lend her 'white child' the money? *Would she?* What she had was mine." As soon as the boat was his he was out of the ten-cents-an-hour class and was his own money man. Or so he construed his change of life after the fact. In his accounts he made the change neat and clean, though it probably wasn't.

His oystering was illegal, because the oyster beds were owned by the big companies; so Jack and his friends went after them vigorously, and they fed the inspectors oysters when they came aboard. Jack was only fifteen, but he had a crew of himself and one other, usually a young man named Spider, and he became a solid member of the oyster-pirate set, consisting of a strong twenty-year-old called Young Scratch, his father, Old Scratch, Big George, Whisky Bob, French Frank, Soup Kennedy, and a few exotic others, including the Queen of the Oyster Pirates, whom Jack stole away from French Frank one summer afternoon. Oyster pirating was a good life, and there was as much as twenty-five dollars a day in it. And there was a moral lurking in it too—he always looked for a moral—since the life led him to alcohol. In this way he broached his drinking theme in the late-life, antidrink book, *John Barleycorn,* saying he grew up hating the stuff, but had learned early that to be respected as a true oyster pirate, one had to compete in paying for drinks in the saloons, after oystering.

The saloon bills made it hard for him to pay back Mammy Jenny, but he did, and did become a good sailor, and did learn what grammar school, one year of high school, and one term of college would never teach him about money: how to make it, and how not to care about keeping it. A few years after the oystering he wrote the real "Swinburne girl"—whose name was Mabel Applegarth, and who had complained to him that he was not a responsible breadwinner—that if he had followed her "conception of duty" he wouldn't have been interested in her or "Tennyson" but only "fitted to enjoy . . . a bunch of hoodlums on the street."

So he was grateful to the oyster pirates. While oyster pirating he even discovered that there was money to be made on the right side of the law. Having been arrested for oystering, he became a member of the Fish Patrol and went forth to arrest others. He was spared the shame of going after oyster pirates by being assigned to the shrimp pirates, who were mostly Chinese with long knives. Jack was very brave at rounding up the shrimp pirates, and for his pains he received as much in the sharing of fines as if he had himself been a pirate.

But when he was very old—seventeen—he decided that he wanted more of the sea than San Francisco Bay. He signed on a three-master for the real ocean, crossed the Pacific, saw aborigines, hunted seal, got drunk in Yokohama, and returned to San Francisco after half a year to discover that he was still expected to be dutiful. "When I returned from seven months at sea, what did I do with my pay day? I bought a second-hand suit, some forty-cent shirts, two fifty-cent suits of underclothes, and a second-hand coat and vest. I spent exactly seventy cents among the crowd I had known before I went to sea. The rest went to pay the debts of my father and to the family."

It was more than he could stand, having money but not much, and being obliged to turn over what he had to the cause of family. For another few years he would not know what to do about such obligations except to meet them when he could and leave town when he could. Bringing the obligations relentlessly to mind were not only the parents and stepsisters but also the "Swinburne (or Tennyson) girl."

Before long he found that he did not have to go to sea to be gone. He could hit the open road—that is, the railroads—and be gone too.

He reported that he had discovered the open road while an oyster pirate, sailing his boat up to Sacramento and listening to the slang of the "road kids and gay cats" of the railroad yards. Their talk about the "bulls" being "horstile" on the Union Pacific, their advice on how to climb on the "blind baggages," and what "mainstems" were best to "batter" became his first lesson in road travel. Then he went "over the hill" experimentally for a few days, the hill being the Sierra Nevadas. But he saved his big road experience until after his return from the Pacific, when he couldn't find a job, and unemployment had become a revolutionary cause.

Jack's sociologist daughter, Joan, wrote a biography of her father, and she has helped to fill out Jack's romantic account of the unemployment marches of 1894. The Panic of 1893 had brought them on, just as it had brought Henry Adams home from Switzerland. The Panic had not only scared the Adamses but had ruined five hundred banks and sixteen thousand businesses. Accordingly, a rich man with reformist notions named Coxey, from Masillon, Ohio, decided to march on Washington and persuade legislators to dispose of unemployment and usury. Soon he had seventeen separate armies marching or riding the rails, all aiming at reaching the Capitol by May Day, 1894. The Californian Coxey army that Jack joined, headed by Charles T. Kelley, was one of the most disciplined armies, yet like most of the others, it failed to reach Washington as a unit. Only Coxey's own Ohio army made it intact, an army of five hundred hounded through Pennsylvania and Maryland by fifty reporters. When it arrived, it marched on the Capitol and watched its leaders arrested for walking on the grass. Modern revolution in America!

Joan London's account accepts without question her father's descriptions of the deadliness of the laboring life and of the strenuousness of his rebellion against it. She became a far more orthodox Socialist than he, but she was a stuffy writer, and one has to go to Jack himself for the *romance* of marching on—or toward—Washington, via boxcars to Council Bluffs, on foot to Des Moines, and by boat on the Des Moines River. Jack reported that it was at Des Moines that Captain Kelley's army "swore a mighty oath that its feet were sore and that it would march no more." The result was that "Des Moines was desperate." What followed makes one of Jack's best dramas, and much of it may have even been true: "We lay in camp, made political speeches, held sacred concerts, pulled teeth, played baseball and seven-up, and ate our six thousand meals a day. And Des Moines paid for it."

The army was encamped next to the stove works, and the city came down to look at it. One of Jack's tricks, when he was being looked at, was to put on a sad face and say sadly that if he had a postage stamp he would write home to his mother. The money for the postage stamp would then appear, he would scribble, the donors would move on, and he would put on his sad face again. He was also good, he said, at collecting old clothes, and when he returned from a collecting expedition on Des Moines's expensive streets, he brought straw hats and derby hats, summer suits and winter suits, starched collars and cuffs. Daughter Joan said, "The camp roared with laughter and rude jests as some of the men paraded around in discarded long-tailed evening clothes and large-checked gamblers' suits," but Jack's prose was simpler. He said that at that point a bright idea hit Des Moines. The idea was to float the whole army down the Des Moines River. That river was not the best river for floating down, but it was a river and it flowed. It even flowed east, or at least southeast, and it flowed into the Mississippi where, if Captain Kelley saw fit, the army could continue floating.

A bright idea. And with the army consuming its 6,000 meals a day, the bright idea filled the Des Moines citizens' minds quickly. They suddenly "inaugurated," as Jack put it, "a tremendous era of shipbuilding." The citizens completed 134 ships in three days, so that the 2,000 stomachs could sail for Washington via Ottumwa and Keokuk, and possibly Hannibal.

The ships were eighteen feet by six feet by one foot. That is, they were rafts. And as they were rafts, they were just the ships for the Des Moines, the Des Moines being one foot deep most of the way to the Mississippi. They were the right ships, and they were there at the right time. The army set sail. Next day the *Des Moines Register* ran a headline, "RID OF AT LAST."

As soon as they set sail Jack was in his element; he commanded a boat and was called Sailor Jack, having been in better boats than these. In a few years he would be ready for the challenge of the Yukon, and he would canoe down the Yukon River through nineteen hundred miles of mosquitoes to the Bering Sea in nineteen days; but now it was the Des Moines. He quickly put his boat out front and aimed to keep it there.

The city of Des Moines had not only provided sixty-six thousand meals when the army was in town, but had also sent twelve thousand extra meals along in the commissary boats. Jack thought that was generous of Des Moines, a nice "precaution against famine in the wilds," but not too generous, since the army had threatened to come back if it starved. "Think what it would have meant," he said, "if we had remained at Des Moines eleven months instead of eleven days." Certainly the twelve thousand meals were not enough to last the army the length of the river. It became Jack's job, because he appointed himself to the job with his nine hustler crewmen, to be a food scout and line up rations from the river farmers for the commissary boats to the rear. Soon his scout boat was half a day ahead of the fleet, and he was busy at scouting. He was also busy caring for the survival of the fittest, the fittest being in the scout boat: "We went down the river on our own, hustling our 'chewin's', beating every boat in the fleet, and, alas that I must say it, sometimes taking possession of the stores the farm-folk had collected for the army."

Hustling their own chewin's was unkind to General Kelley, but Jack said it was not too unkind since they were careful never to take more than they thought they could get away with. They merely kept "the cream of everything." They took the tobacco, sugar, coffee, and canned goods but "resolutely refrained" from taking beans and flour. They were so well off in their scout boat that they boiled their coffee with milk and called it pale Vienna. They were so well off that General Kelley was unhappy about them.

First the general sent two strong rowers in a small boat to catch them, and "they overtook them all right but they were two and we were ten." The rowers told Jack and his crew that they were prisoners, but when Jack expressed "a disinclination" for prisonerhood, they rowed ahead to the next town to find the police. The police lay in wait to imprison them, but Jack emulated Huck Finn and slipped by the town after dark.

Then the general mastered Jack for a day by sending two horsemen forward, one on each bank, to warn the citizens of the "Jack menace." The plot worked, with the result that the "erstwhile farmers met us with the icy mitt" and brought constables and dogs to the scene. Jack tore his pants trying to climb a barbed-wire fence "with a bucket of milk in each hand." Soon he had to retreat and join the fleet. But there was dissension within the fleet, and while the head of Company L argued with the head of Company M about what to do with Jack, Jack slipped out front again, this time with two boats.

Jack's one boat had been fast because Jack ran it, and Jack's two boats were even faster, especially in the shallows, because the two together were a great scientific breakthrough for shallow-water cruising. The boats were lashed together. When they went aground, the twenty crewmen of the two boats quickly massed into one boat, letting the other boat float over; then they massed into the free boat, letting the second float over. It was athletic boating, but it was also science (Jack discovered later that Chinese boatmen, his racial enemies, had mastered the science a thousand years before) and kept them out ahead again. Once, the general, who remained angry, sent three police boats after them, but the police boats foundered in white water, while Jack's athletic boats passed over.

So Jack would have been a fine revolutionary in the unemployment army, if he could have kept at the boat-jumping all the way to Washington, and perhaps through life. After Keokuk on the Des Moines he could have boat-jumped to St. Louis and Cape Girardeau in the Mississippi River shallows; then he could have arranged to be towed up the Ohio River to Louisville and Cincinnati, there perhaps joining with a section of General Fry's army that had been towed toward, but not to, Pittsburgh (General Fry's army never made it either). Jack would have been fine if he could have come boat-jumping down the Potomac at last, over the Great Falls and into the Tidal Basin, to be met there by General Coxey's own army, cheering. But no, Jack's good days with the army were closing. And the good days of that army were closing too.

Kelley's army floated down the Mississippi as far as Hannibal, but the Mississippi was not like the Des Moines. The boats were lashed together, not in pairs but in big groups, and towed like barges. They passed Quincy—and Quincy was a rich town to plunder—but after Quincy food was scarce, morale low. Jack deserted at Hannibal because, he said, of his stomach. He was hungry; he missed the cream of everything.

And after he deserted he found that he was not interested in invading Washington. Instead he took to the rails solo, rode to Chicago, visited relatives in Michigan, rolled on to New York City. And having reached New York City he had no thoughts of rolling south to help Coxey. By then he had just Jack in his mind, and so he rolled to Niagara Falls.

At least he now felt free. He was eighteen, strong, and a master of living well with no commissary. He had nothing to worry about even if the sweatshops all closed.

Except that when he jumped off the freight train in Niagara Falls, still solo, he was arrested.

He was not arrested for walking on the grass or for being a revolutionary, but for having no hotel address. He was taken directly to court, where he was barred from speaking a word as the judge sentenced him, and sixteen others, to thirty days. "It went like clockwork, fifteen seconds to a hobo." He was handcuffed to another prisoner, clanked off to the Erie County jail, shaved, stripped, inspected, vaccinated—and then indoctrinated to a kind of life worse than that of discouraged sweatshop workers. He said later that it would "take a deep plummet to reach bottom in the Erie County pen," and though he was not there long enough to plumb that bottom, he got hints of it; he saw enough to know that at the bottom he had no rights and could be beaten, and starved, and ignored. In his one long month there he saw enough, he reported, to help him arrive at true piety in dealing with the Erie County pen, the piety that ruled his conduct as he left: "I kept my tongue between my teeth, walked softly and sneaked for Pennsylvania."

This was when Upton Sinclair, soon to be Jack's Socialist comrade, was still in school in New York City, having just begun to write potboilers (thus beating Jack into literature) but having yet to join, as Jack had, the "legions of toil" and rebellion. For Jack the jailing was not a useful literary event but his great moment of political truth—or so he thought later—when the romance of the hobo life became tarnished, and he saw the dimensions of moneylessness. He then hurried home to Oakland, where he could be found reading Babeuf, Saint Simon, Fourier, and Proudhon ("property is theft"), as well as Marx. In a reminiscence he claimed he underlined the nothing-to-lose-but-your-chains passage in the *Communist Manifesto* at this time, and it is certain that he did find himself suddenly standing and speaking— age nineteen and in high school—before workingmen in Oakland's city park. He proclaimed capitalism a form of theft.

The idea-romance continued. He was arrested again but was now in home territory, a local boy, so was released rather than jailed. The Oakland paper ran the story under "huge streamers, calling Jack 'the boy socialist.'" His fellow students were impressed. He was on his way.

But to what? It is at this point that the idea-romance runs aground, and the hero is to be seen stranded in his maturing, wondering whether he is a revolutionary or a writer. He doesn't really know about the writing yet, but he does know that whatever he is to be, he is to be in style. He is a Hollywood personality before Hollywood's time, *echt* California. California is his experience-core, where money and fame come and go faster than in other places and where any ideology picks up strange markings. To be eighteen and a world traveler and a jailbird, but in high school, and to be lecturing in the city park on the subject of capitalist thievery, to be all that is to be a fine figure of a Californian. Imagine what New Englander Henry Adams would have thought of him—but then Henry was never good in boats.

Another Californian ten years older than Jack, Lincoln Steffens, was differently stationed in life but plagued or blessed with something of the same inner drive. Son of a rich merchant, recipient of an expensive education, a promising progeny expected by the father to become a solid, money-making citizen, he was still attracted to the world of writing *cum* reform and was to be labeled, like both Jack and Upton Sinclair, one of the muckrakers (the label was devised by Theodore Roosevelt for what we might now call investigative reporters). The muck that Steffens most noisily raked was a political scandal in Minneapolis.

Then there was a third Californian, William Randolph Hearst, whom both Jack and Steffens learned to dislike, but who had the reformist spirit too, and he was for a time thought to be a true radical. As late as 1906 Jack described him with some enthusiasm, in a political novel, *The Iron Heel* (having covered the Russo-Japanese War for Hearst in 1904). But unlike Steffens and Hearst, Jack had no money to start with, and if he was politically confused, it was partly because he was still ignorant of the lives of the rich, not being one of them but wishing to be one. As he matured he suffered his upward-mobility torments right along with his socialist imperative. He spared himself little. First he decided that he was—and he was—too old for high school. In the summer of 1896, at age twenty, he crammed for college until "simultaneous equations and chemical formulas fairly oozed from his ears," took entrance exams, and was admitted to the University of California. There he worked hard for one term, carrying fifteen books about campus and looking harassed. Then he quit.

Second he found himself a series of jobs—the work-ethic call was sounding again from his family—but the last job, in a hot laundry at the same old rate of ten cents an hour, told him again that the work ethic was not for him. What did he want? He wanted freedom of course, but he also wanted real money, and he wanted to make it the rugged-individual way. He wanted to compete for it out in the money wilderness and win it like Carnegie and Rockefeller. He may have said to himself that he wanted to beat the capitalists at their own game, but he did like the game, liked it as long as it was not played as a respectable middle-class game but as a true survival game. Later he described, in Martin Eden, a man who had risen in his job to a steady thirty thousand dollars a year and community leadership, saying of him that there was something "paltry" about the man's career: "Thirty thousand a year was all right but dyspepsia and an inability to be humanly happy robbed such princely income of all its value." Jack wanted the income but not the dyspepsia.

He therefore, third, decided that he wanted to go to sea or into some enterprise with the romance of the sea. But by now he had the "Swinburne girl" to contend with as well as his parents. He admired her brains and culture, but he was perturbed that *she* was perturbed at his unwillingness to settle down. He listened to her, he nearly harkened to her, and if the big chance had not come at the right moment he might have found himself trapped with her and with her possessive mother. The chance came: the gold strike in the Yukon.

He had to go. Even his stepsister agreed, and she persuaded her husband to grubstake him.

The Yukon was perfect because it was both remote and full of gold, but it was also something of an ideological aberration for him. He had joined the Socialist Labor party officially in 1896, and he had a little red card in his wallet to prove it. He had been reading, besides Darwin and Herbert Spencer, all sorts of radicals for a Berkeley course, and he had been busy writing angry letters to the papers against Henry George's single-tax plan—he thought it far too moderate. When the Yukon rush came he had to scrap all those interests.

Joan London said in her biography that he didn't go for gold but for adventure. She was wrong. It is true that he didn't find gold when he reached the Yukon, and it is true too that he had adventures there (and between adventures he read two heavy books he had brought along, Milton and Marx), but he must have gone for gold as well as adventure because he *always* went for gold. Yet the biggest event in his Yukon experience had only indirectly to do with the gold rush. It was his first lunge for writing gold.

He kept a journal up there, and its possibilities enchanted him. He came down the Yukon River goldless and with scurvy, and arrived in Oakland with his brother-in-law's grubstake gone. But he now had words on pages, and plans for a different life.

He was penniless. He pawned his bicycle and his watch. He found no job and was hungry. He took a civil-service exam, passed it, and would have gone to work in the post office had he not then suddenly and firmly decided to be true to his journal. He borrowed a typewriter.

Later he said that he learned his writing trade in the next three years (1898–1900). Before then he had been feeling his way, muddling through, practicing. Now he was earnest, pounding at the typewriter twenty hours a day. He tried poetry, fiction, and social essays. He even concocted, with a new intellectual companion, Anna Strunsky, a novel in letter form about love between two scientific lovers. He went at his new profession as part artist and part entrepreneur, a Horatio Alger in business, burning the midnight oil.

And there was more to his discipline than hours at the typewriter. There was also boxing, fencing, putting the shot, and walking on his hands. And there was the endless mystical search for verbal facility. He left little record of *how* he learned to write—perhaps no writer ever knows—but he did say that the writing apprenticeship converted him quickly from a parlor bumbler to a cultivated man (one who knew proper English). When he described the conversion in *Martin Eden,* critics said the education happened too fast to be believed. Jack defended himself, saying it had happened to *him.*

Certainly the early Yukon stories show his fix on correctness. They were too correct for the Yukon, though the villains at least tended to be more correct than the brave heroes. The villains were effeminate, middle-class "scions of civilization" such as Carter Weatherbee and Percy Cuthbert, who couldn't row a boat or chop wood. They were "incapables." Jack arranged their affairs so they were suddenly stranded in a Yukon cabin to last out the Arctic winter. They couldn't.

Like the Kilkenny cats, they fought with each other "till neither hide, nor hair, nor yowl, was left."

Obsessively he came to describe the process of maturing—to capability or its opposite—and he made it for his heroes and for the good guys a two-stage education like his own, with the hard knocks (unknown to the Percy Cuthberts) coming first to produce capability, and the amenities second to produce beauty (and money). Also important, for the amenities, was the appearance of cultured females. Jack was mythologizing for the magazines with such plots, having an actively indecorous sex life of his own as he did; but he also had the real "Swinburne girl" as a usefully ideal emanation to refer to, plus a librarian, Ida Colbrith, who happened to be poet laureate of California. Jack was ten when Ida took over supervising his reading habits, steering him to Washington Irving and Ouida, then moving him upward to Tolstoy and Dostoyevsky. Years later he wrote her that she had been a goddess to him as a child, and in a late novel she appears prominently, spouting poetry and idealism.

Between Ida and Mabel, then—and with dialectical Anna on his sidelines—Jack as a young man must have thought he had proof that females were basic repositories of the higher things. And although it was hard to locate an ideal female in the Yukon, he managed to do so, presumably in his head. "White Silence" was typical. In that story the female was pure nobility, the daughter of an Eskimo chief. When her white mate was mortally wounded by a large white pine that happened to fall on him, silently, in the great white silence, she mushed on into the future (she was pregnant) without a tear and with the poise of an aristocrat.

Then there was the heroine of a novel written at about the same time, *A Daughter of the Snows*. She was an amazon. She had been foreshadowed in one of the earliest stories, in which "a new breed of woman" was introduced, but that woman had been Mrs. Eppingwell, the name taking much of her Darwinian strength out of her. In the novel the heroine was a Viking, Frona Welse, and she was a good trail breaker too. She liked to let men feel her muscles. She had been bred up in the northland, and as a child she had stolen a dogsled in the dead of winter, and mushed over a mountain. In her there was "no female helplessness throwing herself on the strength and chivalry of the male." She didn't mind swearing, she didn't mind sharing a tent with a strange man, she smiled when splashed by an oar, she was willing to help bail a canoe, and she could "swing clubs, and box, and fence." But she was cultivated too, and a millionaire's daughter, and could quote from Browning's poem *Paracelsus*. She obviously had twice what Mabel or Anna had, and on top of that she believed in what *some* Darwinians were believing, sexual selection. For children she wanted good strong Aryans "with bodies comely in the sight of God and muscles swelling with the promise of deeds and work." She was a scary heroine all around. If ever there was a primal force she was it, but she was an oddity among Jack's females. Most of them were like the "Swinburne girl."

His Yukon males could be equally improbable as they went at their surviving. Probably the worst selection in his first story collection, *The Son of the Wolf,* was a pop-Darwin affair that he sold to the *Atlantic Monthly.* It had in good measure the mix of contemporary ideas that were to become his staple. A bestial "thing" appeared in it along with a good deal of gore, but he also incorporated pedagogy about how to survive. The "thing" did survive. The "thing" successfully made it from "Akatan, which is in the Aleutians: Akatan, beyond Chignik, beyond Kardalak, beyond Unimak," to the Malamute Kid's cabin, and when it entered the cabin it had suffered so much that it was indeed an *it* rather than a *he.* But it was still alive, and after a few good meals it recalled its humanity:

> The thing advanced to the table. The bright flame of the slush lamp caught its eye. It was amused, and gave voice to eldritch cackle which betokened mirth. Then, suddenly, he—for it was a man—swayed back, with a hitch to his skin trousers, and began to sing a chanty, such as men lift when they swing around the capstan circle and the sea snorts in their ears.

What Jack was doing—mixing popular Darwinism with dog-sleds—was not only, as it turned out, an excellent formula for selling books, but it was also a way of literature that, at the turn of the century, seemed natural and right even for writers with weaker commercial aspirations than Jack. After all, Henry Adams himself mixed something like Jack's Darwinism into *The Education.* If *The Call of the Wild* were now to be sent around as a manuscript to New York publishers, my guess is that nobody would want it; nobody would think that such a heavy burden of philosophy and sociology could be sold to an audience—except perhaps an audience of spy buffs, looking for adventure and violence. But when it was written the mix was quite acceptable. Jack was doing the conventional thing in catching the fashionable ideas of his time and wrapping stories around them. His chief problem was that he was catching both Darwinian ideas and socialist ideas, and they were hard to mesh.

He tried to solve his problem by having the Darwinian ideas surface in a different environment from the socialist ideas. In the Yukon, he argued, the social conditions had not yet arisen that made advisable the reduction of natural competitiveness. In the Yukon it was all right for a man or a woman to flex muscles, because survival depended on muscles, on power; but in Oakland life was different. Herbert Spencer told him so. Spencer said that in man's primitive beginnings the affairs of the strong *and* the weak were worked out by having one person, group, or tribe subjugate another, and be in turn subjugated, but that in advanced cultures large consolidations became the norm instead, great national groupings within which subjugation was no longer a healthy Darwinian game, and could be a dangerous menace to the groupings. Jack took this ambiguous Spencer cue off in a socialist direction (most of the capitalists of the time thought that subjugation was perfectly fine, in Alaska, Oakland, and anywhere else) and wrote an essay, published in *Cosmopolitan* in 1900, saying that in modern society competition was destructive; cooperation was the way.

The essay was a breakthrough for him. It won a prize of two hundred dollars, and made him think he was the only Socialist in the country making money while preaching his creed. But for all that it was a lofty, portentously scholarly essay, with none of his stories' luridness, and little style. Also it said little of the intensely racial nature of the great national cooperative consolidations he imagined. In letters he wrote at the time he was more frank.

Between 1900 and 1903 he corresponded steadily with a fellow Socialist, also a writer, named Cloudsley Johns. Johns was an Anglophobe—or so Jack described him—and Jack disapproved. Jack advised him that the English were the salt of the earth. They were also, he added, the ones triumphing over the earth, and that was good. Jack liked the imperialist side of Kipling, and he felt that English triumphs were good for Americans as well as for the English, since the two cultures went together, making for the great consolidation of Anglo-Saxons that Jack was promoting. Anglo-Saxons were, he said, the best of the whites, and the whites were the best of the races. The whites had a deep fraternal feeling, white to white. As Jack put it to Johns, "Let Mr. White meet another white hemmed in by dangers from other colors—these whites will not need to know each other—they will hear the call of blood and stand back to back." When Johns continued to make doubtful noises, Jack reaffirmed the English excellence, adding that they were so because they were not afraid to say so ("No hemming or hawing; we state the bald fact. It is for the world to take or leave"). Johns must then have questioned how Jack fitted his racism to his socialism, for Jack replied firmly: "I do not believe in the universal brotherhood of man. I think I have said so before. I believe my race is the salt of the earth. I am a scientific socialist, not a utopian."

So the salts of the earth were to run their affairs cooperatively, like the Nazis to come, but fight off other colors, other races in the bush—and fight off (particularly) the Chinese at home. That, in Jack's early philosophizing, was *scientific socialism,* and when he looked in the mirror he saw himself as a leader of such enlightenment. (Only a year or so later he visited London's East End, and the English salts lost some of their savor.)

How did the Yukon fit in? The Yukon was where the Anglo-Saxons, if they became soft, could be purified, toughened up again, sometimes. The softening occurred in civilized places, came from too much luxury and too little snow, but it also came from what Jack called—sounding, as he did, rather like Brooks Adams—commercial selection. Commercial selection was wrong-way Darwinism. Adams had proposed that commercial selection put the craftiest rather than the best in charge, and now Jack proposed that commercial selection also watered the good racist blood, leading to "race prostitution" and "race deterioration" since going for a dollar was poor physical exercise for survival. He declared that such social weakness in his chosen race had to be combated by minimizing "internal competition"—that is, competition within the Anglo-Saxon nations—and making "industry yield more and more to the cooperative principle."

Of course the strong Anglo-Saxons could be betrayed by weak Anglo-Saxons, the incapables. Jack worried about *them,* and sometimes he also began to worry about his own capabilities—what would become a headache problem and a "white logic" problem for him. But usually he was self-confident, excessively so, and might have benefited from a small daily dose of incapacity. He also might well have worried more than he did about the ambiguities in his own social convictions. Aside from his racist thoughts, he was personally so competitive, during his best writing years that the Jack in the mirror looked more like Daddy Warbucks than a cooperative Socialist. Early in *Martin Eden* for instance, he described an episode in his hero's childhood that was probably from his own childhood, in which the hero at age eleven had an enemy named Cheese Face, with whom he fought so hard that they were "like two savages of the stone age." Their battling would have been ideologically correct, however, if Jack had not then had his hero bring the savage ethic with him out of the primitive childhood into the hero's own adult writing life. He had the hero give himself a private fight talk: "You licked Cheese Face and you'll lick the editors if it takes twice eleven years to do it. You've got to go on. It's to the finish, you know."

As Jack's intellectual development proceeded, so did his life with women. Mabel he abandoned early, as in *Martin Eden,* because she wanted to make him a dutiful middle-class litterateur. Anna and Bess had appeared out of the mists at about the same time, his brief Berkeley period, and they had filled his life and thoughts until about the time of the writing of *The Sea Wolf* (1904), with Anna as his ideological mate, and Bess as the one he merely married, lived with for three years, and who had his two children. After them came Charmian, though there was some apparent overlap, as well as one or two lesser female presences.

For a time at least Bess must have believed she was his mental equal and was being courted for mind as well as body. Early in the affair she typed his manuscripts, and when he proposed to her she was given to understand that if they were to marry, their marriage was to be one of "affectionate companionship." Biographer O'Connor states that they thought of themselves at the time as "free of illusion" about the romance of marriage and able therefore to "have children and devote themselves to their home and to Jack's career." Jack even introduced his racial thoughts to their proposed conjugal felicity, suggesting that they have "seven sturdy Saxon sons and seven beautiful daughters." This was the period of *The Daughter of the Snows,* when he was hipped on selective breeding, but he was patronizing even then about Bess's function, saying that she was "a comely young woman" who could bear "splendid children." Not much later, during their acrimonious divorce, biographer O'Connor reports that the word he applied was not "comely" but "stupid."

She was not stupid. She was a good mathematician and helped fumbling Berkeley students with calculus. (She had helped Jack with his entrance exams.) She had a precise mind, as Jack in some ways did not. Her trouble was that she did not reach for great concepts and syntheses. She was a clean-cut homebody, unlike Anna. During much of Jack's marriage to Bess, he and Anna were busy collaborating on a dialectical correspondence novel about love, though in their actual relationship they do not seem to have been particularly intimate until the marriage was breaking up. Ironically, it was then that Jack pushed their intimacy, meanwhile withholding from Anna the interesting news that Bess was again pregnant. When Anna found out, she was appropriately indignant—in a long letter at the time she announced (reports Andrew Sinclair) that they were now to be correspondents only—and the letters between them thereafter do show them talking mostly business and ideas. Anna's withdrawal left the road clear for Charmian, who swept Jack into marriage number two the day after his first legally ended.

But Charmian only became material for Jack's mythological mill in *The Sea Wolf,* to be published two years later. Before *The Sea Wolf,* there were three emanations of the Anna-Bess era, all published by Macmillan, where George Brett was Jack's editor: *The People of the Abyss* (his "report" on London's East End), *The Kempton-Wace Letters* (the dialectical love novel), and almost as an afterthought, *The Call of the Wild.* They are such different efforts that they point up well Jack's own uncertainties at the time, but they also show his colossal energy and ambition.

Energy? Ambition? In the deceiving way of still photos, in snapshots the young Jack London appears simply good-looking, conventional, and dull. In a shot taken just before Berkeley he is a complete naïf, wearing a high school sweater and a blank high school face. In a slightly later, young-writer picture he has his hair cropped and is staring straight at the camera, as if thinking thoughts about duty that Mabel Applegarth would have approved. In an early marriage picture he and Bess are posed standing in a calm ocean, water up to their thighs, wearing decorous old-time bathing costumes while hammily flexing their muscles. And in one other picture from the years with Bess he is caught on a couch pretending to be asleep, with one magazine open at his elbow, another above him on a pillow, and his hands clasped as if in prayer (I was reminded of eccentric promotional pictures of Truman Capote). There is no care in his posed expression, no survival urgency, no Spencerian first principles.

Many of the comments about him from early friends are of the same order, not descriptions of a superman but of a friendly, open, gregarious, nice guy. A companion in the gold rush noted piously that Jack's "companionship was refreshing, stimulating, helpful. He never stopped to count the cost or dream of profits to come." And biographer Irving Stone, who was one of the big promoters of the all-American, happy-go-lucky Jack, reported that Jack's tramp friends from the "road" days were always dropping in on him for a glass of wine and a loan, both of which he supplied. Where were Spencer and Darwin, except as hokum, in such a character?

In his writings, even from the beginning, they were there aplenty, but of the three books of 1903, the most modest is *The People of the Abyss*. Let me be perverse and call it, for its modesty, the best. It shows a side to Jack that is not conventional and dull, but not heroic and profound either (except in the last chapter); it is his reporter side.

Even as a reporter Jack was, of course, Jack, and in *The People of the Abyss* he was hardly anonymous. Thus his preliminary description of the book to Brett at Macmillan was amusingly false; he said that it was "simply the book of a correspondent writing from the field of industrial war," and that it "proposed no remedies and devoted no space to theorizing." Those words were hokum, yet the work remains a piece of reportage to be reckoned with. In it he managed to subordinate some of his mirror features to the business at hand. For several years afterward he was unable to do so; he became selves-ridden in ways remarkable even for a California celebrity.

He undertook the East End project when an assignment to cover the Boer War fell through and he found himself halfway to the war— that is, in London—without any assignment. He then gave himself one so quickly that he must have had it in mind beforehand, and he headed into seven hard weeks of slumming: the observation, the research, *and* the writing itself, sixty-three thousand words worth (not including the last chapter), right on the spot. (He was an obsessed word-counter.) Biographer Sinclair observes, and I agree, that Jack had "pre-judged" his subject and had its general shape and direction in mind before he reached London at all. After all, why does a Socialist social reformer think of reporting on the Western world's biggest slum? Yet it should also be noted that when Jack actually confronted the place he wrote several letters home, to Anna, expressing shock. Oakland could not compete. "Everything," he said in letter one, "is overwhelming. I never conceived such a mass of misery in the world before." In letter two he referred to it as "a human hell-hole." In letter three he remarked that he had spent Sunday with "homeless ones, in the fierce struggle for something to eat." And in letter four he summed the shock up: "I have seen men's eyes here, & women's, that I was almost afraid to look in—not because of the viciousness therein, nor the sensuality, or anything of the sort, but because of the utter lack of all these, because of the supreme bestiality or unhumanness." Even for someone who knew what he came to see, the East End was a surprise. In later books his fantasizing could and would proceed wildly, but in the slum book it was effectively moderated by his direct perceivings.

From the beginning his "research" was definitely Jack-style (academic daughter Joan thought the whole thing flimsy), with Jack in slum clothes actively trying his hand at survival. And for the first thirty pages he was still the hero of his own narrative. They are, I think, the best pages, for he did need his own presence, but even in them he showed a respectful awareness of the limits to slum-heroism; this time his genre was nonfiction, and he knew it.

He sought out help in finding a halfway house to retreat to and write in. He picked up a promise of rescue, if needed, from an American consul. He even checked the Thomas Cooke & Son travel people about how to *get* to the East End (here he was hoking a bit), learning that they were ready to advise him on how to journey to any point in the world *except* the East End. Then he hailed a cab and found (here hoking further) that the cab driver didn't know how to get there either. He had the driver take him to a second-hand clothing shop vaguely adjacent to the East End, where a sleazy merchant thought him "a high class criminal from across the water" but sold him what he wanted. So, dressed in his "frayed coat with one remaining button," shoes that had been in a coal mine, and a very dirty cloth cap, he and the cab driver managed to find the East End. There, because of his clothes and his Oakland training, he was taken for a true denizen of the abyss, no longer to be called "governor" or "sir" but "mate."

Or rather, he was taken—after a brief preliminary survey of the slums—to "the most respectable street" in them, "a street that would be considered very mean in American, but a veritable oasis in the desert of East London," where he met a certain Johnny Upright and Johnny's wife, who soon arranged for him to rent a room on the same street. Johnny and wife were affable, wise about the East End, and receptive to Jack in either his slum or civilized clothing, and he was soon ready to be launched.

Before meeting the Uprights, his research had already produced a conclusion—a reasonable one that he would belabor later—about those who belonged to London's middle-class: that they had managed to block the East End from their lives and minds. Johnny and wife now helped him go further, in a passage worth pausing on:

> "In a couple of years" he [Johnny] says, "my lease expires. My landlord is one of our kind. He has not put up the rent on any of his houses here, and this has enabled us to stay. But any day he may sell, or any day he may die, which is the same thing so far as we are concerned. The house is bought by a money breeder, who builds a sweat shop on the patch of ground at the rear where my grapevine is, adds to the house and rents it a room to a family. There you are, and Johnny Upright's gone!"

> And truly I see Johnny Upright and his good wife and fair daughters, and frowzy slavey, like so many ghosts, flitting eastward through the gloom, the monster city roaring at their heels.

> But Johnny Upright is not alone in his flitting. Far, far out, on the fringe of the city, live the small business men, little managers, and successful clerks. They dwell in colleges and semi-detached villages, with bits of flower garden, and elbow room, and breathing space. They inflate themselves with pride and throw out chests when they contemplate the Abyss from which they have escaped, and they thank God that they are not as other men. And lo! down upon them comes Johnny Upright and the monster city at his heels. Tenements spring up like magic, gardens are built upon, and the black night of London settles down in a greasy pall.

Johnny's clarity of thought and statement there was surely Jack's. But what of the passage as a piece of reporting? Jack must have been happy with his image of flight in paragraph two. He may also have liked the mixture, in paragraph three, of sociological generalization and dramatic irony. But was he not overstorying in all three paragraphs?

Defer the question, since his actual descent into the slum abyss only begins at this point. At this point Jack abandons his narrative thread and supplies only disconnected episodes, each worth a chapter.[2] In one he is standing in food lines. In another he is "carrying the banner" (walking the streets all night with no place to sleep), being prodded by bobbies. In another he finds shelter in the "unmitigated horror" of a doss-house. And in still another he spends a day as a migrant worker with "hops and hoppers," earning—with an East End acquaintance—2 and $3/7$th cents per hour and being told at the end of the day that he had received a penny more than his due. He even attends, in his slum clothes, Coronation Day for King Edward VII, (though "the East End as a whole remained in the East End and got drunk,") and listens to comments of the poor upon the pomp of the occasion. In some of the chapters it is the episode that stirs his sociology; in others the order is reversed, and Jack takes a particular subject, like "inefficiency" or "wages," and searches out supporting data. In all the chapters, however, his primary device is reportage on individuals he has met, talked with, endured with; and these interviews—if they may be called that—have a steady ring of truth to them.

An especially memorable meeting is with a seafaring cockney Jack quotes at length—Jack enjoyed the flavor of "blimeys" and seems to have used this particular cockney as a model for Mugridge in *The Sea Wolf*. Another good one is with a dying radical, "embittered and pessimistic," fighting vermin and looking at a wall on which hang pictures of Garibaldi and Engels. Still another is with a carter and a carpenter he meets as they are picking up bits of orange peel "from the slimy sidewalk," and with whom he then spends a workhouse night. He also produces, in passing, many unpleasant little cameos, such as a battle between drunken females ("You'll get this rock on the 'ead," etc.) and a Salvation Army tyrant demanding piety in repayment for a charity breakfast. Admittedly Jack is present in each case, but he is present as reporter, not hero. A cynic might well say that the switch must have been hard for him; the fact is that he made the switch and did it well. He even backed up his text with amateurish but convincingly dismal photographs, of which only one seems to have been a fake, presumably a joke. It is of a vagrant looking remarkably like Jack, and healthy too, being lectured to by a stagey bobby for lying on the sidewalk. In a window above is an advertise-

---

2. The book did not appear in a newspaper, but some of it was published serially, in *Wilshire's Magazine,* before coming out as a book.

ment for "Truth: A Weekly Newspaper." The picture reminded me of Alfred Hitchcock showing up in his melodramas.

Naturally his oyster-pirate, Yukon, and Oakland past helped him carry through the project, helped him play his necessary role. It also helped with his conclusions, some of which could be transplanted, without change other than locale, to his fictions. Like this one, "They possess neither conscience nor sentiment, and they will kill for half a sovereign, without fear or favor, if they are given half a chance. They are a new species, a breed of city savages [bred, that is, by the Spencerian survival principle at work in the wrong place]. The streets and houses, alleys and courts are their hunting grounds."

Reliance on Jack's kind of research for sociological conclusions is not appealing to academic minds like his daughter's, and it seems to have bothered biographer Sinclair too. Yet we have modern versions of Jack in Norman Mailer and Tom Wolfe, who are consistently less well backed by experience than Jack was as they emit wisdom. Also in our time we have much of what might be called junk sociology, beside which Jack's performance seems exemplary. In the new junk the reporter will follow Jack's procedure with Johnny Upright (in the first paragraph of the passage quoted above) but will not announce his own presence. Such a single opening instance, so handled, is a cheat, a lead-in only, and Jack was enough of a sociologist to know better. Arrogant he could be, but he recognized the relevance of acknowledging his perceptions as his own.

But what of all the occasions in the book when he overplayed his role, as in the last chapter? Then he does seem to have been following a bit of his own Hearst-like advice to his friend Johns on how to write: "Out of the many details, many features," he said firmly, "select only the most salient one—but, God, man! when you have selected that one, shove it along for all it is worth." Nowadays we might call this perception shaping.

The last chapter is where he pushes that principle hardest, but interestingly it was written later, back home, and written at the suggestion of editor Brett. Without the last chapter the book's conclusion would have been relatively low-key, for Jack. While still in his halfway house, he had written happily to Anna that he was finished, and he had quoted for her benefit the last paragraph of what turned out to be just the next-to-last chapter. In it he referred to the work of a socialist reformer, a Dr. Barnardo, who had been saving approxi-

mately "nine waifs from the streets" every twenty-four hours, adding
that "the people" had better "learn their East End and the sociology of
Christ" and "follow Dr. Barnardo's lead, only on a scale as large as
the nation is large." The "people" were of course the people of the
beginning of the book who didn't know about the East End, and Jack
concluded that when they learned a few things they would stop "dabbling with day nurseries and Japanese art exhibits"—and stop cram-
ming their "yearnings for the Good and the Beautiful down the throat
of the women who are making [*sic*] violets for three farthings a gross."
It was an angry ending, provoking him to admit to Anna that it might
be worded "too strongly" for serial publication, but it was brief. And
for a high-powered Socialist rhetorician it was not a major intrusion
on the reportage. In the chapter he tacked on later he went much
further.

That was a chapter in which he managed to avoid mentioning
socialism, sticking in "management" instead! In the name of management reform he knocked off Christianity, British imperialism, and
democracy in one sweeping slash, being—despite the comic switch—
the extravagant reformer of old. He quoted Thomas Huxley (whom
Aldous emulated in *Brave New World*): "Were the alternative presented to me I would deliberately choose the life of the savage to that
of those people in Christian London." And he backed up Huxley with
his own experiences with the relatively "healthy and strong and happy"
Innuit Indians of Alaska. The Indians "feasted in good times, died of
starvation in bad, but did not suffer from starvation as a chronic condition," never suffered from a lack of shelter, and "had no debts." But
in England? "There are 40,000,000 of the English folk, and 939 out
of every 1,000 of them die in poverty, while a constant army of
8,000,000 struggles on the ragged edge of starvation. Further, each
babe that is born is born in debt to the sum of $110. This is because of
an artifice called the National Debt."

He then rushed through many other statistics, including a fine
one about the denizens of the *West* End. There are "400,000 English
gentlemen 'of no occupation,' according to their own statement in the
census of 1881." There is amusement in comparing what he said here
with what he had said of the English only three years earlier (to friend
Johns, in capital letters): "NO OTHER AGENCY OF CIVILIZA-
TION HAS BEEN SO POTENT AS ENGLAND'S ENLIGHT-
ENED SELFISHNESS." But he professed now not to be amused, an-

nouncing that "civilization must be compelled to better the lot of the average man."

But how? It must face up to the fact of poor management. Again, how? By instituting new management. He did not at this point mention revolution, and the compulsion part seemed rather simple: "Society must be reorganized and capable management put at its head." So one had only to call up the Harvard Business School. Then the salts of the earth, basically "as strong and vigorous as ever," would be on top again.

The People of the Abyss would be a better piece of reportage without the last chapter, and yet it is a powerful chapter. Also it is a chapter suggesting that when Jack got home from London and thought about what he had seen, some of the confusions of his life in 1902 seemed somehow resolved. He was preparing to become a hero again.

Of his other two books of 1903, *The Kempton-Wace Letters,* with Anna as coauthor, was largely complete before he sailed for England, and it might never have been undertaken—or so it seems to me—if England had come first. Psychologically the trip to England was just one of his many escapes, but in 1902 he had plenty to escape from; the East End experience gave him two months' perspective on his gains and losses at home.[3] The high-toned dialectic of *The Kempton-Wace Letters* would have been hard for him to work up steam about after the East End.

In the book he played the part of Herbert Wace, a young man who was about to be married to Hester Stebbins (presumably Bess), but who was writing loftily about marriage and such matters to Dane Kempton, Anna's sexually confused persona. Dane is a fatherly advice chap who likes to discuss the meaning of love, and he sounds like a motherly advice chap, too. Dane even proposes to give more than advice and to go talk with Herbert's fiancée, Hester, provoking Herbert to say, "Tell her all you wish, you dear old fluttery, motherly, poet-father." At the end the wedding is canceled, and the ex-fiancée is admitted to the book with two high-toned letters of her own, not, presumably, written by Bess. The book was published under a pseudonym and didn't come to much, understandably, until the real co-

3. Home life included life with what came to be called "the gang," bohemians for their time, opening up Carmel. See the Sinclair biography for sexual details.

authors were revealed, and journalists decided that they had a hero's sex-scandal on their hands.

But the third book of 1903, *The Call of the Wild,* was indeed written after the London trip, and its writing at that time is hard to explain, except as diversion. Perhaps classics are like that, and *The Call of the Wild* became one, Jack's own. The easy explanation for his retreat into an earlier Jack is that he thought he still had a little steam left for the Yukon—he had a way of counting the words he had written on each "subject," like someone figuring up his assets in several savings accounts. So he proceeded to mix memories of the East End beasts with Darwin and Dogs He Had Known. He found that all he had to do was look in the mirror, see a heroic Californian dog, and change his costume again.

But this dog, Buck, was different from the old heroic figures, in that he had not been brought up in survival-of-the-fittest country, not even Oakland. He had lived a soft, civilized life at Judge Miller's place in southern California, where the cooperative, civilized morality recommended by Spencer reigned. The soft life had made him flabby and unwary; he would become the model for Jack's well-bred, upper-class human narrator in *The Sea Wolf,* Humphrey Van Weyden. Luckily Buck—and Humphrey after him—was not an incapable. He was big, healthy, and willing; he could learn to be tough, could evolve backward with skill. So when he was kidnapped and shipped off to the Yukon to be a sled dog, he mastered the Law of Club and Fang faster than the other kidnapped dogs.

And when he watched another dog, caught off the alert, torn to pieces by the dog pack, he became wise in wilderness ways on the spot, saying to himself, as if he had been Jack, "So that was the way. No fair play. Once down, and that was the end of you." He instantly resolved that he wouldn't be caught down—good logical thinking on Buck's part.

And predictably, Buck was also logical enough to compare the new morality with the one down at Judge Miller's place, deciding (after a moment of civilized reverence for private property!) that the new primitive morality was, for the present, quite superior. He thereupon went about learning to be cunning and devious, and he slowly reverted to the wildness that was his heritage. One of his most remarkable mental feats was that of recalling his life in Neanderthal days, when he was not only a primitive dog, but his master was a primitive man:

Sometimes as he crouched there, blinking dreamily at the flames, it seemed that the flames were of another fire, and that as he crouched by this other fire he saw another and different man from the half breed cook before him. The other man was shorter of leg and longer of arm, with muscles that were stringy and knotty rather than rounded and swelling. The hair of this man was long and matted, and his head slanted back under it from the eyes. He uttered strange sounds. . . .

Truly Superdog. And at the end of the story he became known as the Ghost Dog of the wilds, a dog of legendary strength and cruelty who had settled in as a leader of the Yukon morality, a leader of wolves, not dogs. By this time Jack was being called "Wolf" by his friends, and he would soon plan to build a great house in back country and call it Wolf House. So we can safely discount the long and mechanical sequel, *White Fang,* he turned out three years later, a quickie that reversed evolution yet again, having a wolf become civilized. With *The Call of the Wild,* plus his experience in the East End, Jack was now ready to put aside ordinary beasts in favor of three fictions about the leaders of beasts, leaders of packs.

Somehow the years 1902–1903 had mixed his many melodramatic experiences with desire, as in Eliot's famous line. For the power of fame was now coming his way, and he did desire it. Also his mind was ready for it, attuned to factoring, to trying different combinations, to churning out words methodically. He took time out briefly from factoring in 1904, to cover the Russo-Japanese War, and this time he not only made it to the war but also became something of a hero for disobeying Japanese regulations for journalists. The war produced no book from him, only an increase in his antagonism for the "yellow races," but it didn't slow him up either. The production process of writing was now built in. No matter what he was doing, or where, he carefully allocated his daily hours. The discipline held him together.

And now his old socialist mission renewed itself. How, he must have asked himself, *did* one go about being *sensible* about effective, efficient "management"? The answer emerged for him twice in two years, in two novels: *The Sea Wolf* and *The Iron Heel.* And it emerged again (after a lapse during which he sailed halfway around the world in his own ship, *The Snark*) in *Martin Eden.* What he produced in these works were, in effect, six different management answers, in the form of five male characters and one malicious managerial combine or oligarchy.

Jack London buffs have argued extensively, in the pages of *The Jack London Newsletter,* about when Jack first read Nietzsche, but everyone agrees that Nietzsche helped shape *The Sea Wolf.* Nietzsche's Zarathustra, having declared the death of God, announces that man has to replace Him: the role for the Superman. To do so, man has to "break up the good and just." He had been "born and bred . . . in the lies of the good"; the good had taught him "false shores and false securities"; but now he has to venture out on the high seas of life on his own. When he does so, then "cometh unto him the great terror, the great outlook, the great sickness, the great nausea, the great *mal-de-mer.*" But he must fare forward anyway, must break up the good and the just that have heretofore "radically contorted and distorted" everything. The passage presumably inspired the setting on Wolf Larsen's ship (though Jack had himself been on such a ship), and certainly it inspired the character of Wolf Larsen. It probably also lay behind Jack's decision to have as his first-person narrator a shang-haied, seasick, upper-class character who had been born and bred among the lies of the good, Humphrey Van Weyden. Luckily Humphrey is, like dog Buck,[4] capable of learning, of rising to reality's demands. As for Wolf Larsen, he is the Nietzschean Superman, though later in the book Jack decides to compare him with Milton's Satan. He beats up everyone handily (breaks their arms, *snap snap,* renders them unconscious with a quick pinch on the neck) and insistently ridicules conventional beliefs. Jack has Humphrey admire and despise Wolf,[5] but steadily submit to him until suddenly, about halfway through the tale, a female appears aboard—having been conveniently salvaged from a shipwreck—and the tables begin to be turned. She bears a striking resemblance to Charmian, and she quickly helps Humphrey see that Wolf is strictly the enemy. Meanwhile Humphrey is, like Buck, getting stronger and more wary, and his new powers are reinforced by Wolf's strange, rapid decline. For Wolf, it turns out, is a mortally sick man, and his sickness, which begins as headaches, moves on to blindness

---

4. Wolf Larsen's ship is called, after Buck, *The Ghost.*

5. The relationship between these two Jacks is, before Charmian's arrival, suspiciously like that between Joseph Conrad's ship captain in *The Secret Sharer* and a communing stranger who comes aboard, like Humphrey, in the night.

and progressive enfeeblement. It is at this point that Nietzsche's Superman has to take on some of the imperfection of Satan—doomed with the wrong cause.[6] He even gives Wolf-Satan a murky older brother—Moloch?—for one must remember that Jack took both Marx and Milton with him to the Yukon—who chases Wolf around the Pacific for various misdeeds and seems to be trying to out do Wolf as Satan. Between the avenging brother and the encroaching illness, Wolf hasn't a chance. Soon Humphrey and his fine new life-mate escape the *Ghost,* and after primitive trials on a deserted Aleutian island, they have it out with the enfeebled Wolf (who conveniently becomes shipwrecked there) and carry the day. The girl and Humphrey then head back (unlike Buck) to civilization.

Obviously Jack was factoring at a great rate in the book, but the factors were both symbolic forces and people Jack knew. He had an unusual capacity to merge the abstract with experience, and *The Sea Wolf* shows this talent even when the plot is muddy. It was an instant success, and with it he began to receive the big royalties that would follow him the rest of his life.[7] (Money-minded biographer Irving Stone reports that he made more than a million dollars and could never keep any of it.) Further, with *The Sea Wolf* he began to be a celebrity, not only as a writer but also as a Socialist. It was primarily as a Socialist that he undertook *The Iron Heel*—though that book gives us some fascistic notions of socialism.

In it the central factors or forces are, first, a *good* Nietzschean Superman by name of Ernest Everhard, and second, a seedy collection of capitalist villains which is only super by virtue of being an economic and political combine. Everhard has all the qualities of Wolf Larsen except evil. He is constantly in the parlors of the rich or on platforms. (In 1906 Jack was himself constantly in parlors and on platforms, speaking social truths to America's equivalent of London's West End.) In other words, Everhard's scene of action—set ahead to the year 1932—is not the wild ocean but civilization, and it is in civilization that he runs up against the Law of Club and Fang, as exercised by the capitalists who resist him.

6. Jack has Wolf discuss Milton's Satan with the new female, describing him as a "free spirit" who "cared to serve nothing" and "stood on his own legs." The female declares Satan the first anarchist, and Wolf cries, "Then it is good to be an anarchist!"

7. Jack had not made great royalties from his dog book, since he had accepted flat fees for both magazine and book publication.

He doesn't win, but he doesn't develop headaches either. He is jailed. The socialist movement is crushed—but then keeps threatening rebirth. His loyal and true mate is now the book's first-person narrator, and she keeps writing until page 303, where there is an abrupt conclusion in the form of a final footnote (the book is also loaded with footnotes elsewhere):

> This is the end of the Everhard Manuscript. It breaks off abruptly in the middle of a sentence. She must have received warning of the coming of the Mercenaries, for she had time safely to hide the Manuscript before she fled or was captured. It is to be regretted that she did not live to complete her narrative, for then, undoubtedly, she would have cleared away the mystery that has shrouded for seven centuries, the execution of Ernest Everhard.

Irving Stone thought it one of Jack's great books. Max Lerner was dazzled by its prophecies. Nikolai Bukharin singled it out as the one American book worth listing in an extensive socialist bibliography, and the editor of a good collection of Jack's political writings, Philip Froner, described it as "masterly and unforgettable." These comments were, of course, made in the historical context of the rise of fascism; they praise Jack for his ideological prescience, and I agree with them. Perhaps the book should even be revived. Yet it goes quite against fashions in the novel these days. Even a sympathizer will probably find Everhard a bore, and the rich hear-no-evil, see-no-evil hypocrites he does battle with merely comic. The work emerges as a laborious instance of factoring. Missing is the experiential Jack to give it life, the simpler political Jack of the first-draft *People of the Abyss* and the artful but modest Jack of this truncated villanelle "The Worker and the Tramp":

> Heaven bless you, my friend—
> You, the man who won't sweat;
> Here's a quarter to spend.
>
> Your course I commend,
> Nor regard with regret;
> Heaven bless you, my friend.
>
> On you I depend
> For my work, don't forget;
> Here's a quarter to spend.

Ah! you comprehend
That I owe you a debt.
Here's a quarter to spend.
Heaven bless you, my friend.

Somewhat before writing *The Iron Heel,* Jack was taken up by
Upton Sinclair, who read *The People of the Abyss* to *his* mate, Meta.
Jack in turn took up Upton, whose meatpacking epic, *The Jungle,* so
impressed him that he wrote a ten-page polemic in its favor and damned
the Chicago newspapers that were maligning it. Sinclair and he had
little in common—and particularly they did not have drinking in common—but mutual admiration for their similar literary politicking
stirred them to friendship. Soon Upton contrived to make Jack the
president of an organization that Upton had created, the Intercollegiate Socialist Society, and Jack was to be found in the summer of
1906—at about the time of *The Iron Heel*'s publication—addressing
that organization in Madison Square Garden. He came to the meeting late (from Yale, I believe, where he had also been speechifying)
and performed theatrically to great cheers, being charming and revolutionary at the same time. Stardom was his, and this dangerous condition soon began, in its American way, to kill him.

He had been having trouble being a superman for some time.
(Biographer Andrew Sinclair made a thorough study of his physical
ills and is a good source.) His frailties began with shingles and scurvy;
he suffered several fractures and was eventually lamed (at an unspec-
ified date he "virtually gave up walking"), and he developed a rectal
tumor he wrongly thought malignant, as well as an unsubstantiated
fear that he had syphilis. Sinclair declares that the accumulation of
misfortune produced in him, beginning about the time of *The Sea
Wolf* "a morbid worry about his physical condition that would end
only with his death." It must have been partly to combat the "worry"
that he undertook the voyage of *The Snark,* but *The Snark* trip gave
him a strange tropical sickness—intensified by alcohol—that must
have helped modulate the healthy heroism he was factoring of himself
in *Martin Eden.*

The trip was a disaster from the time of the ship's construction.
When complete it was still riddled with defects, and as it was launched,
it was dropped and damaged. When Jack and Charmian set sail from
San Francisco on it in April 1907, it was still defective and had, as a

bonus, an equally defective crew of landlubbers. Yet it had cost Jack thirty thousand dollars up to that point, and bill collectors nearly stopped him from casting off from the pier. The voyage to Hawaii took a month. *The Snark* nearly foundered, and it was reported lost but made it and then set forth for the South Seas refurbished with a new engine, a new crew, and new money from Jack's writing *about* the voyage. Every morning Jack was to be found forward, writing his daily thousand words. He was now doing *Martin Eden,* but he was increasingly handicapped by "the sickness." Part of it was a painful skin ailment, which caused layers of his skin to peel off. There was also a "nervous disturbance," which, declared Stone, also began to affect his mind. "His persecution mania returned, there was a conspiracy against him, people were trying to prevent him from completing his voyage around the world." Whether this was mania or truth, he was suddenly in the hospital in Sydney, and the voyage of *The Snark* was over.

In the summer of 1909 he arrived back in San Francisco, saying to reporters that he was weary and had come home for a rest. He was also nearly bankrupt and had lost his public glow. But *Martin Eden* was probably the better for his reverses, though in his happy moments the hero Martin was presented, as of old, as every inch an Aryan wonder, and ideologically a perfect Spencerian:

> . . . he got into bed and opened "First principles" [Herbert Spencer's best-known work]. Morning found him still reading. . . . He learned that evolution was no more theory, but an accepted process of development; that scientists no longer disagreed about it. . . . And here was the man Spencer, organizing all knowledge for him, reducing everything to unity, elaborating ultimate realities. . . . There was no caprice, no chance. All was law.

With Spencer leading him, Martin, on good days, could do absolutely anything with his mind. He could even make rational connections between his two great loves, women and sailing. In fact he could connect "love, poetry, earthquakes, fire, rattlesnakes, rainbows, precious gems, monstrosities, sunsets, the roaring of lions, illuminating gas, cannibalism, beauty, murder, lovers, fulcrums and tobacco." Did such wonderful connecting powers need more than Spencer behind them? In a later book, *John Barleycorn,* Jack said no, he never drank until he had finished his thousand words for the day, even on *The*

Snark, but he might have been bragging. For he *was* still bragging, still setting everybody straight on the nature of society and the universe, the way his character Everhard had done in *The Iron Heel.* He was still a master theorist of force, a steamroller of logic, except that this time he was also looking at, and occasionally writing about, his lesser self and giving Martin some of his lesser qualities.

Martin was not physically sick, as Jack had been on *The Snark,* but soul-sick, will-sick. And he was particularly sick of his writing life, the factoring part, the part that made him wish in vain that the world would recognize him not for his hoked-up stories but for a great thoughtful essay he had written that was loftily entitled "The Philosophy of Illusion." The world kept ignorantly reading the stories; the money kept ignorantly pouring in, but Martin had grown weary of his success. Partly he was weary because he had found a new and masculine soul-mate who was a fine poet *without* such success, and lo! the poet had committed suicide, leaving behind a great neglected epic.[8] But mostly he was weary because he was himself now convinced that the world had no place for truth and beauty. On a sudden impulse he set sail alone on a big passenger ship, to remove himself from the rat race. The first night from port he climbed out a porthole, dove into the ocean and swam down, down to the depths, his final act of superman will.

In *John Barleycorn,* Jack described at length the gloom that came over him while drinking, and the gloom was like Martin's. He called it his "white logic," and said that when the white logic was upon him he was convinced that all man's struggling was for naught. The account rings true.

At any rate, having killed off Martin, Jack himself lived another eight years, and he mostly kept the white logic under control. He wrote his publishers businesslike, dispassionate letters and told them about the quantities of words he had on hand for the market. (After the voyage of *The Snark* he had eighty-one thousand words on hand about the voyage, fifty-two thousand more left over about the Klondike, and fifty-three thousand about the South Sea Islands. How many of these words were written on the voyage itself, aside from

8. The model seems to have been George Sterling, with whom Jack—according to Sinclair—was in love. Sterling remained alive to attend Jack's funeral but committed suicide in 1926.

those in *Martin Eden,* is not recorded. And of course the figures have a Superman look about them.) Then he went on the wagon, at which point he wrote *John Barleycorn* and managed to pretend that the white logic had gone out of his life.

The editor of the excellent four-volume *Bodley Head Jack London* thinks that *John Barleycorn* is Jack's best book. I'd say not. It contains fine autobiographical matter, and reads wonderfully, but is thin. It skims over Jack's deepest troubles.

Right after it came the sudden catastrophic loss of Wolf House, the most ambitious of his undertakings, far beyond the building of *The Snark.* It was part of a ranching project, and it was no socialist enterprise either. It was a castle, his San Simeon. It took years to build; it was made out of the best stone and the best lumber, and it was enormous. It was for Jack and Charmian to live in, above the crowd, and Jack must have thought then that they *could* live above the crowd, since he was making seventy-five thousand dollars a year. The trouble was he was spending one hundred thousand dollars. He remained confident throughout the building, or pretended to be, and kept at his thousand daily words. A few days before they were to move in, the castle burned down.

It was *then* that the white logic came over him in earnest. He took out his grief in drink. He wrote terrible letters to daughter Joan, whom he accused of having deserted him when he needed her. And he cooled on Charmian too. Of Charmian he came to "realize," said Stone, that at the age of forty-three she was still a child, "preoccupied with infantile details," someone he could not rely on. It was the beginning of the end.

He put up a front for a time. He paid the contractors in full and set out to dispose of his indebtedness. He kept at his daily words, he tried to fight off the bottle, he corresponded with editors and publishers, he worked on a terse, moral-terrorist novel, anticipatory of James Bond, *The Assassination Bureau Ltd.* (never finished, though it was later published with a tacked-on conclusion), and he went to the length of resigning in a huff from the Socialist party. Of that he said that he had always been a fighting man and the party was no longer a fighting organization (the party had gone pacifist about America's participation in World War I), but the truth was that the fight had gone out of Jack. He had known for a long time that he was not like Wolf Larsen or Ernest Everhard but like Martin Eden, and he had presumably even become suspicious of some of Martin's idealism—about truth and beauty, for instance—but I agree with biographer Sinclair that suicide is too complicated to be blamed, neatly, on something fuzzy like disillusion. At any rate, in November 1916 he took an overdose of morphine sulphate and atropine sulphate—the dive down.

Lessons in American social thought lurk here, but whether they can be tied to this unusual individual, Jack London, is another matter. Jack was a pre-Hollywood star with all the infirmities of that breed, but what still distinguishes him, I think, from the breed was the extent of his commitment to his various radical and social science enthusiasms. Not that our star system has bred only conformists. In the thirties, in the McCarthy period and through the whole of the Vietnam period, there was plenty of dissent evident among the big names, and in either of those American moments, Jack could presumably have been found orating, picketing, and writing polemics. Yet his abiding commitment—aside from his bursts of social energy—seems to have been to the fierce, relentless logic with which he endowed his supermen. A foolish commitment it may have been, though the thinking climate of Nietzsche, Spencer, and company certainly encouraged it, but it was his self-faith; he believed in it; it was part of the real Jack. And it was a part of him that does not, somehow, fit with his activism and entrepreneuring.

The seriousness of it is visible in a gruesome way even in his last work, the unfinished potboiler *The Assassination Bureau Ltd.* On the surface the book seems just a forerunner of James Bond and now Stephen King, a bit of fantasy violence in the big bad world of national leaders. But the head of the "bureau"—another one of Jack's logical supermen—turns out to have a connection with Jack himself in 1916. After beginning with the assassination of a police chief responsible for much brutality in the labor struggles of the period, and moving to other powers, rather like the evil capitalist oligarchy of *The Iron Heel,* this superman follows his own logic into his own life, and on page 122 of the book—which is as far as Jack got with the manuscript—the loyal members of the bureau are gloomily weighing their chief's orders to assassinate him. Since Jack did then take his own life we can speculate that he was thinking about doing so as he wrote. There seems to have been, as usual, a face in the mirror for him to reckon with.

Here is not, to be seen, at any rate, a conventionally factored relationship between best-selling fantasizer and his products (though I grant that Edgar Allan Poe bears looking into on the point), and it is here that Jack's dissent gains rather than loses stature, here that his distrust of the conventional pieties of his culture appears as not just good box office.

Of course, in our time his particular brand of super-think seems archaic, our time being the age of "the end of ideology" as well as of the diminution of social thinkers like Herbert Spencer. Jack was like a good many social beings walking the earth at the turn of the century, who could talk reality incessantly while the meat burned on the stove. He was like Axel Heyst in Joseph Conrad's novel *Victory*. Heyst was a prototypical late-Victorian hard-facts man. When asked by a Mr. Tesman what he was interested in, Heyst replied, "Facts. There's nothing worth knowing but facts. Hard facts. Facts alone, Mr. Tesman." Wandering through the islands he became known as hard-facts Heyst, but the attribution was a joke; those who called him that really thought of him as a utopist, a perfect gentleman and a mooner. He mooned about the Java Sea; he talked about good and evil like a theologian, and he could not bring himself to pay any attention to mundane daily affairs, he lived in the mind. Clearly Conrad put a lot of himself in Heyst, but Conrad was not bragging. He was setting up for critical inspection the cloudy ideals that, in the period before World War I, marked the realists infallibly. For Heyst shared with half the hard-facts thinkers of Europe the same abstract notion of a hard fact. And he shared it with Jack too, who was probably closer to Heyst than was Conrad himself.

Jack liked Conrad, and when he read *Victory* in 1915, he wrote Conrad about it, telling him that though he had appreciated his work for years, the new book was so fine that it had caused him to lose a night's sleep. "On your head," he concluded, "be it." Surely Jack saw himself in Heyst, who in his happy days was a social optimist and world-saver, but who at the end of *Victory* discovered, as Jack had discovered by 1915, that all his victories had been hollow.

THREE

The Fixed Ideals of Upton Sinclair

Upton Sinclair (1878–1968) was two years younger than Jack London. He grew up, as Jack did, with the fifty-seven early varieties of Socialists. He lived long enough, as Jack did not, to see some of the social reforms for which he worked hardest put into law, and he also lived long enough, as Jack did not, to see what happened to socialism in Germany and Russia. Worse, he lived long enough to become a much more predictable thinker than Jack, though this essay will limit itself to his early life largely. He was a more conventional Socialist than Jack, but he made up for his ideological plainness with political fervor and with peripheral eccentricities of comic dimensions. He admired Jack, but from the distance of one who disliked and feared drink. He forgave Jack his capitalist sinning, and thought it was capitalism, and not Jack himself, that destroyed Jack.[1]

If Upton had been more understanding about *Upton* he might have imagined that it was obsessive socialism—and whatever psychic unrest underlay it—that destroyed his own literary talent, by making him into a political hack.

Oddly, that scholar of American radicalism, Daniel Aaron, did

1. Anyone wishing to write about Upton Sinclair will be kindly treated by the Lilly Library, University of Indiana in Bloomington, but will be depressed by the six tons of Sinclair material in storage there. I haven't been there for some time, but I suspect that in most years the tons still rest quietly. My primary sources for this essay, aside from the Lilly "file," are two biographies: *Upton Sinclair: A Study in Social Unrest* by Floyd Dell (New York: AMS Press, 1927); and *Upton Sinclair: American Rebel* by Leon Harris (New York: Crowell, 1975). Then there are Sinclair's own ninety books (of which I have read, I think, twelve) including *The Autobiography of Upton Sinclair* (New York: Harcourt Brace, 1962); and the autobiography of his second wife, *Southern Belle*, by Mary Craig Sinclair (New York: Crown, 1957). Daniel Aaron's *Writers on the Left* (New York: Harcourt Brace, 1961) provides useful background material.

not describe Upton as a Socialist in his authoritative volume, *Writers on the Left,* published in the early sixties. He said instead that Upton was politically unclassifiable, a unique figure, and put him aside. Upton was still alive when *Writers on the Left* was published and must have been offended at the neglect, having spent most of his adult life classifying himself as a Socialist and doing so even after he resigned from the party proper (he did so in the same year that Jack did, 1916, because the party had taken a pacifist position about World War I). From early in his life he seems to have been sure that he did not want to be what Aaron made him, unclassifiable. He discovered socialism when he was in his early twenties, and having done so he immediately wanted the Socialists to persuade him, as he put it in his autobiography, that they existed. In 1902 they did, and the persuasion stuck.

My guess about Aaron's demurral is that he read Upton's autobiography and decided that he had—as with so many autobiographers—an unreliable narrator on his hands. At many points Upton's account is impressive for its psychological omissions. Despite his efforts at frankness he does not come clean about his relations with his parents, and though he is always eager, as was Jack London, to mention the economic struggles of his childhood that led to his radicalism, he is most choosy about other data. Still, his account appears honest as far as it goes, and perceptive too; and since it is an extensive record of the progress of impietism in an interesting mind, it is not, I think, simply to be discounted. His summary of his early political development and "conversion" well represents his usual focus. In it he said that before he saw the light he was like many another American idealist. As he put it, "From the age of seventeen to twenty-two I faced our system of class privileges absolutely alone in my mind; that is to say whatever I found wrong with civilization I thought that I alone knew it, and the burden of changing it rested upon my spirit." With his spirit so laden he thought of the big movements around him, Bryanism and populism, as "vulgar, noisy and beneath cultured contempt." Converting to socialism changed him, made him into a genuine American political animal, always busily getting out the vote and looking hopeful even though, as a Socialist, he did not often have much to be hopeful about. He arrived at his socialism, he reported, "through the psychology of the poor relation." He was Baltimore-southern, which meant that he had a little of the old plantation in him, but a little also of northern capitalism. The capitalism was not in the immediate, nuclear family, but off in the lives of cousins and uncles, particularly of his Uncle Bland. Uncle Bland had a big four-story Baltimore townhouse with the customary marble steps, and Upton, an only child, spent many of his childhood days there. His own parents' house was not a house at all, but a series of tenements where as a child he "slept on a sofa or crossways at the foot of his parents' bed," and where sometimes at night he had "an exciting chase for bedbugs." It was the southern connection that made him, though poor, well bred. He was a "nice little boy," he reported, who had been brought up with "good cooking and good manners." He had to dress himself like a toff on Sundays and he "never buttered the whole slice of his bread." Also, his efforts to be *not* nice backfired. At the age of eight he started a cigarette given him by a big boy on the street. He lit it and was going quickly to the devil when another boy told him to watch out because a policeman was coming to arrest him. He threw away the cigarette and "ran and hid in an alley." He never smoked thereafter, and in reporting on his subsequent purity he did not even notice how inadequate his explanation for it was. He merely said that he had better things to do, such as learning to be, like Jack London, financially responsible early. He had taught himself to read at the age of five, "before anyone realized what was happening." Then his mother realized what was happening and began to help him with it. She had to do it alone because the father was off selling whiskey and drinking it. The father was small, plump, chivalrous, gentle, and genteel, the son of a captain in the Confederate Navy. Brought up after the Civil War in a "ruined" family, he didn't like Yankee hustle. He was a rotten salesman, and he came to live in the past, dreaming of the old South of "slaves and estates." He fell victim to the demon rum, with the result that both his wife and his son—again Upton's account is simply too pat—had their lives "poisoned by alcohol."

The father's drinking, together with the father's dislike of books, were the expressed chief sources of Upton's early complaints, but Upton insisted that despite them he did not actively rebel against the father; the father was simply too pathetic a figure to be angry with, and in his decline he was replaced as a villain in Upton's mind by the rich Uncle Bland. Uncle Bland was kindly rich, did a great deal for his nephew, and received as thanks the nephew's lifelong dislike of the monied. It was Uncle Bland who brought him, said Upton, the bad news about money, that it ran America.

Then there was also Grandfather Hardin, his mother's father, who was a railroad tycoon attracted to terrapin and other beasts. (Upton remembered a live terrapin in the backyard being approached by a Negro servant planning to cut off its head.) He carved "unending quantities of chicken, ducks, turkeys and hams" at the end of a long table, leaving Upton's serving to last because he was the youngest. When Upton's father was broke, Upton found himself living with the Hardins or the Blands, and when the father decided to move to New York, Upton was in a position—according to his own account—to have stayed behind and grown up with rich relatives. His decision to endure parental penury was a hard one, and crucial. The parents made the move when he was ten, and as soon as they made it his social consciousness began to bud. They lived all over Manhattan, from East 12th Street up to West 126th, with several way stops. They were always in money trouble, but on Sunday mornings he was expected to be a "devout little Episcopalian," and wear "a pair of tight kid gloves and . . . a tight little derby hat," as they walked down 5th Avenue to a fashionable church. He had been a frail child until he was perhaps ten and had not gone to school at all until the New York move. Attending his first class in the city he found that he had to avoid looking fashionable before his classmates, who "didn't like Fifth Avenue dudes wearing silk hats and kid gloves." Later he remembered a teacher as tough as the students, a "jolly old Irishman" who threw chalk at the students who troubled him and cracked their knuckles with a ruler. And he remembered also learning to try to be a tough himself, by raiding grocery stores to grab a few potatoes and "roast them on bonfires in vacant lots." To a friend who complained that he had been such a serious boy that he never played, he replied in a defensive letter that he had played football and baseball in the vacant lots, "shinny" on roller skates, and a game of pitch on roofs, where the boys of the neighborhood threw clothespins at people passing below. But in another account of his early days he put on his socialist hat—which was also an extremely prudish hat—and declared that while the survival of the fittest made some sense as gospel for the physical side of man he could not see that there was a chance for "genius, beauty, dignity and true power of mind . . . to survive in the insane hurly burly of metropolitan life." This last remark was made by an elderly Upton trying to reconstruct his youthful thoughts, but even when he was young and Episcopalian, and inclined to throw clothespins, he was—if he did say so himself—something of a genius, with power of mind and a sense of beauty that *deserved* to be saved from Darwin, money and New York. He was also wiry and quick, and must have been lucky too, but what seemed to have helped most was his determination, grit, resolve. Against all the capitalist rules of the time, he was to become a sort of socialistic Horatio Alger.

Later he thought in a modern way that his sex life might have done it—that is, his non-sex life that kept him out of museums for fear of seeing nudes, and made him, despite "storms of craving," much repressed. But whatever it was, he had it, a will to get on. When he went to school at age ten he disposed of eight grades, he reported modestly, in two years, having trouble only with arithmetic, which his mother had never taught him. "This branch of learning," he said, "so essential to commercial civilization, had shared the fate of alcohol, tea and coffee; my mother did not use it, so neither did I." After putting the arithmetic in its place he went on so rapidly in the other courses that he was ready for college at age twelve. The City College of New York "was in reality a high school," but even so he could not be admitted at twelve. He repeated the last year of grammar school, then lied about his age and entered City College at fourteen.

It was at City College, where he stayed five years, that he discovered perhaps half of the vices of American education—finding the other half later at Columbia, where he did graduate work—and thus built himself a sound base for writing an angry book about education later, *The Goose Step.* He was already a bookworm, having read dozens of adventure stories of the old dignified kind, and now he set to reading in earnest. He didn't, however, pay much attention to his courses after the first week, because by then he had read all the texts and had nothing to do in class but write verses and draw pictures of teacher. Instead he took the class reading lists, and worthwhile clues in the preliminary lectures, and went off to follow them up on his own. His favorite writers were Dickens, Thackeray, and Shakespeare, and he thought he liked Carlyle until he discovered that Carlyle was a terrible Tory. Also he tried to learn a number of languages, including Greek and Latin, but he discovered that the teaching of languages in the college was so poor that he did better on his own. He had a passion for memorizing words as soon as he ran into them. Each morning as he shaved he would run through a word list in his mind, and eventually with no help from anyone he had a reasonable reading facility in Italian, French, and German. He also tried his hand at chemistry, physics, history, drawing, and philosophy. One of his steady complaints—a curious complaint from someone as rigid as he—was that the teachers were incurably authoritative and dogmatic. He had a Catholic English teacher whose way of promoting the faith was "to set a class that was 60% Jewish to work learning Catholic sentimentality disguised as poetry." (This teacher described Milton as "a dangerous disturber of the peace of Europe.") Then there was the Jesuit who shouted at him, "Mr. Sinclair, it is so because I *say* it is so." All in all, CCNY and Columbia were as hard to survive in, by his account, as the New York streets themselves, but he managed. At Columbia he even managed to beat the system financially. He registered as a special student, and discovering that the rules allowed him to drop courses and begin others without extra charge, he proceeded to sample forty courses over four years while paying tuition for only one term's worth. He didn't earn a master's degree that way, but he picked up an education.

Also while in school and college he picked up three heroes who speeded his arrival at revolution: Jesus, Hamlet, and Shelley. His first biographer, Floyd Dell, reported on these that Jesus was a hero for him because he threw the moneychangers out of the temple; Hamlet was a hero because he was "a prince of the spirit" who had been "cheated by the world out of his inheritance—the poet's natural inheritance of beauty and happiness"; and Shelley was a hero because he knew that the poets were the true legislators. But Upton, looking back, did not take his heroes as seriously as Dell did. Of his early Hamlet fetish he later complained that it displayed him as "an advanced case of delusion of grandeur, messianic complex, paranoia, narcissism, and so on to the end of the line."

At the time of his love for these heroes he was living in penury with his parents—CCNY had no dormitories, no campus—reading furiously through the night on his bed, and eating cheap food in the cheapest places (a way of life that he later blamed for his continuing stomach troubles). He was also, suddenly, writing. He was not writing in the mode that would come to be notably his, the investigatory and political mode of *The Jungle,* and he was not writing as if he were Hamlet or Shelley either, but he was warming up his amazing writing machine, and writing, like Jack London, to make money.

He began at the moneymaking, he said later, when he made friends with a boy his own age—sixteen or seventeen—who had just had a story accepted by a magazine. Upton thought that if a boy named Simon Stern could write and sell a story Upton could do so too, and so he wrote his first one. It was a story about a pet bird. He knew about pet birds, having made a practice of taking young birds from their nests and raising them; so he put one of these birds into an adventure, making it serve "to prove the innocence of a colored boy accused of arson." (Upton did not in his memoir describe the nature of the proof: the story itself is not in the Sinclair memorabilia.) He sent it to *Argosy,* which accepted it and paid him twenty-five dollars. The money converted him to hacking. He raced into it not to change the world—that came later—but to pay for a separate room for himself away from the parents ($1.25 a week) and "a clean collar and other luxuries" ($.25 a week) plus two meals a day ($3.00 a week)— all for writing stories that began with lines like these: "It was early in the month of February, in the year 1804, along the northern coast of Africa. A small vessel of moorish rig was speeding over the Mediterranean waves, urged onward by a fierce gale."

Then he hurried into short stories for children, made a little there, and casually discovered—a momentary diversion—that he could make more money, and faster, by writing jokes. So he wrote jokes. He wrote "tramp jokes, mother-in-law jokes, Irishman jokes, and so on," and was paid one dollar apiece for them. He wrote them in church, in class, at lunch, and while dressing. He wrote each joke on a separate scrap of paper and numbered it and kept a record of when and where he had sent it. Then he tired of jokes, and later when people accused him of having no sense of humor he blamed his joke period. He went back to stories.

And how he did write. He was nineteen. He went into adventure stories and war stories for the pulps, beginning with a pulp called the *Army and Navy Weekly* (price five cents) that commissioned him to do a thirty thousand-word novelette every week for forty dollars. He did several novelettes at this pace and price, writing under the pseudonym of Lieutenant Frederick Garrison, USA, and taking as his occupation "killing Spaniards." He thought nothing of "sinking a whole fleet of Spanish torpedo boats to make a denouement." Then he switched to other publications and increased his pace. There he was, still in college, still a minor, yet for a number of months he kept two stenographers working full time. That left him, he said, mornings for Columbia, and for practicing the violin. He liked hacking. He was making sixty dollars a week, and he was using his talents for other purposes than those devised by the slow minds at CCNY and Columbia, where the only person he met who seemed to him to have talent was not a writer but a musician, Edward MacDowell. It gave him pleasure to be putting on paper a quantity of English words equivalent, he figured, to the works of Sir Walter Scott, while being told by one of his English teachers—one who wanted him to write little themes about college athletics—that he knew nothing about writing English. There was little wrong with his English by then. It was fluent and clear but (inadvertently) comic, as in the passage below from a novelette he wrote, called *A Prisoner of Morro* (price ten cents, 1898), under the pseudonym of Ensign Clark Fitch, USN. In it a young naval officer named Cliff is discussing with a Mr. Faraday a bad man named Ignacio.

> "You may have heard about one of his exploits."
> "Which one is that?"
> "He made an attempt to assassinate Rear Admiral Sampson."
> "Oh yes, I heard about that," said the officer. "The admiral told me about it himself. I believe you were the person who interfered."
> "I had the good luck to be standing near," said Cliff modestly. "And of course I sprang between them."
> "And the spy stabbed you?"
> "Yes. In the shoulder, but he did not hurt me much."
> "He must be a desperate man."
> "He is. That stabbing business seems to be a favorite trick of his."

In his autobiography Upton boasted that he could write that sort of thing by the yard but that he soon "came to loathe" such hackwork and took steps to become a serious writer. What he did not say was that as a serious writer he continued to subordinate character (and what any character in the world might ever say to any other character in the world) to matters that he felt needed to be talked about. Whether he hacked or wrote seriously his art remained one of statement, not of people.

He groped, however, for the serious with adolescent intelligence and energy through his first three full-scale novels, all written before he was twenty-five. Adolescence was, he reported, a long trial for him—his severer critics have suggested that he remained permanently adolescent—and his desperate need showed itself sexually as well as economically. For the control of sex he would "leap out of bed in the morning and plunge into cold water." For the appeasement of his poverty he would think dark thoughts about Uncle Bland and display some of his early socialist feelings to his conservative mother:

> Mamma, there is, whether you quite believe it or not, a God in heaven . . . who once said, so we believe, Thou shalt not covet thy neighbor's house, nor his etc. Possibly there may be a higher motive in this world than love of money, a higher motive than getting it. . . . Let me tell you, sweetness, that I would not take Uncle Bland's wealth if it were offered me today.

His new seriousness extended to the milieu he found he needed for the act of creation. He began seeking out pastoral retreats, and for the first two novels, *Springtime and Harvest* and *Prince Hagen,* he rented or simply occupied a number of shacks in Quebec and northern New York. The novels were remote and romantic, like the settings he chose for himself, but the second one moved in gingerly on the capitalist scene by borrowing characters and plot fragments from Richard Wagner's *Der Ring Des Nibelungen,* a five-part immensity about gold and greed. The novel was born, Upton said later, "of the playing of the score of Das Rheinold [the first part of *Der Ring*] to so many squirrels and partridges." It had a cast of dwarfs from the bowels of the earth (where all the gold was) and of Wall Street brokers. The head of the dwarfs, Prince Hagen, moved in on Wall Street and captured the place. Upton himself appeared as a commentator in the novel by the name of Virtus Semper. He observed the prince's actions with disapproval and finally said to him, "Does it ever really occur to you how pitiful it is for a nation to center its whole life on the digging of gold?" The prince replied, "No, I can't say I ever thought of it." The prince was a strong believer in social Darwinism, and when he gained Wall Street control he observed philosophically, "Life is the survival of the strong. I care not if it is in the jungle, or the city, it is the warfare of each against all." Luckily Upton was able to arrange to have the prince killed by his own runaway horses.

During the writing of the first two novels he suddenly became accompanied in his various pastoral shacks by a girl; and when she came to live with him full time he built himself a platform at some distance from their living quarters, where he composed all day, scarcely moving. He *couldn't* move. The platform was so small he couldn't stir from his chair on it without falling off. He was like Saint Simeon on his pillar.

The girl, a childhood friend, had renewed their acquaintance by reading his manuscripts and declaring them wonderful. Upton described their romance in a later, embarrassingly autobiographical novel, *Love's Pilgrimage*. If that book was even half right about his views about sex and marriage at the time, the girl, Meta Fuller, had found herself no bargain. True, she had been the one to come to him first, full of literary purrings, but he took her advances at face value and quickly converted their affair to something she certainly hadn't planned on, that is, a reading-and-discussion group. They read Green's *History of the English People* to each other in the evenings, and sometimes Corydon (Meta) "would have to go and plunge her face into cold water to keep her eyes open."

But they were young, and thought of themselves as very modern. They decided to marry, without benefit of clergy or officialdom, by reciting to each other their own vows. Thyrsis (Upton) had already indicated to her that since he was a genius he expected that she would serve him as such; but in their marriage vows the service obligations were made out to be reciprocal. She said, "I take thee, Thyrsis, to be the companion of my soul. I give myself to thee freely, for the sake of love, and I will stay as long as thy soul is better with me than without. But if ever this should cease to be I will leave thee; for if my soul is weaker than thine I have no right to be thy mate."

Thyrsis replied in the same fashion. Thus married, they went on reading Green's *History*. Some months later they traveled to New York and, becoming legally tied, settled into a tenement. Upton then went to see a doctor about his stomach trouble. The doctor asked him how his marriage was going and Upton responded:

> "We're just—brother and sister."
> "But—why did you get married?"
> "We got married because we wanted to study, . . ."
> "And how long do you expect to keep that up?"
> "For a good many years—until we've accomplished something, and until we've got some money."
> "I don't wonder your stomach's out of order."

Meta was of course not the radical idealist she had seemed to be when she read the early manuscripts, but she did know something about love and now introduced Upton to it, with the result that she instantly became pregnant. They discussed abortion learnedly but were afraid of it. The baby was born and became, for Meta, a singular burden in the primitive, group-discussion life that Upton favored (at one point it nearly died of malnutrition in a cabin not far from the Princeton library). Soon Meta was spending much of her time at home with her parents, hearing the parents tell her what a fool she had married. Meanwhile the fool was writing his third novel, *The Journal of Arthur Stirling*.

The Journal of Arthur Stirling was the novel to end the romantic and literary novel mode he had settled on earlier, but to write it he still demanded romantic isolation for the creator. In early spring he dug in on an island in Lake Erie, where "the icy gales blowing through the tent" almost froze him to his chair. For some days he could not get back to the mainland at all, and had to live on "dried apples and saltine crackers." He shot a crow but couldn't eat him, and a little later he laid plans to shoot a deer but became absorbed in his reading. The deer came up behind him, scared him, and rushed off into the brush, "twenty feet at a leap, and me pulling the trigger of an uncocked gun." It was a long year, writing of Arthur Stirling. Upton worked fourteen hours a day, sometimes not moving from his chair for hours, and so he suffered from his now usual indigestion. He went to a country doctor, who told him to let his food be digested "by the contents of the stomach of a pig." The doctor's proposal was the first of a series of eccentric remedies and diets that he experimented with for decades, and though it didn't work the thought appealed to him as an "advanced idea." As for the character of Arthur Stirling, that was an advanced idea too. Arthur Stirling was Upton himself, preparing for a new life, a life of social engagement. In the novel Arthur Stirling put up with the indignities of the world's neglect of art as long as he could (neither of Upton's first novels had sold at all), then committed suicide, leaving Upton a clear road into the future.

How seriously Upton was himself thinking of suicide at the time is not clear, but after he had finished the novel he at least felt that he could joke about it. He joked by arranging to have a notice printed in a New York paper reporting Stirling's death by drowning in the Hudson River. The hoax helped him sell the book, but annoyed reviewers when they found out that they had been had. Meanwhile Upton, having disposed of his old self, and having put his wife and child momentarily aside, was now ready for socialism.

The European literary traditionalists to whom American writers

paid their respects in the nineteenth century had always decreed that
writing was genteel, but many rebellious Americans starting with Whitman were not respectful of such views, and if there was one point
upon which most of them could agree it was that gentility was a big
part of what was wrong with the country. Gentility was manners
without substance; it was hypocrisy; it was Huck Finn's aunt. Hence,
thumbing the nose at gentility became a familiar American game for
decades, starting with Huck himself and working up to intellectuals
like Ezra Pound and proletarian writers like Mike Gold. Jack London
with his celebrations of violence and the hard life was also an antigentility gamesman. All Socialists had to be. And in his genteel way
Upton was too.

But the ways of playing the antigentility game were many. There
were for instance, those who attacked the soft *lives* of the genteel, and
there were those who instead went after their soft *language,* the fuzzy
euphemistic language of writers like Henry Van Dyke, who wrote
mistily about truth and beauty and culture. Neither Jack nor Upton
criticized the language. They had both been brought up with verbal
gentility as the starting point for the writing act. They had been taught
the traditional literary forms and subjects at school. They had been
told what was polite and what was abusive speech, what was correct
and what was incorrect grammar. In sharp contrast to the poetry
rebels (Pound, Williams, and so on) and the prose rebels (Stein, Dos
Passos, and Hemingway) they never found the occasion to carry their
rebellion as far as the word. Perhaps they were simply born too early
to do so, since for both of them their writing manners had been shaped
before the usually announced dates of modernism (such as Gertrude
Stein experimenting with "cubist" sentences in 1907 and *Poetry* magazine beginning in 1912). But even if they had been born later they
probably would not have become good *literary* radicals. Aesthetic
modernism fared with them pretty much as it later fared with the
Socialist realists of the USSR. Modernism was wrong, they thought,
because it didn't reach the people. It was individualism rampant. It
was anarchic and antisocial. Jack London's biographer Irving Stone
(*Sailor on Horseback*), was himself a popular writer, and he was most
insistent that Jack was a great literary radical. He claimed that Jack
had been the one who had really set the American short story in motion and also the one who brought American fiction to focus on common humanity. But whatever Stone was thinking of, he was not think-

ing of Jack's reforms in terms of Jack's words, sentences, conventions. Jack was a Victorian verbally, and capitalized on familiar, genteel form and constructions, with plenty of room for ministerial discursiveness. *The Call of the Wild* was thoroughly traditional in this sense. For all its thematic ferocity it was slick magazine matter, the kind in which modernists found bourgeois softness, found parlor manners instead of what Ortega y Gasset called "lived reality." But Jack, like his best-selling biographer, was not ready to find the softness there. He would not have sold many copies of *The Call of the Wild* if he had.

And Upton was no literary revolutionary either. He too wanted to reach the people and wanted to reach them with ideas as well as art. He threw up his hands at formal innovation like free verse and stream-of-consciousness syntax. Bred up among southern cousins, he was possessed of a traditional gentility deeper than Jack's, and he was never able to outlive it. One of his best books, written in late years, was traditional stem to stern and showed very well where his literary heart lay. It was a reconstruction of Richardson's *Pamela,* bringing Richardson's heroine up to date. Upton put Pamela, a poor country girl, among evil modern capitalists rather than evil nobility and had her write home about *them.* He kept the eighteenth-century female virtues but moved the locale to modern California.

So when Upton had Arthur Stirling commit suicide because Arthur was too literary, he did not thereby dispose of the leisurely traditional novel genre with its talky moments and high moral tone. He simply disposed of aesthete Stirling himself so that he could get on with "social justice." (Late in life he declared that those were the two words written on his heart.)

His first venture after *The Journal of Arthur Stirling* was a transitional effort for him, a Civil War novel, *Manassas,* that mixed history with social fervor about slavery. It was a windy bore, but it set the stage for *The Jungle* (1905), in which for the first time he moved directly to the contemporary social scene. The occasion for writing *The Jungle* was a strike at a Chicago meatpacking plant, about which he first wrote a short piece for the socialist paper, *Appeal to Reason,* under the heading, "YOU HAVE LOST THE STRIKE. And Now What Are You Going To Do About It?" The editor of *Appeal to Reason* was enthusiastic about Upton's enthusiasm and proposed that he do something at length about "present day wage slaves" comparable to what he had done with Negro slaves in *Manassas*. He offered Upton five hundred dollars for prepublication serial rights.

Five hundred dollars was big money to Upton. He accepted, hurried to Chicago, and became an investigative reporter for seven weeks. He lived his role just as Jack had done in London's East End. In fact Jack was his model, since *The People of the Abyss* had appeared six months earlier, and Meta and he had read it together. He wandered about the packing plants "dressed in his usual cheap clothes and carrying a dinner pail." But unlike Jack he did not then make himself the hero of the work. Instead he concocted a strong proletarian immigrant for his hero, a hard worker who was, with his large family, new to the city and the language, and especially new to the ruthlessness of American capitalism. He then imposed his own Chicago experience upon the immigrant life, an experience which had been stunning.

He had seen the hogs killed, had heard the squeals as they were killed, had felt that the squeals somehow stood for the whole tragedy of hog or worker in Chicago, being "the squeal of the universe" against injustice. He had seen bad meat thrown in with good or dumped on the floor to be run over by rats. He had watched inspectors being bribed not to notice, and he had watched the workers doing their jobs under conditions unsafe and unsanitary, with no job protection whatever. He had also watched the peripheral business people—the storekeepers and tenement owners—join with the meatpacking bosses in what he quickly concluded to be a classic instance of social injustice against the whole worker population. He had watched all this, and so sat down with his usual intensity to put it down. Hundreds of pages.

The dialogue was sometimes as stilted as in the pulps he had written, and the emotions were sometimes lush and hokey, as in his first two novels, but the center of *The Jungle* was new. The center was what he had personally experienced, and it was a good tough center. As Finley Peter Dunne said of the book when it appeared, "It shud be taken between meals" and not by "maiden ladies contemplatin' their first sea voyage." It earned Upton a quick thirty thousand dollars.

Among those to praise the book was Jack, who had admired *Manassas* while Upton and Meta were admiring Jack's *People of the Abyss,* and who now sent forth a loud socialist blast, in *Appeal to Reason,* against the capitalist press, which he declared had joined in a conspiracy of silence against the book. Then there was Teddy Roosevelt, who, much taken by the book, invited Upton to the White

House for lunch, instituted an investigation of the meat-packing industry—an investigation that confirmed Upton's findings—and soon had Upton as a difficult, indefatigable pen pal. (TR rapidly tired of Upton's letters, and remarked to a publisher that he wished Upton would let him run the country for a while.) As for the press, it was not silent long about the book; 1906 became a triumphant year for muckraking and produced the passage of the first Pure Food and Drug Act. Upton would never do better, and in retrospect *The Jungle* remains a phenomenon worth studying both for the social forces contributing to its success, and for the curious turn that Upton's literary talents took in it, a turn that proved to be definitive and final for him, a turn to a single-mindedly activist notion of what a novel should do and be.

The social forces were the complicated turn-of-the-century money forces that had depressed Henry Adams and had produced a variety of political reactions from the socialist party itself and a whole spectrum of union movements, to Bryan's populism and Roosevelt's trust-busting. The forces had also created a great wave of journalistic muckraking, led by such writers as Lincoln Steffens, Ida Tarbell, and (in fiction) Frank Norris. In this atmosphere Upton surfaced as a thoroughly political animal in 1905, when he formed an organization known as the Intercollegiate Socialist Society and persuaded Jack, whom he had just met, to be front man and president. The organization was a significant entity for some years, giving Upton his own political machine to direct and keep oiled, and effectively pulling him away from his platforms in the woods. Naturally such involvement came to direct in some measure his literary energies. *The Jungle* was the first clear instance of the effect of such involvement, and for all its tedious old-world story-tellingness it was a new phenomenon on the American novel scene.

The novelty of it may be seen by comparing it with Frank Norris's *Octopus* (1901). The two books are superficially similar, both being addressed to a contemporary instance of social injustice (Norris's revelations about railroad price-fixing were a model for Upton's handling of the meatpackers), and both being obviously based in their authors' fierce social convictions. But Norris's convictions never drove him into the political arena with Upton's fervor, nor did they lead him to subordinate his novel-making to his thesis-making. In *The Jungle,* on the other hand, the meat-packing scandal, together with its larger implications about monied America, ran the whole novel show. Upton's seven weeks of research in Chicago gave him a view of a Lithuanian wedding, an immigrant family's daily tenement life, and of course the many hardships of a laborer's working week. It did not give him, perhaps because he wanted no such gift, any feeling for the special and private feelings and thoughts of those upon whom he modeled his fictional characters in *The Jungle*. He only saw representative immigrant problems before him on the Chicago streets, and he duly created representative problems for representative persons in the novel. If anything his political obsessions served to aggravate the mechanical qualities of character and plot that he had relied on in his hacking days, though the mechanics were now different. The mechanics were now simply the socio-political mechanics of labor unrest in Chicago in 1904–1905, rather than the white-hat black-hat mechanics of the Spanish-American War, and they were not much more convincingly human. Upton had conceived the sad story of *The Jungle*'s hero, Jurgis, as a story of ideological conversion; so hapless Jurgis was not only obliged to suffer all the tyranny of the meat-packers, but obliged to obey Upton's political needs too—that is, finally obliged to turn Socialist—at which point Upton simply abandoned him in favor of a thirty-page terminal academic discussion of the virtue of socialism. Upton's biographer Leon Harris tells us that Upton was never happy with his resolutions for either Jurgis or the novel, but there they are. Norris could never have used a character as Upton used Jurgis, yet Upton seemed not even aware of the transparency of such usage. Such usage became the norm in the dozens of Sinclair books to follow, and such usage eventually doomed him on the American literary scene.

Still, Upton's blindness to the damage that an ideological imperative can do to the human complexities out of which great novels mostly grow was at least matched by the blindness of the press to those imperatives, as they were displayed in *The Jungle*. *The Jungle*'s worldwide fame and influence would have constituted a complete triumph for less ambitious promoters than Upton, but for him its success was—and understandably—clouded by the reporters' diversionary accounts of its meaning. What he most particularly wanted from *The Jungle,* recognition and acknowledgement of it as a *socialist* document, was what he did not get. He had conceived of the book as more than a muckraking book, and he had placed great store not only on Jurgis's developing awareness of socialism, but also on the final thirty-page discussion of socialism. Did the press recognize those elements of the novel? Not at all. For the press Jurgis's politics and the last thirty pages didn't exist, and for the press the main Sinclair thesis—that what was happening in the meat-packing establishments was not an isolated abuse but central to the ways of American capitalism—didn't exist either. The reporters simply ignored his dearest convictions—as reporters persist in doing with similar books to this day—and dwelt instead on the book's particular muckraking revelations, such as Upton's discovery that some of the beef coming out of Chicago was tubercular. As Upton put it, "I aimed at the public's heart, and by accident I hit it in the stomach."

But he didn't mean that *he* hit it by accident. He meant that the press hit it for him.

In a later book about the press, *The Brass Check,* he developed a metaphor to describe the reporters' handling of his writings and life. He said that for all the big things he was aiming at—I will call them his major social impieties—the reporters would erect a cement wall, but that for the trivialities, and for the statements by him that they could turn against him (especially later, when his marital troubles became national news) they would open a great channel. The trivial or bad would then be instantly transmitted to the public, sometimes, he said with pride, as far as New Zealand.

And then there was also Teddy Roosevelt's predictable deafness to Upton's socialism. For Roosevelt, Upton's socialism was fanaticism. Where, then, were the intelligent readers willing to take the book, for better or worse, as it was written? Too many of them were not in America but Europe, where cool-tempered, sweepingly general discussions in plays and novels had become conventional. In America such sweep seemed awkward, sometimes comic, and Charlie Chaplin liked to parody Upton's manner by making world-shaking statements with an expressionless face, keeping his mouth fixed in a thin smile. That smile dominated *The Jungle*'s last pages, but it was a smile that the odd Europeans seemed to like.

Wearing that smile, Upton would go on from *The Jungle* to investigate the oil industry, the coal industry, the press, the universities, the churches, Henry Ford, Andrew Carnegie, and many others. He would back solid causes and fringe causes. He would churn out thousands of pages of what he would himself describe as propaganda. He would maintain that what he was doing was a normal way for a literary man to conduct himself. And he would send the thousands of pages off to important people for comment. His second wife, Mary Craig (of whom more in a moment), reported that for such efforts he received from H. G. Wells an inscribed book, "To the most hopeful of socialists from the next most hopeful," and from G. B. Shaw a letter telling him, "When People ask me what has happened in my lifetime I do not refer them to the newspaper files and to the authorities, but to your novels." Of course Wells, Shaw, and their kind had plenty of opponents too, but they were not washed out by the literary powers, as was Upton by the New York and Boston publishing houses.

The Jungle's thirty thousand dollars came and went rapidly, as all of Upton's monies did. He spent it on some horses and a commune. The commune was known as Helicon Hall, and Upton created it at just the time that Jack was building his ship to sail around the world. ("You are building a yacht," wrote Upton, "and I a colony. I wonder which costs the most money, and takes the most time.") It was a commune with forty adults consenting, according to Upton's own prescriptions, to "cooperate in the essentials and eliminate the unessential," to use the shower before entering the pool, "treat children as playmates and equals rather than playthings and pets," and to free themselves, by putting their money in the common pot, "from most of the occasions of bitterness which exist elsewhere." It was also a commune where there was a good deal of talk of free love, and where Meta had several real affairs, including one with the "tramp poet" Harry Kemp that seems to have done much to destroy her marriage to Upton. When the commune broke up—or rather, burned down—the newspapers decided it had been a vile love nest, and with that scandal—which seems to have been as maliciously reported as Upton claimed—some of the shine went off Upton's reputation from *The Jungle*. His books poured forth but the commercial publishers were leery of him, thinking him an opportunist rather than a serious social reformer (he tried to be both), and driving him to the practice—which he was to continue erratically for the rest of his life—of publishing and distributing his own books. The combination of an unfriendly press and a harassing separation from Meta did not improve his writings. A characteristic book of his for the period—before he married Mary Craig Kimbrough in 1913—was *The Moneychangers* (1908), a much thinner book than *The Jungle* containing a villain modeled on Pierpont Morgan, who would have done well in one of Upton's early pulps. There was "not a man in Wall Street who could live for twenty-four hours if Dan Waterman went after him in earnest," Upton wrote, and sent Dan instantly after several financial victims as well as several beautiful females. Then he had Dan take out after the book's innocent heroine, luring her to his yacht with him and unexpectedly (to her) making love to her. Luckily the hero arrived in a rowboat in time and called her name outside the closed cabin door. As she described the tense moment to the hero later, "When you called my name, he dropped me and sprang back. I never saw such furious hatred on a man's countenance in my life."

As for the other characters, they walked around in their social roles only, and they thought about money day and night. They were essentially caricatures of Social Darwinists. What they liked most was a "good vigorous hatred," and they cultivated that hatred, put it to the service of destruction, and thought of it as the "highest reach of civilization: It is the survival of the fittest in a new form. You study your victim, you find out his weaknesses and his foibles, and you know just where to plant your sting. . . . You choose your allies carefully and you surround him; then when you get through you go after another."

In this novel Upton was describing the story behind the story of the Panic of 1907, and though he was not wrong about the kind of financial actions that produced the panic, and though he did not end his novel with a thirty-page panel discussion, he certainly overplayed his political hand. What he and his hero had seen during the 1907 Panic filled him, he said, "with dismay, almost with terror," and he determined to fight it all his life. How? In the last line of the book he revealed his own (not his hero's) life plan. "I am going into politics. I am going to teach the people."

A better book of the period was his autobiographical novel, *Love's Pilgrimage,* the work describing, among other things, his early platonic affair with Meta. When he came to write of the birth of their child he was unusually explicit for the times, with the happy result that he had another *cause* on his hands, which he characteristically proceeded to exploit. As became his steady practice he circulated copies to scores of important people and publicized their more vehement replies. Some of them found him magnificently daring, others thought that about his own wife he could have been more reticent, and an English bishop "begged" through his secretary to return the copy of *Love's Pilgrimage,* which "he had no desire to read or possess." But the book had the merit of being a gesture away from propaganda and toward literary spaciousness. Jack was delighted with it at first, and his reaction to it makes an interesting introduction to Upton's lifelong "people" problem and how to make them live, beyond their messages, on the page.

Jack read early pages of the manuscript and wrote that it was a "hummer." It was going to be "the rawest, reddest meat that has been slammed at any American publisher in the last five decades." Then he read more of the manuscript and went silent. Three years later he explained himself unpleasantly, saying that he could not feel close to Upton because of Upton's attitudes, as expressed in the book, toward sex.

Their exchange took place at the time of the appearance of Jack's antidrink book, *John Barleycorn*. Upton wrote Jack to say that he was delighted with the book and with Jack's public announcement that he had reformed, adding that his own antipathy to drink had always made it difficult for him to get on with other men, including Jack, because he felt "outside the gang." (In the letter he even blamed his ignorance of Meta's nymphomania on his isolation.) Jack wrote back an unpleasant and distant "Dear Sinclair" letter saying that no, it wasn't drink that had come between them but "your sex-poise, or sex-attitude. . . . It is so foreign to me that it keeps me out of touch with you. In short it's a temperamental lack of touch." Upton replied with thin-smile coolness, "I think that you will find that my work is gradually changing . . . as to sex," and they became friends again, at least to the extent that Jack then wrote an introduction for an anthology of socialist verse that Upton edited. Yet the subject of his sexual innocence and insufficiency wouldn't go away for Upton. He was stuck with it, because by this time he had found a woman to replace Meta, one who was as convinced as Jack was that he knew very little about women. She seemed to like him for it.

Mary Craig Kimbrough was of a good southern family that was convinced she had gone slumming when she lit on Upton. After all, she had attended the Gardner School for Young Ladies in New York, where the school receptions offered, said the brochure, "opportunities to meet the millionaires of the world's richest city." In her later accounts of Upton she was extremely patronizing about the shabbiness of his appearance when he was courting her. She persuaded her family to tolerate him because he had good southern blood, and she professed to see him as a little boy who needed to be taken care of.

Still, she had enough romance in her to be genuinely attracted by his enthusiasms and by the continuing political uproar that he managed to stir up around himself. After their marriage she picketed with him, campaigned with him, wrote ferocious letters to the papers with him, and when he took arms against no less a person than John D. Rockefeller she was delighted to walk up and down with him in front of the Rockefeller Tarrytown estate, to make that rich man aware, wrote biographer Leon Harris, of "the inequities and injustices of ignorant and outdated industrial practices." She also, however, tried to help him understand women and bring that understanding into his novels. There she became something of a meddler. The book she meddled with, *King Coal,* was based on Rockefeller's rough handling of the Ludlow mining strike in Colorado, where strikebreakers had set fire to workers' tents and killed fourteen women and children. It was a fierce tract but it was a novel too. Upton sent his first version of it to the editor at Macmillan who had accepted his Civil War novel, *Manassas.* George Brett was also Jack's editor there—and he had been good to Jack, sending him urgently needed advances in the middle of the Pacific—but he was by no means sold on Upton. He had turned down *The Jungle,* and lost a mint there, but he was still unpersuaded that the genre that Upton had created for himself was properly literary. He therefore rejected *King Coal,* telling Upton to "bear in mind that it is a *novel* you are writing and not a work of history or controversy." Upton was crushed, and would have been more crushed if he had known what biographer Harris uncovered in the files decades later: a letter that Mary Craig wrote Brett at the time, saying that she agreed with him.

Craig even asked Brett to suggest a rewrite to Upton, which Brett did. And then Craig looked over Upton's shoulder during the rewrite, paying particular attention to the characters of the women in it. She must have bothered him with her industry, for he wrote Jack a sad and tired letter in the middle of the rewriting, saying that he had been working too hard, that he wished he knew Jack better so that he could get criticism from him, and then adding, "Craig insists on fussing with me over my female psychology. She insists that I can't portray women—and I have no doubt you'd agree with her."

Upton's letter to Jack proved to be even sadder after the fact, since it was the last letter between them. This was 1916. Jack was dead in two months.

Of course Upton's problem with female characters was only part of his genre problem. Brett accepted the revised version of *King Coal,* but the acceptance did not mean that thereafter Upton had a steady commercial publisher, except in England. His editors and friends were almost unanimous in telling him that he should lay off the propaganda and get to the noveling. His most interesting confrontation on the subject of the novelist's role and function came with Sherwood Anderson. He had written Anderson, also in 1916, with the intention of getting Anderson's signature on a socialist proclamation. Anderson replied with a letter that sounded remarkably like an Anderson story.

> My dear Sinclair:
> Your letter set me thinking. It was a cold snowy afternoon in Chicago. I left my office at four and started to walk home across the city. A man with a withered hand ran down a stairway out of a tenement. He had no overcoat and his clothes were thin. The blue veins on the back of his withered hand were ghastly blue. He saw me looking and stared into my eyes. His lips mumbled words.

Nor was the man with the withered hand sufficient local color for Anderson. He then added a middle-aged policeman and a young girl, who had a small romance on the street as he observed them, and who also "mumbled words."

> . . . Man, you seem to see and feel them socialists as things apart. You ask me to pity and understand socialists as you might ask me to understand the Arabs and Chinese.
> Truth is, Sinclair, I'm married to a socialist and when I vote I vote that ticket myself but if I thought the fact of my doing so set me apart in the way your letter suggests I'd quit in a hurry.
> Really I'm tempted to go at you hard in this matter. There is something terrible to me in the thought of the art of writing being bent and twisted to serve the end of propaganda. Why should we as writers be primarily socialists or conservatives, or anarchists, or anything else . . .
> I do want to see writers quit this drawing themselves apart, becoming socialists or conservatives or whatnot. I want them to be something of a brother to the poor brute who runs the sweatshop as well as to the equally unfortunate brutes who work for him.
> Won't we be better served thus? We are terribly young. We haven't even begun to understand our own American life. As writers can't we leave politics and economics to the more lusty throated ones and run

away, one by one, into the streets, the offices and the houses—looking at things, trying to write them down. . . .

It was some years before Upton worked up an adequate reply to Anderson's attack, but when he did so he did so publicly and unsmilingly in *Money Writes*:

> Suppose that Anderson in his letter had written to me, "Yes, of course, I see the class struggle. How could any clear-sighted man fail to see it? How could any honest man fail to see lt? How could any honest man fail to report it?" Would he then have become the white hope of the intelligentsia, as he is today? No indeed! The way to be a genius of the Freudian age is to write, 'How are you going to understand anyone or anything?' When the intellectual reads that he slaps his leg and cries, 'Aha, here is sincerity! here is naturalism! here is the real, elemental, primitive, naive! Here is something Russian! here is cabbage soup! . . . take the 13 volumes of Sherwood Anderson and analyze the characters: men and women who cannot adjust themselves to any aspect of life, cannot live in marriage or out of it, cannot make love, cannot consummate love, cannot restrain love . . . and always, everywhere, over and over again, the one repressed artist personality making agonized efforts to state *himself* in words.

Yes, Upton did have a strange "sex-attitude," as Jack put it and despite the social eloquence of the outburst above, the "over and over again" annoyance with love in it is most conspicuous. Furthermore the annoyance kept cropping up in odd places where one might have expected of him only coolness and rational poise. In the year after Jack's death, for example, Upton amazed the editors of the then-new socialist magazine, the *Masses,* by displaying high puritanical rage at the magazine for printing a story by Floyd Dell that was not, Upton said, about free love but "just smut. . . ." Dell, who was one of the editors and had always thought highly of Upton, was so struck by Upton's eccentric response that he became very curious about the man—and ten years later wrote a biography of him. The biography, though kind, dwelt constantly on Upton's puritanism, and concluded that Upton's imagination "was securely barricaded against real life." Biographer Harris, working on Upton from a distance but with the great quantities of evidence (from the Bloomington file), came to the same conclusion in 1975.

There is no doubt that behind the cool rational facade lurked a real eccentric, and the eccentricity cannot be ignored. He was, most particularly, a food and health nut, and tried on diets and physical training programs the way most people try on clothes. After taking the pig-pepsin in Canada for his unhappy stomach, he experimented with vegetarian dishes, all-meat diets, and plain fasting, and he also went in hard for "fletcherizing," even traveling a good distance to meet Dr. Fletcher himself and discuss with him the wonders of thorough chewing. He also conducted a learned argument by mail with a famous Yale economist, Irving Fisher (in whom Ezra Pound would later find interest), discussing with him not economics but diet. He visited as well with John Harvey Kellogg, the author of *The Itinerary of a Breakfast* (being a "popular account of the travels of a breakfast through the food tube . . . and of the obstacles it sometimes meets") and the builder of the Kellogg cereal empire. After spending some time at Kellogg's Battle Creek Sanitarium, trying out its dietary specialties, he wrote Kellogg that though he admired the sanitarium, "the cooked vegetarian diet is the worst diet that human beings can possibly follow." He added that Kellogg was in effect spiritually bankrupt for pretending to run a health resort while manufacturing "Health Chocolates and Sanitarium Sugar Cookies."

Then there was his interest, late in life, in what he called "mental radio," that had him attending seances and trying to figure out how a certain Pole named Ostoja could cause "a thirty-four pound table to rise four feet in the air." His most exciting psychic experience was a short conversation he had with Jack, who came back from the dead to tell him, via a medium (Craig herself!), that he (Upton) was "one of the three living writers who will be remembered." Jack did not say who the other two were, but he asserted that Upton was, of the three, the only one being read in Europe. Naturally Upton drew a book out of the seances, *Mental Radio,* but his attraction to the seances, other than as grist for his writing mill, resembled his susceptibility to food fads. Always behind his cool rationalism there were strange whirrings, some explicable as promotion stunts (from this distance *Mental Radio* seems thoroughly hoked up), but most of them genuinely based in his relentless, soul-slaving, flesh-saving, world-saving idealism.

Was his literary aesthetic a strange whirring too? Most of the American editors he dealt with certainly thought so, and most of his literary acquaintances thought so too. Even Ezra Pound, who wrote him that he had long admired his "cannonade," added, "I think you are at your best when you are LEAST trying to put over any particular idea. . . . If you get the thing written down, it does its own talking, and has more effect than any labeled preaching."

Yet Upton did have defenders for his labeled preaching, mostly abroad. If we put aside his eccentricities we can, I think, see him as an American manifestation of a mostly un-American tradition of literature, a tradition probably best represented in his time by those two British admirers of his, Shaw and Wells. Shaw and Wells were frequently criticized for the same failings as Upton—T. S. Eliot said that Shaw was "never really interested in life," and both Henry James and Joseph Conrad went after Wells for his ideological urgencies—but of course neither Shaw nor Wells was ever short on replies to such complaints. (And they had plenty of supporters.) The general line they took was that their critics were incurable *artistes* and therefore themselves not interested in life. The Shaw-Wells prescription for avoiding excessive aestheticism was to take pride in the role of journalist. Shaw announced that "journalism is the highest form of literature," adding that the writer who writes for all time "has his reward in being unreadable in all ages." Wells had his doubts about Shaw as a journalist (so did many others, including Ford Madox Ford, who remarked that Shaw did not record facts but invent them), but he too took the line that journalism was a way out of the aesthetic box: "Long ago, living in close conversational proximity to Henry James, Joseph Conrad and Mr. Ford Madox Hueffer, I escaped from under their immense artistic preoccupations by calling myself a journalist. To that title I adhere."

Wells and Shaw had a vision of the literary-journalistic act that can be said to be still with us in the debased form of novels and plays about Washington and big money by journalistic muckrakers, but both Wells and Shaw avoided the muckraker label by placing, on top of their journalism, another 'ism. They were, as was Upton, Socialists; they were, as was Upton, concerned with social criticism that went beyond tainted meat and crooked deals. But such concern in their work was attended to by a substantial audience, as Upton's dissertations on big issues were not. They did not suffer the isolation that Upton in his own country somehow achieved.

Was it that their dissertations were better dissertations? Or was it that America was just not receptive to such dissertations, especially anti-money dissertations? Perhaps the answer is yes to both questions. Anyway it seems clear that by the twenties Sherwood Anderson's put-down of Upton was of the order of a national literary vote against him, and whether he deserved it or not he certainly felt it.

So what did he do? Unable to sell his "novels" and straight polemics to big publishers, or his theories of what a literary man should be doing for a living to the critics, he kept publishing himself, and tirelessly publicizing himself, and tirelessly wearing his thin smile. Then in 1924 he announced to Craig that he was going to muckrake world literature *itself.*

He then did so in two volumes, *Mammonart* and *Money Writes,* one of which has already been quoted from here (his reply to Sherwood Anderson). The critics' response to the books was mostly shock, with Floyd Dell writing that *Money Writes* was "a God-damned lie," and Sinclair Lewis (who had been a sort of janitor, years before, in Upton's commune) saying, "My God, Upton, go and pray for forgiveness, honesty and humility!" Yet the books, though notable for extravagance of statement, do not seem shocking now. *Mammonart* was a breezy, angry literary history purporting to show who had been, down the ages, the impious speakers of truth, and who had been the slavish spokesmen for money and power. Dante had been a writer of truth, a muckraker, but Shakespeare had been a super propagandist for the enemy, "the crown and glory of the system of class supremacy," whose very name had become, since his death, "a magic word used by every time-server in the place of straight thinking and the reality of life." (Perhaps Upton borrowed his Shakespeare polemic from Shaw.) On the other hand Shelley was fine, "the supreme glory of English letters" because he "attacked class privilege, not merely political but industrial." Unfortunately, since the time of Shelley the literary scene had deteriorated. Of contemporary figures he had not much to say—he was saving them for the second book—but those he mentioned he managed to dislike, except Frank Norris, whose *Octopus* had "electrified" him, Ambrose Bierce, whom Upton described as a moral writer despite his hatred of socialism, and Stephen Crane, whose chief trouble was that he had taken up socialism for only two weeks. Not surprisingly, one of the important villains of the book was the popular writer Richard Harding Davis, whom he described as a typical sycophant of the "rulers." He reported having met Davis once. The man had rushed up to him to say, "You write books because you really have something to say, while I only write to make money." Upton was taken aback and said nothing, but Davis reaffirmed his plight: "It is true, I know it, and so do you." In the second volume, *Money Writes,* he went after the slick writers chiefly (Anderson, whom he attacked, was a distinguished exception) and took on the "central power-plant of Fascism in America," the *Saturday Evening Post,* under George Horace Lorimer, where Booth Tarkington and Zane Grey thrived. Upton described the two as the chief representative bootlickers of the "masked forces" of American corporations.

> Once Mr. Tarkington fooled me—I thought he was on the way to growing up. He wrote a novel called *The Turmoil,* telling some truth about our industrial squalor; but alas, the rebellious young hero performed the established fictional duty of marrying a pure girl of the leisure class, and living happy ever after upon the income of his father's greed.

And of Zane Grey, Upton observed that he had met *him* at a party and told him, "I make my heroes out of the same fellows that you make villains of." The remark, he said, astounded Grey, even though in a novel called *A Desert of Wheat* he had "portrayed the industrial workers as degenerates and criminals whose occupations were burning barns and crops, and abducting beautiful heroines." And who was the chief villain, according to Upton, among the literary critics? Upton chose no other than William Lyon Phelps—and Pound must have sympathized. Phelps, of Yale, had been Jack London's defender once, in 1906, when Yale authorities had threatened to keep Jack from speaking there, and Phelps had declared that Yale could not afford to be so cloistered; however, his vapid opinions in popular magazines since then had annoyed Upton, who had come to dislike the whole of Yale anyway, objectified, he thought, in the person of William Howard Taft, and dedicated to capitalism as its religion.[2] Phelps was evil because he was a literary hypocrite, one who could praise dead writers or foreign writers for qualities that merely frightened him at home. Thus, said Upton, Phelps had been full of praise for Dostoyevsky who, had he been alive and in America, would have been no more likely to be admitted to membership in Phelps's club than Theodore Dreiser.

Biographer Harris was, like all the other critics, unhappy with

---

2. "Capitalistic exploitation is Yale's religion; and you will note that in all its essentials it is identical with the religion of Rasputin and Tsar Nicholas, who blessed the icons of the lumber-interest people just as Yale's chaplains bless the flag when American Marines set out to shoot up natives in the West Indies and Central America for failing to pay their interest on the bonds of J. P. Morgan and his Yale trustees."

Mammonart and *Money Writes,* and explained Upton's trouble psychologically:

> It must have been an essential of Sinclair's sanity, or perhaps of his very life, to believe that his own failure as a poet was not due to a lack of artistry but rather to the state of society. Therefore, none of his other books seem to have been more necessary for him to write than *Mammonart* and *Money Writes!* None are so burdened with his worst fatuities. But he published both although he knew, even without the repeated warning of his friends, that these books would call down the scorn of enemies, friends and critics.

Yes, both books were sour grapes and probably were "necessary" for Upton, an obsessed man at the time, in much the way that Ezra Pound's works in protest of usury were necessary for Pound in the thirties and forties. Yet to say that about the books is to avoid the literary issues lurking behind their venom. The complaints in them about the emptiness of literary America remain telling, though Upton's literature remains suspect. His shadow will continue to darken the American literary scene, particularly in connection with the Anderson dispute. To Anderson's assertion that the lusty-throated ones should be left to handle the world, Upton kept saying that to do so was to leave the world to the apostles of greed, that is, the monied Social Darwinists (late in life Upton kept telling Truman, FDR, *everybody* that). And while his complaint can be answered with withdrawal-ism it is not thereby removed. It outlives Upton.

But Upton himself managed to outlive, if not his complaint, at least some of his intensities about it. In the thirties his fortunes improved. He had learned the hard way that perhaps after all socialism did not exist in America, with the result that when the depression set in and a good many literary competitors were learning to be leftists, Upton ran for governor of California on the Democratic ticket! His political savvy was impressive at the time, and he didn't lose by much (and of course, he was positive that he didn't lose fair and square). But his son David, now grown and a good Socialist, was shocked and telegraphed him from New York, "ALMOST COLLAPSING GRIEF INSANE OPPORTUNISM IS IT POSSIBLE YOU HAVE LOST ALL INTEGRITY AS MAN AND SOCIALIST STOP LEADERS HERE THUNDERSTRUCK." Then, aside from the near-miss in California he finally found a formula for commercial publishing success in his Lanny Budd series, and while the son might well have sent him another telegram about *that*, he probably would not have kept Upton's thin smile from softening a bit, growing mellow. Lanny Budd was a ridiculous hero but right down Upton's alley. He was immensely rich (how interesting that Upton should have given his alter ego wealth) and he was, like Upton, an aggressive optimist, taking on all the available great forces without blinking, and becoming a constant intimate, as Upton always wished to be, of world leaders. He was also, like all of Upton's other characters, an ideological prop, one upon which Upton decided to hang a complete history of modern times. Lanny showed up everywhere, knew everybody. He was not only a Hitler intimate (having witnessed his tantrums and ego trips), but he also knew Goering and Hess. For years he was also a secret agent for FDR and sent him major reports on the state of the world daily (FDR read every word). Then, moving to the Truman administration, Lanny talked a good bit with Truman about the USSR, telling him that he had discussed socialism with Stalin personally and left the consequences of the conversation up to Stalin. "The words I spoke to him," said Lanny to Truman, "would have moved any true socialist." And for amusement Lanny played Mozart sonatas with Einstein. And for drama Lanny persuaded a friend to write a "Dear Oppie" letter to the atomic guru Oppenheimer, so that Lanny could watch—as of course he did—the show at Los Alamos. Lanny was also on the scene for most of the other big shows of the century, from the forming of the United Nations to the Nuremberg trials. Upton found Lanny useful not only for getting his history written, but also of course for mouthing his own confident solutions to most human troubles. All in all the Lanny Budd books were perhaps closer to straight journalism than Upton's earlier work, that is, to journalism of the big-picture sort like John Gunther's best sellers of the time, such as *Inside Europe*. In fact they seem to have appealed to the same audience as Gunther's. Upton's biographer Harris reported on a number of public figures and journalists who complimented Upton on the series[3] (there were eleven books in all), but he mentioned no praise from literary lions except Bernard Shaw.

3. Harris, for instance, quotes Ladybird Johnson saying she "gained a more vivid recollection of foreign affairs (the rise of fascism and the American involvement in World War II) through the adventures of Lanny Budd than from reading the newspapers!"

When Upton died at the age of ninety a picture of him in the *New York Times* showed him standing beside a pile of his ninety books that stretched above his head. The *Times* reported that in an interview a year or so before his death he had listed for the interviewer his ten greatest accomplishments: cheap and inspected meat, an end to wage slavery in Colorado mining camps, helping found the ACLU, better newspapers, spurring an interest in psychic phenomena, his EPIC (End Poverty in California) campaign for governor, his Lanny Budd books, his democratic influence in Japan (not mentioned by Harris), his founding of the College Socialist Society with Jack London, and his campaign against drinking. Quite a list! But conspicuously missing was his effort to turn the American literary community around. For of course he hadn't turned it around, and he hadn't been accepted by the community. He hadn't even won a Pulitzer prize, though the Pulitzer naturally gravitated to journalistic fiction.[4] As a *New York Times* editorial was quick to point out on his death, "Upton Sinclair was not and is not considered a towering literary figure. . . ." Upton would have smiled his thin smile at that judgement and perhaps been offended by it even while knowing it to be correct. But whether he took offense or acknowledged his literary limits he would not, I am quite sure, have wanted to rewrite a word. From start to finish he had always had other causes than literature.

---

4. Harris reported that *Boston,* his two-volume novel about the Sacco-Vanzetti affair, was seriously considered for a Pulitzer, but rejected.

FOUR

William Carlos Williams and the Puritans

In the early days of the leftist magazine the *Masses,* Upton Sinclair wrote a letter to its editors to make what became a steady complaint from him about modern poetry: the line divisions made no sense. He asked the editors to print a poem by a "so-called modern poet" but print it as prose and offer a prize to any reader "who could divide the prose into lines in the same way that the poet had done." The editors didn't take him up on the project, but three decades or so later in 1951 he still had the project in his head when a review of two books by William Carlos Williams appeared in the *New Republic.* Upton wrote a two-page letter to the editors this time, and at the beginning he made a good summary of his trouble with the modernists:

> Poetry began to be modern about 40 years ago, and first I gave up looking for any rhyme, and then I gave up looking for any rhythm, then I gave up looking for any melody, any beauty, any wisdom, any sense.

Then he came back to his narrower complaint about line divisions, by damning six Williams lines quoted by the reviewer:

> Like a cylindrical tank fresh silvered
> upended on the sidewalk to advertise
> some plumber's shop, a profusion
> of pink roses bending ragged in the rain—
> speaks to me of all gentleness and its
> enduring.

Why, Upton wanted to know, shouldn't "a profusion" *begin* a line, since it was beginning a clause, rather than ending one? He saw no reason for throwing away "the elemental rules of sentence structure, and the physical facts of the human lungs and vocal chords."[1]

The editors printed the letter with a line at the end: "Poets, speak up!" A few poets (and critics) then did speak up for about two months, with one or two trying to provide Williams with a rationale for his line breaks, but with most sharing Upton's opinion that no rationale would do. (No rationale from Williams was printed, nor from the reviewer, M. L. Rosenthal.) There the controversy ended, with Upton's problem—and related problems like the strange backward logic of the simile in the lines—still rankling. Poor Upton, he wrote poetry too, and though it was old-fashioned it sometimes appeared in the *New Republic*. Here is a sample (1926), in which all the lines (except the first) end as both syntax and rhyme used to like to decree:

An Evangelist Drowns

What's this? A terror-spasm grips
My heart strings, and my reason slips.
Oh God, it cannot be that I,
The bearer of Thy Word, should die!
My letters waiting in the tent!
The loving messenger I sent!
My daughter's voice! my mother's kiss!

1. William Carlos Williams published nearly fifty books. Not as prolific as Upton Sinclair, he was luckier with publishers, or rather one publisher, James Laughlin of New Directions. Laughlin took him on in 1937 and handled everything after that. He also reprinted earlier works, and has kept everything in print. All the Williams books have close autobiographical connections but these two New Directions books are the most useful: *The Autobiography of William Carlos Williams* (1951) and *Imaginations* (1970), a collection edited and introduced by Webster Schott and containing, among others, two crucial early works, *Kora in Hell* and *Spring and All*. Then there is a perceptive study, *William Carlos Williams: The Knack of Survival in America* by Robert Coles (Brunswick, N. J.: Rutgers University Press, 1974) plus two biographies other than my own: Mike Weaver, *William Carlos Williams: The American Background* (Cambridge: Cambridge University Press, 1972); and Paul Mariani, *William Carlos Williams: A New World Naked* (New York: McGraw Hill, 1981).

My short biography here is not a condensation but a by-product of my research for *William Carlos Williams: Poet from Jersey* (Boston: Houghton Mifflin, 1974), which was completed with the constant help of James Laughlin and the Williams family, starting with William's widow, Florence Williams, who died in 1976, and moving to his two sons, William and Paul. For information about William's misfortunes with the Library of Congress "consultantship" I refer the reader to my own pamphlet, "William Carlos Williams: The Happy Genius of the Household" (1984).

> My pulpit notes on Genesis!
> Oh, count the souls I saved for Thee,
> My Savior, will thou not save me?
> Ten thousand to my aid would run,
> Bring me my magic microphone!
> Send me an angel, or a boat . . .
> The senseless waters fill her throat.

Bill Williams would probably have been amused by Upton's lines, and certainly Ezra Pound, his guru in modernity, would have sympathized with their intent, since Ezra himself liked to indulge in light satiric verse when there was a good target at hand like an evangelist. The trouble with Upton was that his social impieties did not extend to his aesthetic, and especially not to free verse, while the impieties of Ezra and Bill began there.

No, not quite. At least for Bill there was a brief literary period when he thought he was a traditionalist and a disciple of Keats. He had a slim volume printed—with his own money of course—of archaic verses that Keats would have burned instantly but that at least stopped lines where Upton wanted them stopped. A sample

> Love is twain, it is not single,
> Gold and silver mixed in one.
> Passion 'tis and pain which mingle,
> Glistering then for aye undone.

So one theory to explain how Bill went to dividing lines peculiarly has to be that after his slim volume appeared he was as depressed as Keats would have been with it, hence set out to do something, anything, different. (Ogden Nash explained the wild lineage that made him famous with a similar argument: he had tried to write good verse and failed; so he set out to write bad verse and succeeded.) But the other theories to explain him as poet are more complicated and take us back further.

His father, an Englishman, met his mother, a French-Dutch, Sephardic Jewish Spaniard, in Puerto Rico, and married her in, of all places, Jersey City. They then moved to the little town of Rutherford, New Jersey (just west of the Palisades), for the birth of William, and from there the salesman father commuted daily to Manhattan on the Hoboken Ferry. A second child, Edgar, was born a year later, and soon came to act as if he were the elder child. Meanwhile the father's mother, Grandmother Wellcome, who was to figure prominently in Bill's poems but seems never to have been convincing about where the name Williams came from, moved in with them, and the father's business prospered sufficiently to finance travel and a sensible education for both children. (For Bill that meant a year in France at age fourteen, two high school years commuting to Horace Mann School near Columbia University, and then a shift directly into medical school at the University of Pennsylvania.)

But the father was a remote, stiff, traveling man (though known to have read Shakespeare aloud in the parlor once or twice), and the mother was an unhappy artist-dreamer. She had been to art school in Paris, so she dreamed of living in Paris rather than in a dull little town. Also she was angry at the presence of her mother-in-law, and only intermittently content with being a mother at all. Accordingly, the grandmother played a parental role in Bill's early life, though it was the mother who pushed him into medicine. (Her brother was a successful doctor in Puerto Rico.) The medical decision was one that Bill actively questioned during the years of his medical training, internship in New York, and then early practice as a general practitioner at home.

Those were also the years when he tried his hand at being Keats,[2] but they included the years at Penn, years when he met three important modernists: Pound, Hilda Doolittle, and artist Charles Demuth. They were years when he was not only unsettled about his future but also insecurely aware that he had managed to omit an ordinary undergraduate education. He found himself taking courses in biology and anatomy while Pound, across the quadrangle, was deep into Provençal verse; and he was dealing with the sick and maimed in tough New York hospitals while Pound was picking up a master's degree in French. Also, he was not well read in the literary classics, in history or philosophy (he remained a poor reader all his life). He might or might not have learned much from four years of the liberal arts, but their omission was hard on his morale, making him feel like a redskin among palefaces.

2. In his autobiography Bill claimed to have written a little free-verse poem while still at Horace Mann, but the date for it is suspect. Here is the poem: "A black, black cloud / flew over the sun / driven by the fierce flying / rain." Bill ridiculed the poem later for having the rain driving the clouds—a good point—but he didn't complain, as Upton would have, about the line divisions.

His younger brother, Edgar, helped to make him feel that way. Edgar went to MIT, and Edgar distinguished himself academically; Edgar won an architectural *Prix de Rome* while Bill was struggling as an intern. Edgar was the success story in the family, and he didn't mind making Bill know it.

And Pound helped to make him feel inferior too, though he could also be kind and conscientiously encouraging. Pound was an eccentric scholar and something of a scholarly fraud when he put his mind to it, but he was aggressive in his knowingness, usually adopting the role of pedagogue with his friend. And by 1909—he was twenty-four—he could lord it over Bill—who was twenty-six—not only because of his learning but because of his new placement in the world. He had moved to London; he knew everybody who was anybody. He wrote back to Rutherford telling William to get out of that "hole in the wall."

It was Pound chiefly who brought the impieties of modernism to Bill and Pound who provided much of the intellectual ammunition needed for both of them to attack the pieties, that is, such matters as the tradition of the verse line. Yet it was Bill—and many years later Pound declared it to be so—who of the two came through with the first genuinely modernist piece of verse, a little thing full of archaisms, and conventional in its line divisions, but nonetheless new, a breakthrough. Pound paid tribute to it in 1965 when his own first book of poems (*A Lume Spento,* 1909) was reprinted, a book he then described as a collection of "stale cream puffs." They were written, he said, while Bill was moving ahead with "The Coroner's Children."

Pound was wrong about the title of the poem and the date but not about the spirit of it. It is a good poem and, oddly, one that even Upton might have approved. Here it is.

> Hic Jacet
>
> The coroner's merry little children
>   Have such twinkling brown eyes.
> Their father is not of gay men
>   And their mother jocular in no wise,
> Yet the coroner's merry little children
>   Laugh so easily.
>
> They laugh because they prosper.
>   Fruit for them is upon all the branches.

> Lo! how they jibe at loss, for
>> Kind heaven fills their little paunches!
> It is the coroner's merry merry children
>> Who laugh so easily.

Its rhythm and line structure are not radically irregular, and do not represent what Bill would soon be experimenting with, but the rhyming of "brown eyes" and "no wise" is handled in an offbeat way (the "wise" receives only light stress), and of course "branches" and "paunches" also jar slightly against each other. As for the short last line of each stanza, it is a positive dissonance, not at all a conventional refrain line. Such prosodic regularity as the poem possesses is muted and combated. And the resultant grittiness is itself an achievement.

But the poem's prosody is presumably not what Pound was impressed by, as he compared it with his own poetry of the time. His own was musically finished yet a poetry of traditional subjects and second-hand perceptions of the subjects, while the subject of "Hic Jacet" was novel and was treated (as Pound was soon to preach) "directly." It is not a poem out of Keats or Shakespeare but a poem out of doctoring, a poem out of the world of money, a poem hardly revolutionary but certainly a poem ironic at the expense of things as they are. Most of all, it is a poem of Bill's own experience. It is based in his medical immediacies.

Soon such a base would become his staple. He was to be a master of, and in his sometimes incoherent way an advanced aesthetician of, the immediately experienced in art. Pound's brand of modernism would not be like that. Between the two of them the complexities of the modernist phenomenon appear dramatically, and they are formidable.

But in the transition period represented by "Hic Jacet," Bill had plenty of his own complexities to contend with. He was entering medicine with a small office in his parents' front hall; he was getting married, against his father's wishes, to Flossie Herman after a long engagement; and he was feeling his way artistically, with little confidence, feeling his way in both poetry and drama. Even the poetry and drama contended against each other in him, with his dramatic past lodged in Philadelphia (where he had appeared in a number of university productions, mostly musicals), and his new poetic gropings being supervised from London by Pound. His dramatic experience told him of the importance of the conventional, the predictable, the formulaic, whereas poetry pulled him the other way. Between 1910 and 1913 he actually wrote several plays—never published—that were thoroughly old-fashioned, yet they contained little islands of rebellion, and revealed some of the troubles inside him.

In one play, *Betty Putnam,* the scene is set in old Salem, and the heroine, Betty Putnam, is thought by the Puritans to be a witch because she writes poetry! She escapes burning at the end by the skin of her teeth but not through any aid from the wicked father. The biographical connection is a bit obscure but tantalizing, and it would have been firmer if Betty had only been a *modern* poet. She was not. She was a busy rhymer.

In the other play, *Sauerkraut for the Cultured,* the cast contains a *good* father (the model seems to have been Bill's future father-in-law), and two sons competing for one female. The scene is also historical, placed in Nieu Amsterdam, but the two sons seem most contemporary; that is, they seem like Bill and Edgar. Bill and Edgar had indeed competed for a female, the older sister of Flossie (Charlotte), and when Bill lost the contest he turned around and proposed to Flossie instantly. (Later Edgar lost Charlotte too! She married another.) The play's lowbrow denouement involves a lamp-design contest for the two suitors: to design the proper lamp to hang in front of the good father's home. The sophisticated brother proposes a fine lamp "of hickory . . . turned into elegant curves" to be hung out by the curb, but the simple plain brother proposes a simple lamp on a simple nail hung right next to the front door. The winner?

Bill gave the lamp prize to the sophisticated brother, and the girl to the simple plain brother. Was the girl Charlotte or Flossie? No matter, the playwright's sympathy for the simple lamp on the nail was clear enough. And in poetry in the same period he wrote a long piece, "The Wanderer," that enforced and elaborated on his position.

"The Wanderer" is a poetic hybrid, mostly in rough iambic, that reaches both forward and back in Bill's development, and is perhaps best looked at here not as a poem so much as a psychological puzzle. It is a rambling affair in several parts about a loner, the poet himself, confronting a new world that is not at all clean and orderly, and not at all beautiful, confronting it under the tutelage of his muse, an old harridan (sometimes posing as a seagull!), who gives him a tour of his own native surroundings, and especially of the banks of the Passaic

River (which runs through Paterson, Passaic, Rutherford, and then Newark). And who is this poet's muse?—Bill tells us, in a late commentary on the poem, that he modeled her after Grandmother Williams Wellcome.

If a poet had to have a relative for a muse he could do worse than choose someone like Grandmother Wellcome, but she would remain an odd choice. She was ugly, she was tough, she was not in any conventional sense poetic. If she brought her poet an aesthetic it was an aesthetic of the ugly or at least of the brutally real. Certainly the poem shows us plenty of turn-of-the-century, garbage-can realism, with the river and the living bodies around it described as filthy and stinking, with "the faces all knotted up like burls on oaks," and with half the workers of Paterson on strike and starving. Yet the poem also shows us that the poet's odd muse is inspiring to him. She is "electric," she is a truth-bearer, and she is the person in his life best equipped—because of her toughness and capacity to cope—to answer the key question that the poet asks himself in the poem, how should he be "a mirror to this modernity"? All in all she well knows what her poet needs and will thrive on, knows his secret springs of talent.

During William's long engagement to Flossie Herman he wrote her occasionally about those springs, trying to tell her that she didn't yet quite know the man she was planning to marry. In one long letter, when he was in Germany for a year taking medical courses (and when he thought Flossie was going to leave him for a man with money) he elaborated on the dark side of himself that he called his "strange me," the secret side that his muse liked and encouraged: "I have warned you that I am melancholy, I am weak, I am wild, further I hate religious creed, and all dead forms and I will never yield to them. Yet I am conscious of my own worth and I tell you my heart is no small thing. If you refuse me I can and will work alone." Those are the words of a romantic in his gloom, facing a world, including Flossie, that he thinks does not understand him, and is not likely ever to understand him. Actually Flossie, living through many difficult years with him, came to understand him very well, but in the period of the writing of that letter—which was also in part the period of "The Wanderer"—he had little assurance that she or anyone else understood him. The poet felt alone with his muse on the dirty riverbank of life. He was beginning to think that he understood modernity, but he had no confidence that anyone else would believe that he did or see that he did. He was too far out. He was finding poetry and truth in the wrong places, at least not finding them where others had found them. Not even Pound could really imagine the stuff of poetry existing in industrial northern New Jersey, or in the life of a harassed general practitioner living just off Main Street in a sedentary bourgeois town.

But his muse *could* imagine him finding poetry and truth there. In "The Wanderer" she in effect told him not to wander but to settle for where he was settled and make the dirty Passaic his inspiration.

At the point in the poem where the muse tells him this the tone of the poem changes. The river scene suddenly becomes a pastoral scene (and indeed Bill, an amateur painter, did one or two landscapes of the Passaic where it is leafiest), and the reader is left with the pleasant momentary fantasy of the Passaic as Wordsworthian and lovely. That river was a deep one for Bill and he would write about it all his life. It was the mirror of modernity for him, far more than any technical poetic considerations such as imagism and free verse.

Late in life, after a series of heart attacks, Bill's "strange me" took the form of periods of manic-depression, and in retrospect his early moody moments, as seen in his letter from Germany, seem of that cast; yet his moodiness, though severe and lifelong, is easy to overemphasize, or at least emphasize without attention to his self-control, which was good. Any writer, to write, withdraws. There is no other way. Bill withdrew at the drop of a hat, withdrew suddenly from his patients during office hours, withdrew in his mind from Flossie while she was reading to him in bed, withdrew while driving along the street. He had a great capacity to stop everything, grab his prescription pad (or any paper handy, including toilet paper), and write something, some momentary observation. He also had a great capacity to stop the writing and go right back to office, wife, driving. His essential *steadiness* in living his double life was perhaps his most remarkable characteristic, and surely that steadiness was built on something stronger and more positive, more affirmative in him than his undoubted tendency to melancholy. He was gregarious, boyish, impetuous, and full of enthusiasm. He liked to eat and drink. He liked to shock and amuse. He liked women, and he liked male parties where men talked about women. He liked gardening and baseball. He liked Broadway plays, beach weekends, cats, gadgets, and gossip. So let us not let the "strange me" run away with him.

But let us not forget it either. Anyone adopting an aesthetic stance as eccentric as his was (for the time) must be looking for an escape of some sort from the dailiness, and indeed he was. He was looking for it for psychic as well as aesthetic reasons, and he had a metaphor for his search. When he tried to escape from the dailiness he was, he said, *stealing*. He was stealing time mostly, but he was stealing freedom too, freedom not only from doctoring but from marriage and children. Some years after his marriage he wrote a rather nasty little poem, "Le Medicin Malgré Lui," in which he described Flossie as his "Lady Happiness" and said that if he were to perform as she wanted him to perform he would instantly wash the walls of his office, build shelves for the office, clean the bottles in the office, and put the journals and articles of the office in order. He would also grow a beard and cultivate a "look of importance." He would do all these things because Flossie's mode of life demanded such actions from him, but he would not be wholly happy as he did them, since he sometimes wanted to have something in his head other than a "white thought."

The alternative to the life of white thoughts is of course the stolen life, and that is well described in one of his very best early poems, "Danse Russe":

> If when my wife is sleeping
> and the baby and Kathleen
> are sleeping
> and the sun is a flame-white disc
> in silken mists
> above shining trees
> if I in my north room
> dance naked, grotesquely
> before my mirror waving my shirt round my head
> and singing softly to myself
> "I am lonely, lonely,
> I was born to be lonely,
> I am best so!"
> If I admire my arms, my face,
> my shoulders, flanks, buttocks
> against the yellow drawn shade—
> Who shall say I am not
> the happy genius of the household?

The early years of his marriage, especially after the births of his two children (in 1914 and 1916), were troublesome for him as the "happy genius." They were years when stealing away was not at all easy to do, yet it was crucial to his art and even his health ("when I can't write," he once said, "I'm a sick man"). They were also, not surprisingly, the years when his aesthetic took shape, an aesthetic heavily dependent on the stealing process.

It was an aesthetic having as the first step in creation the liberation of the artist from every habit, routine, convention, rule, every prescriptive white thought that surrounded him. Bill had a story—which he told in the "Prologue" to *Kora in Hell*—to describe the mode and significance of such liberation, a story about his mother when she visited Rome. There she was as a tourist, being duly led about by the usual guides to the usual places, but one day she broke loose. She went out on the town on her own, became lost, arrived back at her hotel late and exhausted—and serene. She had had, she said, the best touring day of her life. Free of the guides, she had seen Rome. Similarly, said Bill, the poet had to free himself from the poet guides before he could begin to see the world truly with his own eyes.

His little freedom code was of course not his own private one for creation, though he applied it well to his problems in Rutherford. The code was also to be found throughout the arts of early modernist days, a time for steady talk of scrapping everything and starting over. In literature it came to be described in many ways (not long ago it was labeled the art of "de-familiarizing the overfamiliar"[3]). Also it came to be a common code among painters—and Bill lived with painters, as much as poets. There was Picasso's recommendation, for instance, that the painter first "assassinate" the forms he chose to paint, so that he could then put them back together again in his own way; there was Kandinsky's word that the painter should deliberately improvise, that is, go out of his way to avoid all preliminary plans, forms, concepts, and just *paint;* and there was also Marcel Duchamp's exhibitionistic game of *finding* art, much as Bill's mother found Rome. The code was visible all through the exhibits at the famous Armory Show in New York in 1913, a show of great influence upon Bill and his painter

---

3. See Ambrose Gordon's "In the Daylong Rain: The Visible in Hardy's Poetry"— *Southern Review,* Summer, 1981. Gordon found interesting instances of defamiliarizing techniques in premodernist lines by Hardy that seem, at first glance, quite conventional.

friends in Greenwich Village, as he also indicates in the prologue to *Kora in Hell,* which is perhaps the best source for Bill on Bill as an artist. If Ezra in London had not been preaching to Bill in Rutherford, by letter, the importance of making it new in poetry, Bill would have learned it from Marsden Hartley (who brought him the Kandinsky gospel), Charles Demuth, Charles Sheeler, and Duchamp.

For an improviser the creative impulse is apt to be stirred up by something ephemeral or something noticed in passing. Like a sunset, the creative moment, when conceived *as* a moment, is over and done with the next moment. What does the artist do then? Duchamp, practicing his found art, reported that he walked into a hardware store, purchased the first object his eyes settled on, an axe, took it home and hung it up—but what then? He was done for the day. Similarly the imagist poet has a pattern thrust upon him by his art, that of searching out his isolate image, working out its small verbal destiny on the page, and then going on to something else. Improvisatory art does not *have* to be so limited, but it does not offer easy ways of moving on after the creative moment, does not suggest ways of fitting the moment to other moments. Instead it encourages small, self-contained works for a single page, or for a lonely place on a museum wall.

And for Bill, stealing moments haphazardly, the isolate small poem, bred from a single moment of seeing, was the natural product of his whole way of life. His little poem "The Red Wheelbarrow" is probably his most famous poem, and also perhaps his most characteristic. Not many readers of anthologies know that it is part of a sequence of poems and prose passages gathered together in a book called *Spring and All,* but they would not benefit greatly by the knowledge. The book sequence is extremely loose (as will be seen), and the little poem is a complete creation on its own.

As a complete work, however, sitting on a page and surrounded by nothing but whiteness, it is a tough item for an orderly mind to contend with. Darwin for instance would have been stunned by it. No systems man looking for connections will find them (he will have to invent them). The poem may well seem to him to be like a single stuffed bird in a glass case, a frivolity, a piece of intellectual barbarism.

The Red Wheelbarrow

so much depends
upon

a red wheel
barrow

glazed with rain
water

beside the white
chickens.

Obviously the poem opens itself to a variety of interpretations by those who seek to *fit* it, somehow or other, into a meaning-scheme beyond itself. It could be a poem recommending the plain lamp on the plain nail. It could also be a poem recommending that we pay attention to the thingy world around us (a few years after the appearance of this poem, Bill's aesthetic battle cry was to become, "no ideas but in things"). And other interpretations could readily be put forward—and *are* put forward, wildly, whenever the poem invades a classroom—since the poem does not explicitly contain instructions for limiting interpretation.

On the other hand it certainly doesn't encourage a meaning-hunt. Like a sunset again, the poem is, if looked at in the way that a painter might look at it, a visual composition of colors and textures. Hanging in a museum as a painting it would not make anyone think to deal with the wheelbarrow symbolically. It would instead command attention to the contrasts between the hard sharp lines of the wheelbarrow and the soft lines of the chickens, and the glossiness of the red against the chickens' dull white. Such visual components are enforced on the page by the line divisions, which Upton would have detested. They are arbitrary (having none of the syntactical logic that Upton looked for) but symmetrical and neat, giving the sentence of which the poem is composed not only a shape on the page to which the painter-mind can point but also giving the sentence exactly what another poet with a quite different view of modernity, Gerard Manley Hopkins, was always seeking too, that is, instress, its own peculiar, individual balancing of word-forces. All in all, as a composition, its chief mark *is* its distinctiveness as simply itself. A familiar wheelbarrow has been defamiliarized and left alone, a curio, and on that aloneness, in the end, "so much depends."

It is a discordant impulse, this reaching for distinction, because it goes against all the social and intellectual obligations that an individual is burdened with, obligations to adjust, conform: pieties. But as Dos Passos said to his young friend Rummy, the way to thought itself—if one can distinguish it at all from conditioned reflex—may well be to combat such obligations. In the case of Henry Adams the area of combat was with his colleagues in the humanities, whose classical conditioning made them unable, he believed, to think clearly about such matters as the laws of thermodynamics. In the case of Upton Sinclair—and erratically of Jack London—capitalist conditioning to the morality of property rights was the area of combat, and both Sinclair and London cerebrated hardest when they were busy asserting alternative social values. As for Dos Passos himself, he too of course raged against property in his youth, but he raged more steadily, and longer, against the ogre of conformity itself in modern life. Among all these figures Bill was obviously the least *thoughtful,* in the sense of rational. His conformity to the doctor's life, and to life in Rutherford, though sometimes grudging, was lifelong, and it pushed his dissenting modernism into a corner of his mind dedicated to the intuitive, the immediate, the spontaneous. His thought emerged in disorderly bursts—in his expressive forms, his syntax, and in his jumpy prophetic pronouncements. Said Pound of him, "He was the most incoherent bloke who ever gargled."

But he was not alone, among modernists, in incoherence. Many of the practitioners and promoters of the modern set up the artist as prophet, as intuitive truth-bringer. Some of them even enjoyed being called mad. But there were good minds among, or in conjunction with, the mad minds, and the cause of making literature a serious business rather than a handmaiden to conformity was backed by a diverse assortment of talent. In that wildness Pound himself, despite his obsessions and the resultant incarceration, was essentially a rationalist.

Was Pound also a first-rate mind? The arguments about him are not over yet, but the evidence we have tells us that he was a mix of genius and mountebank. He was a first-class egotist, poseur, and dramatist of himself and his causes. He was a scholar with a lust for pretending to more knowledge than he had, and in half a dozen languages. He was a loud missionary of the Light as he saw it, and by the thirties he was driven to missionary excesses that alienated even his old friend "Bull." But if we put aside his intensities—or their consequences—it is possible to see him as one who knew as much as anyone about how to run, rationally and coherently, a revolution from a garret. As an editor and a propagandist he not only pushed his revolutions—first of the word and then of currency—with great vigor, but he also told everyone he knew to do likewise. He was a born crusader, and crusaders may be mad but they are often rational too like mad scientists.

Bill was also, sometimes, a crusader, but he was no good at it. And by staying in Rutherford for life he was remote from the places where crusading might be effective (though he did like to frequent Greenwich Village). All his life he was busy writing for little magazines hidden away in places like Rutherford, magazines with circulations of a few hundred, magazines that came and went like the seasons. And until late in life—unlike Pound who had the great of Paris and London in his sights—he had no other audience. Maybe in the long run his isolation was a help as he explored his freedom aesthetic, but the long run was not what he could see when he was writing. What he could see until he was about sixty was that his work was neglected. He could see himself regarded, if at all, as a minor, second-rate poet and thinker, an assessment that did much to stir up his "strange me."

His "strange me" told him that if he were to live up to the literary destiny that he dreamed of for himself he would have to do it by himself, and so he practiced over a long period, when he was feeling dry and uncreative, a kind of forced automatic writing. He drove himself to write something every day *anyway*, in sickness and health, in hope and despair; and as he did so he also drove himself to ignore continuities, forget about meaning, just get something down.

He found the process purgative and liberating, and by 1923 he knew what he was at, to the extent that anyone practising randomness can ever know. Though it made no splash at all, *Spring and All* now stands as sound testimony to the process. It is, as a complete whole, as radical a piece of modernity as are the individual poems swimming in it, of which "The Red Wheelbarrow" is number twenty-two.

The book is also testimony to the dark sentiments of his strange me when he wrote it. At that time his marriage, his doctoring, *and* his writing had been going poorly for some years. He was a bitter, angry man. He was also a man with extramarital affairs darkening his white thoughts. In the earlier book, *Kora in Hell,* he had suggested murkily that he was having trysts in secret places and being plagued by conventional disapproval from wife and community. In *Spring and All* he let up on the personal life and concentrated on the literary life, but that was a swamp too.

On the surface the book was arch and semicomic. It had to be. It was a celebratory volume in praise of spring and creation, succeeding the wintry *Kora in Hell* and another little volume whose title gave it away, *Sour Grapes,* but the comedy was a thin veneer. As he said later he was "disturbed" at the time. He was disturbed about (and jealous of) the successes of Pound's friend Eliot with *The Love Song of J. Alfred Prufrock* and *The Waste Land,* but he was more disturbed by his own failures. He was disturbed because the big world was simply not liking his poems. Here is his own rendering of the world's opinion of him, on page one of *Spring and All* ". . . the poems are positively repellent. They are heartless, cruel, they make fun of humanity. What in God's name do you mean? Are you a pagan? . . . Rhyme you may perhaps take away but rhythm! why there is none in your work whatever. Is this what you call poetry? It is the very antithesis of poetry. It is antipoetry." In those lines he could well have been imitating Upton Sinclair speaking. He had his work cut out for him if he was going to do with the book what the title proposed, write something ending his winter of discontent. So to arrive at the new season he decided that he first had to destroy the old season thoroughly. In the opening five pages he did. He annihilated "every human creature on the face of the earth," leaving nothing "but the lower vertebrates, the molluscs, insects and plants." Then on pages six and seven he readied himself to build the world over again, and discussed the curious fact that, though his imagination had destroyed everything, everything was about to spring up again "in the likeness of that which it was."

Suddenly out of such whirlings, like a pearl in an oyster, came poem number one, one of his best ("By the road to the contagious hospital"). It was a poem describing the coming of spring in earnest. Then further moiling, followed by poem two. And so on. In all the book contained twenty-seven discrete poems, mostly separated from each other by wild prose. Was the wheelbarrow poem illuminated by what preceded and followed it? Not greatly. It was preceded by a weak poem of the same size and shape and followed by a two-page prose meandering about the arbitrariness of "the fixed categories into which life is divided." One could argue that *Spring and All* as a whole is a parody of such dividings, a parody that Bill enforces by comic false numberings of the different sections—but to say that is not helpful. (And later he did not object to throwing out the prose entirely and keeping the poems.) Essentially the book is twenty-seven poems in the prose thought-soil out of which the poems sprout. So the book is an object lesson in the disorderly processes of the imagination. It is also an affirmation of the processes, but tentative and partial.

The word "imagination" sent Bill into some of his muddiest statements, but he would not let the word, and its relation to "reality," go. He would not have denied that *Origin of Species* was a work of the imagination, and he sometimes insisted that there was discipline as well as letting-yourself-go at the root of any imaginative act. But when he did so he was not talking about logical rigor. His distrust of systematic thought was matched by his own weakness at that activity, and he was as distrustful of scientific and academic orderings as he was of their conventional literary equivalents (metaphor, analogy, narrative, traditional verse forms). For him imaginative rigor was something mystical; words wouldn't describe for him what it was, but he was sure that when a poem or a line was right the spontaneity of creating it had been matched by precision, exactness. As he indicated in his late poem *Paterson,* he liked the paradox:

> It is dangerous to leave written that which is badly written. A chance word, upon paper, may destroy the world. Watch carefully, and erase, while the power is still yours, I say to myself, for all that is put down, once it escapes, may rot its way into a thousand minds, the corn become a black smut, and all libraries, of necessity, be burned to the ground as a consequence.
>
> Only one answer: write carelessly so that nothing that is not green will survive.

Whatever the imagination was, it was the singular lonely soul's contribution *to* reality, and that soul's vision could always be depended on to be more real than a collective vision. A weak person was one who "shrank from an imagination that would sever him from the rest," while a strong person did not shrink, but was ready to deal with the wheelbarrows, all of them, on his own.

It followed that "composition"—and when he used the word he was thinking in artistic terms—was a basic tool of the private imagination as it worked on reality. A composing artist did "exactly what every eye must do with life," that is, imbued it with "his own personality." In recent times such subjective composing had progressed, he said, through "the impressionists, the expressionists, Cezanne" and finally arrived at much more abstract paintings such as those of a favorite of his, Juan Gris, in which wheelbarrows and the like were not recognizable as such. Bill's own wheelbarrow was a wheelbarrow all right, but what made it a wheelbarrow that "so much" depended on was its relationship to the other forces in the composition and to the viewer-composer. Those who looked in the poem for another, conventional kind of meaning—taking it for instance as an expression of the virtues of the simple life—were, in his view, the poet's enemy. They were not ready to take the poem on the page for what it was but wished it to conform to *their* expectations. Bill's resentment of such thinking ran deep, and it is the key to what he meant by imagination. For him imagination was the private soul's faculty for achieving its own integrity, its truth.

Imagination, so construed, was also the key to his other big book of the twenties, a prose history book. *In the American Grain* is the only book of his in which he managed to play down aesthetics. Unlike Pound he did not often take it upon himself to reform civilization as well as poetry and language, but in *In the American Grain* he came close. It is a book with a social thesis. It is a book of heroes and villains, about twenty in all, all explorers and developers of America, from Eric the Red to Abraham Lincoln, a book in which the heroes are, uniformly, besieged opponents of conformity, while the villains are enforcers of it, that is, puritans. After *Spring and All* Bill took a year off from medicine to write *In the American Grain*—and to take a trip abroad to remind himself (and Flossie) that Rutherford was not the world—but he did not take a year off from his anger. He focused that on puritanism. As far as he was concerned puritanism was everywhere, even before the Puritans. He had read and liked D. H. Lawrence's polemics against the "anti-life" gospel of American Puritans, and he was immersed, like all of literary America, in the antipuritan sentiments of the Jazz Age; but closer to home he felt the puritanism around him like a death cloud, in his own family, even in his own psyche.

First of all it was in his father. Though the father had read Shakespeare in the parlor, Bill thought of him as a poetry-hater, and he wrote in his autobiography of a dream he had had in which the father had come down the steps to him from his New York office and said to him, "You know all that poetry you're writing it's no good." Bill even had a poem about the father, "Adam," a poem describing a man who had lost all the joy of life to duty and "the death that duty brings so mincingly."

Then the puritanism was in his brother Edgar. Edgar had successfully given in to society's demands and become important, and something of a prude with a slight British accent. After the father's death Edgar, though the younger, had taken over the father functions in the family. And like the father he had not been happy with the poetry revolution that his brother was conducting nor happy with his brother's frankness in print about sex. He tried to persuade Bill to remove a paragraph from his autobiography in which Bill said that he did not intend "to tell the particulars of the women [he had] been to bed with or anything about them or the men either, if [he had] been to bed with any." (Bill removed only the part beginning, "or the men.")

Even his mother, Elena, who was no prude, had enough of the puritan in her to say of one of his books that it was "all sex, sensual, no love the sublime." Bill put the family complaints together with his sense of an America given over to decorum, prohibitionism and a sticky work ethic, put them together and came out feeling a martyr for free thought. He felt his martyrdom most when he sensed the presence of his *own* puritanism, which kept seeping through.

For instance, he played the puritan himself on his trip abroad in 1924, while he and Flossie were visiting the free artist spirits over there that he wanted to admire. He found some of them derelict in their literary devotions—not Pound apparently—and he was most of all annoyed by James Joyce in a Parisian cafe who, rather than settling in for a "profound discussion," kept singing Irish songs.

Then on the medical side he was particularly disgusted, while attending a conference in Austria, with his own American colleagues, "a smoking, story-swapping crew," who were "blatant ignoramuses," not bothering their heads about medicine as a science but looking around for skills they could turn into cash.

All these tensions in him made him feel like an outsider as poet *or* doctor. They produced the heavy thematic drive of *In the American Grain,* an odd piece of historical revisionism. Over and over again the biographies in the volume show America, the new world, being settled and won by brave, independent explorers who sought out with love and violence its newness, its fresh, virginal being. And over and over again the explorers found themselves up against the old world, its staleness, its hypocrisy. Eric the Red was a pagan murderer, but he was strong in his own right, frank and open, while the Christians opposing him and chasing him across the seas had no such inner strength. Cortez was also a man, though of violence, to respect for *his* respect for the new world; so was Daniel Boone, who "took the lives of the beasts into his quiet, murderous hands." Then there was the French Catholic explorer, Père Sebastian Rasles, who urged the Indians to their violence—"Did one expect the Indians not to be fighters? Not Rasles at any rate." The violence was most to be condoned when it was sexual, Raleigh "plunging his lust into the body of the New World," and De Soto listening to the land speak to him saying, "You are mine and I will strip you naked. . . . Down, down to me."

Best of all there was Aaron Burr, who found himself a genuine female, an Indian princess, and was "immoral as a satyr." Burr of course had the extra merit of having killed Alexander Hamilton, whom Pound once called "the prime snot in American history," and Bill also placed him high in his puritan rogues' gallery.

It was not virtue in these violent men that he admired, but naturalness, that is, fidelity to their own natures. The twenties were great years for rediscovering naturalness, via Nietzsche, Freud, Lawrence, and a good many other apostles of breaking loose and being one's self. *In The American Grain* was a social document of its time in its message: Thou shalt be natural. What Bill chiefly did to his explorers, to make them what he wanted them to be, was to leave out their institutional and national-cultural missions, reducing them to their driven individual selves.

He could well have just read the first page of *Thus Spake Zarathustra,* where Zarathustra comes down from the mountain and, having learned that God is dead, wishes to be a man again. Bill's explorers came down from the mountain too, the mountain of inherited ideals, national imperatives, conventional convictions; and in that move they showed their manliness.

Coming down from the mountain Bill was also, at least for some years, a descent into prose. In the early 1920s, before *In the American Grain,* he wrote a supercharged parody, *The Great American Novel,* of the pretentious fictions he saw around him, and after finishing *In the American Grain* he turned to an autobiographical novel, *A Voyage to Pagany,* that described his trip abroad in 1924. His prose grew firm and direct, and by the late twenties he was truly down from the mountain and writing short, naturalistic sketches of his patients and friends, sketches that caught their speech and gave forth with their feelings directly, without commentary. He had trouble publishing some of them in magazines because they were not rounded off, not resolved in conventional ways as editors wanted them to be, but they were solid and true. One of the published ones was so true that when it appeared he was sued for libel, fifteen thousand dollars worth. He wrote in his journal at the time that he was probably going to be driven into bankruptcy, and would have to write a best-seller quick, but he was saved from that, settling out of court for five thousand dollars (and his friends found him a poetry prize worth twenty-five hundred dollars). Later he said in his autobiography, "Floss of course was marvelous, but she let me have it all right." She had reason to. He had written the story down as he heard it from a friend, not even troubling to change names.

Robert Coles said good things of these stories in a series of lectures at Rutgers in 1974 (later published as *William Carlos Williams: The Knack of Survival in America*), and for talking about them in an unliterary way he was sharply criticized in the *New York Review of Books* by an English teacher critic, Helen Vendler, whom Bill would have rushed to call Eliotic. He said they showed Williams as a superior social observer of the kind that more sociologists and psychologists should wish to be. He said that he had persuaded "inner city youths" to read Bill, and that their response had been "frank, pointed, insistent" because they knew the world that Bill was writing about and were moved by the truth of his account. The *New York Review* critic seemed to be against having the stories seep down to the level of such responses, but she need not have worried. Neither the stories nor the poems have seeped down much to the unliterary so far, nor have the stories (now collected in a volume called *The Farmer's Daughters*) been greatly celebrated even by the literary. Yet Coles's liking for them is just. Together with perhaps two dozen of his short poems they may well be his most exciting work. Apart from the faithful observings in them they show well the unfettered writing ease he reached for, the ease of writing fast, without thought. At his best the stories have the artless art of good photography.

But up on the mountain, and fettered, was T. S. Eliot, Pound's hero and William's villain. Bill seems not to have met the man, or corresponded with him, though Pound stood in the middle as close friend of each, but beginning about 1920 Bill spoke and wrote about Eliot constantly, never with approval. (Eliot, more decorous, seems to have made no public statements at all about Bill, and his silence must have meant that he disliked Bill's work but did not wish to offend Pound.) Bill called *The Waste Land* "the great catastrophe to our letters." He said that Eliot's criticism "returned us to the classroom just at the moment" when poets were moving toward an art "rooted in the locality which should give it fruit." He said that Eliot had "no creative intelligence whatever." And during World War II he even suggested—in a poem called "Exultation"—that there was merit in the German bombing of London because there were so many Eliotic qualities in the character of the English people that *deserved* bombing. Eliot's success obviously had much to do with Bill's rancor. So did the academic tone of his criticism, and the intellectually referential character of both *The Love Song of J. Alfred Prufrock* and *The Waste Land* (both asked of the reader the kind of liberal arts background that Bill did not have). But beyond the envy there was a big cultural assumption of Eliot's that went against the Bill grain.

For Eliot the modern wasteland was waste because it lacked a spiritual center, being given over instead to the tyranny of blind material forces, especially money forces. (Eliot took some of his money cues, as did Pound, from Brooks and Henry Adams.) But for Bill the blind forces were not nearly as dangerous as the rational forces, the forces *for* spiritual order. Not that he liked blind forces. Not that he liked the monied. He could be as angry as either Eliot or Pound about the effects of American materialism upon the quality of American life and literature, and he was much more democratic than they about the quality of life lived by the unmonied, the uneducated common people. But the evils of the blind forces were for him less important than the evils of institutionalized values, values he felt Eliot, and sometimes Pound, stood for. For Bill there were very few collective values that were not inhibiting to the private creative intelligence.

He was a poet-anarchist by deep conviction, a believer in the artist making his own world. When he acknowledged allegiance to outside forces it was only to the outside of his own lived life, only to the real and true of the local, the at-hand. Bill devoted the major long poem of his life, *Paterson,* to this anti-Eliot theme.

And as in many such cases of literary conflict the poem owed a great deal to the enemy that the poem was fighting, Eliot. It not only picked up some of its inspiration from reactions against the man, but it also inadvertently asserted the formal merits of *The Waste Land,* asserted them by imitation. *Paterson* was anti-Eliot, but it was put together like *The Waste Land* as a kind of collage of cultural observations. And it was also built upon the assumption, shared by *The Waste Land,* that past and present are of a piece. In its subjective beginnings, however, *Paterson* seems to have preceded Bill's anger at Eliot, going way back to "The Wanderer" (1912–1914), when his grandmother muse had told him to root his poetic life in the environment of the Passaic River valley, stench and all. The muse of "The Wanderer" had specified the culture that he was to look at in *Paterson* thirty years later, his own local, industrial "hole in the wall." At one time he thought to focus his poem on Newark rather than Paterson, but with either he was close to home, as Eliot, writing of London, was not.[4]

Of course Bill's hole in the wall was not much like London, and his complaints about what was wrong with the Passaic River valley did not resemble Eliot's about London. Over and over in *Paterson,* Bill kept saying that almost everything in his home culture could be blamed on academic, institutionalized orderings like those to be found in Eliot. For at bottom *Paterson* was a pastoral epic, in which an earlier, happier time for mankind, a time when man communed with and was a part of the nature around him, was set up against the modern fall from grace, a fall brought about by the false thinkers.

It was the thinkers (like Eliot) with their minds "like beds . . . always made up" who had "subverted" natural thought and separated man from the world around him. It was the thinkers who had brought about man's divorce—a key word—from nature. Luckily Bill did have a solution for divorce, and for the fall from grace. Unluckily the solution involved getting rid of the Eliots.

Of all the kinds of modern divorce that he brought up in *Paterson* the most important was man's divorce from his own natural language— again to be blamed on Eliot. Bill's metaphor for natural language was the great waterfall at the western edge of the city of Paterson. His

4. Eliot was not without respect for the local, and the first draft of *The Waste Land,* before it was altered according to some of Pound's suggestions, was much more a parochial London poem, much less international and cosmopolitan, than the final version.

hero, personifying the city, had become deaf to the waterfall; he had a stone ear; he could not any longer call the fall's language his own, any more than Americans could still call the American language their own. He was with H. L. Mencken here, and he corresponded with Mencken for some years, approving of a remark Mencken had made to him in the thirties, that "the great majority of English teachers avoid common speech as if it were poisonous." To the extent that Eliot was like the English teachers and had gone English, he was a conspirator against American ownership of their own language.

The divorce from natural speech was just a part of a larger language complaint. All through the writing of *Paterson*—which began in the late thirties and proceeded, through its five and a half books, until his death in 1963—Bill was a man of rages against what the intellectuals were doing to the country. He set up shop as a latter-day Rousseauist and took aim against those, always like Eliot, who had given up not only the American language but the language of humanity, the language with which one man—as distinguished from one specialist or picky logician—spoke to another.

His language complaint was really directed at establishment intellectuals as a whole, and what they as cultural leaders had done to stunt the natural development of human understanding. As a sample of the damage they did he often brought up the wrongheadedness of a French teacher in Rutherford who flunked his son Bill in French right after Bill had spent a year in France learning French the natural way. The Rutherford French teacher wanted Rutherford French and would accept no substitutes. Similarly the academics of other disciplines wanted order of their own making to be the life order of their students. They could not see the inward, organic nature of healthy human maturation.

In the thirties Bill had written a series of essays collectively entitled *The Embodiment of Knowledge,* which took off from son Bill's experience with the French teacher and was the ideological base for *Paterson*. In it he blamed the love of fixed categories and prescriptions by scientists, philosophers, and educators for most of America's ills, and he asserted that poetry and poetic methods, those he conceived as organic—were an alternative to their false doctrines. *Paterson* then became a kind of demonstration of the organic mode, his primary exercise in dropping the puritan fetters. He gave its random shaping principle on page one:

> To make a start
> out of particulars
> and make them general, rolling
> up the sum, by defective means—
> sniffing the trees,
> just another dog
> among a lot of dogs. What
> else is there?

He was so sold on the virtues of randomness that when he found himself revising and reordering the first book of *Paterson* he was annoyed with himself, and he wrote a friend that he had worked on it too hard and too long. He thought it had "no flow." He said, "Diarrhea would have been a little better." Yet even the first book was, by most standards, haphazard. He went to the historical archives in Paterson—sometimes he had a young assistant, Kathleen Hoaglund, go for him—and excerpted long newspaper clippings and passages from local history books describing what seemed to him to be interesting Paterson lore: of a tremendous sea fish caught in the river beneath the falls, of a suicide (or was it murder?) over the brink of the falls, of a dwarf with an enormous head. He took such passages, added to them unrelated passages out of letters written to him by friends, and scattered them through his own poetic text like the fillers in *Reader's Digest,* but they occupied more space. He even turned over to Hoaglund some of the cutting and placement decisions for his collage, while he busied himself with the poetry itself, and walked about the mountain west of Paterson learning the feel of the place.

His tree-sniffing way of art was good, he was convinced, because most of the best and worst of life was random too, unplanned. One did not, could not *quest* after beauty, or felicity in experience. Instead one happened on it while driving through the world, happened on it as in the following poem, excellent Bill but sure-fire confusion for students.

> The Right of Way
>
> In passing with my mind
> on nothing in the world
>
> but the right of way
> I enjoy on the road by

virtue of the law—
I saw

an elderly man who
smiled and looked away

to the north past a house—
a woman in blue

who was laughing and
leaning forward to look up

into the man's half
averted face

and a boy of eight who was
looking at the middle of

the man's belly
at a watchchain—

The supreme importance
of this nameless spectacle

sped me by them
without a word—

Why bother where I went?
for I went spinning on the

four wheels of my car
along the wet road until

I saw a girl with one leg over
the rail of a balcony

As for truth, its discovery was always also random, coming mysteriously out of the inert:

Say it, no ideas but in things—
Nothing but the blank faces of the houses
and cylindrical trees
bent, forked by preconception and accident,—
furrowed, creased, mottled, stained—
secret—into the body of the light!

Planted in the collage of *Paterson,* book 1, was a quotation from a letter to Bill from Pound that was a key to Bill's aesthetic difference with Eliot as well as Pound: "Your interest is in the bloody loam but what I'm after is the finished product."

There it was: finder versus maker. They had argued the difference for decades without seeming to see the bigness of the difference, since they had also seemed to agree on so much. They had agreed to dislike conventional prosody, poetic subjects, stock poetic responses, and the institutions that promoted stock responses. They had agreed to like sharpness and integrity of detail, and independence and openness of mind. Especially they had agreed that the artistic act was a serious human business, not just a pastime. And communing as they did on the seriousness of poetry they had managed to ignore their difference mostly, right through to World War II when Pound's social credit mania put him on Radio Rome preaching against the war (and mentioning Bill's name, bringing the FBI to Bill's door). But the difference was there.

Pound's was a rational mind that worked in deductive fashion *down* to his poetic materials (did so despite his imagist pretensions), and fitted them together piece by piece to make what he hoped would be a clear, architectonic whole. In writing *his* life epic, the *Cantos,* he managed in the end to make it look jerrybuilt, but the end belied the first intent, the intent of an orderer who thought—or so Yeats reported—that its architecture would appear clear and firm when he reached Canto 100.

Bill had no such orderings in him. He took verbal camera shots of his wheelbarrows and pasted them into a scrapbook. What he had instead of an imposed order was a body of opinion sitting in his head that he had picked up (naturally, randomly) over the years and was stuck with. The opinion moved in on the wheelbarrows more often than it should have; *Paterson* was more of a tract than he thought it was, but it was not an ordered tract. It was a tract despite itself, a tract opposing tracts. At its best (as in book 2, a description of a summer Sunday afternoon in Paterson's mountain park) it marched the reader through the world with eyes and ears open, receiving, enjoying presentness. At its worst it was pretentious, with opinions making the wheelbarrows over into more than they could be.

Perhaps Pound was his chief false teacher here, leading him away from the wheelbarrows that were his strength, to the abstractions that he couldn't, and didn't want to, keep on a leash. Anyway *Pater-*

son was an uneven performance, both as a work and as a display of the author's beliefs. Why did it take hold so? The fact is it did, and the circumstances of its taking hold are curious.

There is no way of understanding success or failure in Bill's literary life without first and always putting him into the island-like world of the little magazines: *Poetry* (Chicago), *Blast, Others, Contact, The Dial, The Little Review,* and the rest. Some of them were well financed, and some were shoestring things (Kenneth Burke said, "The print shop in the cellar is the only way"), but they all had small circulations and great hopes, they all were angry about commercial publishing, and they all gathered unto themselves writers who knew what a mess the world was in and had decided to make a go of their art *without* the world. Bill found himself in those circles early, and for decades afterward he alternately thanked his stars for giving him honorable, unmonied literary mates and cursed his stars for putting him out of play. (When in the early thirties he became disillusioned as an editor of *Contact* he wrote a friend, "We shit away every chance we have by putting out little piddling magazines here and there.") The magazines were not created to *be* piddling, nor published to enforce their contributors' littleness, but they achieved those ends often. In the thirties Bill moved into his fifties and he was *still,* in the main, a little magazine writer. It didn't please him.

Also by then he had published ten books, and he had been forced to subsidize most of them. Then James Laughlin, the founder of New Directions, came on the scene in the late thirties and changed things. With modest success, and without asking for Bill's subsidy, he published the first story collection, a novel about Flossie, and a volume of poems; but still the little magazine aura hung about Bill. He had become the magazines' patron saint, and corresponded with the editors of over a hundred of them, complimenting them, encouraging them, sending them work of his own, and occasionally letting off steam at their futility, their permanent littleness. Only with Laughlin's publication of the first book of *Paterson* in 1946—Bill was then sixty-three—did the national press begin to pay him heed, and only then did the academics he had been raging against begin to notice him. So his anti-intellectual being had a right to be well pleased when he was given an honorary degree by the University of Buffalo, an award by the American Academy of Arts and Letters (for book 2), and the National Book Award (for book 3). Most of all he had a right to be pleased to be discovered, suddenly, by poets younger than himself. They and the academics, reading *Paterson,* saw in him what somehow or other his own generation of poets—except for a few—had not.

A change set in, a renewal perhaps of the first modernist revolution, the one that had started Bill, Pound, *and* Eliot on their careers. But now the guns were pointed at Bill's targets. He was the romantic among his poetic peers, and the young poets caught up with his romance in the fifties.

Romantic?—So many descriptions of a romantic have been offered up to the god of definition that one more can do no harm. Bill was romantic in many of the usual ways—he was a Rousseauist about education, a Don Juan about women,[5] and a Shelleyite about poetry's power to change the (puritan) world—but he went beyond his fellow romantics in his faith in another process of change, the one constantly described in his writings of taking the raw world and somehow digesting it instantly. If he had been a mystic he would have had visions, he would have received illuminations, but he was not a mystic in the usual sense; he was a practical, hardheaded general practitioner. His faith in intuited order was a quirk in his mental makeup, but it was something he had been nourishing since 1912. He took that faith into the writing of *Paterson* with the naïveté of a boy, and in doing so he really did break new romantic ground. With *Paterson* he tried to show that a long work, a big panoramic work of literature could be written without a preconceived order governing the writing of it. He tried to show that one could *find* an epic.

Duchamp, Kandinsky, and the other painters who had promoted improvisatory freedom in the early modernist days should have been pleased by *Paterson,* for the work came out of their preachings, as did much of the work of poets who began in the ambiance of imagism. But no other poets—except perhaps Louis Zukofsky, a friend who wrote a big obscure long poem called *A–12* in the thirties—tried to carry the collage principle as far as Bill did. *Paterson* was comparable to many large modern murals, like Picasso's *Guernica,* but since it was a literary collage it had the handicap of not being viewable all at

5. "Women!" an autobiographical character in his play, *Many Loves,* says, "With their small heads and big lustrous eyes. All my life I have never been able to escape them."

once. How did a reader see it as a single composition, catch the relations between images, comprehend the whole? *Was* there a whole?

At the time of Bill's death the work was spread over 250 pages, and by then even the loose four-book plan he had started with had been abandoned.[6] Of book 5 he wrote,

> I have been forced to recognize that there can be no end to such a story as I have envisioned with the terms I had laid down for myself. I had to take the world of Paterson into a new dimension if I wanted to give it imaginative validity. Yet I wanted to keep it whole, as it is to me. As I mulled the thing over in my mind the composition began to assume a form which you see in the present poem, keeping, I fondly hope, a unity directly continuous with the Paterson of *Paterson 1 to 4.*

The operative words there are those connecting the shape of the poem with his own feel for the shape. He was looking, he said, for unity on *his* terms, wholeness as it was to *him;* and in doing as he was going well beyond his nearest collage models, *The Waste Land* and the *Cantos,* in asserting a private wholeness only. *Cantos* had a thematic structure struggling to control it, a structure dredged up in part from Brooks Adams's book, *The Law of Civilization and Decay,* where the good cultures were set against the bad cultures, and the present illuminated by the past. *The Waste Land* had that structure too, plus a submerged narrative sequence holding it together, the quest for the Grail; and of course it was relatively short. From the beginning *Paterson* on the other hand had only such shape as a scrapbook or miscellany has, a shape created by the whims of the scraps collector.

Here, then, was Bill's greatest romance with intuited order.

In reviews of the first books of *Paterson* some of the rigorous New Critics thought they saw more order than that, and joined with the intuitors in praise, but by the time of books 3 and 4 they had changed their minds. Randall Jarrell for instance was excited by the first books, but then withdrew into his earlier judgement of Bill, that he was "a very good but very limited poet," being "notably unreasoning"; and a British admirer of Bill's short poems complained of the work's random "kaleidoscopic quality." Luckily for Bill the rigorous critics were

6. "Part One introduces the elemental character of the place. The Second part comprises the modern replicas. Three will seek a language to make them vocal, and Four, the river below the falls, will be reminiscent of episodes—all that any one man may achieve in a lifetime."

outnumbered. Principles that had triumphed before suddenly needed a new triumph over Eliot, uptight artistry, and English Departments. *Paterson* gave them their occasion.

So by the fifties *Paterson* was in, and Bill was established as a literary household word. Perhaps it was too bad that his triumph should have come for the least readable of his works, but triumphs can be like that.

His fortunes after the war were not all good, not nearly. In 1948 he had a heart attack, the first of a series. And in 1952, having been invited to take the honorary post of poetry consultant at the Library of Congress, he was accused in the public press, by the editor of a little poetry magazine, of being a Communist, and the Library of Congress then treated him with suspicion and kept the post from him. The accusation was a red herring in all respects—certainly Bill's literary views were poison to party thought—but the episode, coming on top of his ill health, made his periodic depressions sharper. For a time in 1953 he was put in a mental hospital on Long Island. Meanwhile he had retired from medicine, and son Bill had taken over the practice.

Yet, remarkably, he wrote steadily through the fifties, and turned out, aside from *Paterson,* a number of his most positive poems, including a fine love poem to Flossie ("Asphodel, That Greeny Flower"). He gave readings at many colleges. He let himself be interviewed at a radio station in New Haven, where he made remarks about old Ez that were full of his younger mixture of anger and warmth toward the man. And he worked hard at a verse form he had devised for himself—he called it his variable foot—that he thought was absolutely the best ever, as important as cracking the atom. It wasn't (and Upton would have been happy to say that it wasn't), but it was a happy shift for his spirit, giving his verse lines air and white space on the pages and a music absent from his earlier work. Here is a passage in the form, from "The Sparrow," a passage showing not only the form but also the basic, sparrowy Bill himself.

> . . . Even the Japanese
> know him
> and have painted him
> sympathetically
> with profound insight
> into his minor

> characteristics.
>> Nothing even remotely
> subtle
>> about his lovemaking,
>>> he crouches
>> before the females
>>> drags his wings,
>>>> waltzing,
>> throws back his head
>> and simply
>
>>> yells !

But his best happiness must have been, in his last years, his reception by new forces in poetry—Lowell, Ginsberg, Levertov, Olson, Creeley, and many others. He had stayed young somehow, and they could see the youth in him and admired him for it. In turn he admired them and learned from them. His Rutherford solidity kept him from Zen, kept him from pulling up stakes, kept him dutiful, but it did not keep him from admiring their revolution against the New Criticism, against academic poetry in the Eliot vein, and of course against all possible forms of puritanism. After all, the revolution had also been his.

When he died in 1963 the ceremony at the cemetery, in the rain, was brief but marked by the arrival, late, of a carload of admiring revolutionary poets from New York, dressed in ill-fitting black suits. Son Bill said the skies opened and brightened when they came.

Now nearly three decades have gone by since his death, and the skies have not been open and bright for poetry. *Paterson,* for instance, has been taken over by postmodernist academics and cleansed of its antiacademic polemics, while the rest of poetry has been cleansed of any general ideas at all.

Yet the Williams presence is still bright. He could have been wrong about randomness, and he could have been wrong about Eliot, but he was not wrong about what it is *like* to be struggling to be a free artist against the conditioning forces of the modern world.

Rationalist H. G. Wells probably would have put him among those writers with "abundant but uneducated brains" who have no "central philosophy" but are "impulsive, uncoordinated, willful," but Bill wouldn't have minded. He felt he had to be a barbarian to begin to be his own man.

FIVE

The Lost Humanist Republic of John Dos Passos

John Dos Passos sold an essay to the *New Republic* in 1916, when he was still at Harvard, that informed everybody what was wrong with American literature: It was too nice. It was rice pudding. It had none of the depths of true tradition in it, since its traditions were all borrowed. And it had none of the future in it either (except in Whitman), since we were a people far too content with our "steel and grain and oil" to allow our writers to dream well. Dos Passos said, "I defy anyone to confine himself for long to purely American books without feeling starved, without pining for the color and passion and profound thought of other literature. Our books are like our cities; they are all the same." After his harangue he recommended Dostoyevsky for good reading.[1]

1. All the letters and autobiographical writings of Dos Passos referred to and quoted here are from—except where otherwise indicated—his "informal memoir," *The Best Times* (New York: New American Library, 1966); and a collection of his letters and diaries entitled *The Fourteenth Chronicle,* edited by his biographer Townsend Luddington (Boston: Houghton Mifflin, 1973). The main books in the Dos Passos canon are of course the three parts of the trilogy USA: *The 42nd Parallel, Nineteen Nineteen, The Big Money,* which are available in paperback (Boston: Houghton Mifflin, 1963). His earlier novels mentioned are *One Man's Initiation,* 1917, reprinted with a reminiscent memoir by Dos Passos (Ithaca, N. Y.: Cornell University Press, 1960); *Three Soldiers,* 1921, reprint (Boston: Houghton Mifflin, 1964); *Streets of Night* (New York: George H. Doran, Inc., 1923); and *Manhattan Transfer* (New York: Harpers, 1924). Then there were two travel books: *Rosinante to the Road Again* (New York: George H. Doran, Inc., 1922); and *Orient Express* (New York: Harpers, 1927). Also in 1927 there appeared in pamphlet form his Sacco-Vanzetti report: *Facing the Chair: Story of the Americanization of Two Foreign Born Workmen* (New York: Oriole Chapbooks, 1927). Then there was a late "chronicle," *Chosen Country* (Boston: Houghton Mifflin, 1951).

The major biography is *John Dos Passos: A Twentieth Century Odyssey* by

Some years later, having published a number of books himself, and having also been active with a number of urgent causes, including the cause of the Sacco and Vanzetti Defense committee, for which he wrote a 150-page tract, Dos Passos was still convinced that American literature was rice pudding, but he now thought he saw a way of making sure that his own work would not be. In his introduction to *USA* (a trilogy finished in 1938, the first book of which had appeared in 1930) he was melancholy for a page about the insufficiencies of his own individualism—which had only led him to the discovery that "one bed is not enough, one job is not enough, one life is not enough"— but then he switched determinedly over to describing the social, communal alternative, for a writer, to one bed, one job, one life. It was not the alternative of political activist, but that of recorder, recorder of the stories and speech of family and tribe.

Perhaps his introduction to *USA* was pretentious, since he proposed in it that he personally catch not just the speech of family and tribe but of the whole nation; yet in the book itself he did undertake to do just that, and the undertaking was impressive. He was thinking big in a land where the literary folk tended, he thought, to think small. And in doing so he was running the risk of giving in to undisciplined consensus-thinking, the kind that led to books "like our cities . . . all the same." In other words, he was caught on the horns of the great American dilemma, trying on the one hand to catch the spirit of the divine average and on the other to retain his own moral and intellectual integrity. The journalist in him—and he was a good journalist— reached for the divine average; the literary man in him reached for independence of thought.

When he wrote *USA* he was still in what may be called, loosely, his radical period (in 1937–1938 he had a bad time, personally and ideologically, in the Spanish War, and never thereafter had anything to do with *any* kind of socialism), but from the beginning of his radicalism he was the kind of thinker that the Communists labeled anarcho-individualist; that is, he was a solitary soul uneasy in the

---

Townsend Luddington (New York: Dutton, 1980); but there is also a Twayne volume, *John Dos Passos* by John Wrenn (New York: Twayne, 1961); and *Path to USA* by Melvin Landsberg (Boulder: Associated University Press, 1972). Two important survey books that I have also referred to elsewhere are *The Great Tradition* by Granville Hicks (New York: Macmillan, 1935); and *Writers on the Left* by Daniel Aaron (New York: Harcourt Brace, 1961).

presence of collective enterprises, uneasy no matter how insufficient his "one life" sometimes seemed to be. His early life-story was not of one with deep social commitments—though he kept looking for them—but of an isolated, idealistic wanderer. In fact, in one of his early letters he said to a young friend, "I always envied Satan in 'Job' who was coming from 'going up and down the earth'—don't you want to go up and down the earth?" Or, as he later described his own unsettledness, he wanted "to paddle up undiscovered rivers, to climb unmapped mountains." Like Henry Adams he was always "frantic to be gone."

That unsettledness made him hard to classify, and in the end damaged his reputation. For the literary folk—to whom increasingly, as he aged, he could pay only lip-service as he moved farther and farther away from the novel form into his own brand of reportage—he was often just a journalistic curiosity who indulged in interesting modernist tricks, but to the journalists he was a curiosity too, a literary phenomenon in their midst. Though his greatest virtue may have been that he did not fit comfortably anywhere in the specialist world into which he was born, that world has had trouble, as always, acknowledging the virtue.

At the beginning his isolation was that of an only child[2] who was also an illegitimate child. The illegitimacy did not keep him from either parent, but it made its mark. He spent four years, out of his first ten years, abroad, where his parents could travel freely together, and when he attended Choate School in Connecticut he was still not officially a Dos Passos, but John Madison.[3] His mother, Lucy Madison, was a southern lady whose unmarried years with his father were erratic and debilitating, and when she was finally able to marry him she had a series of heart attacks. She died in 1915 after three years as an invalid, during which young Dos sometimes took care of her and sometimes, from school, wrote her loving but helplessly patronizing letters, letters calling her "Baby" and "dear Princess," letters of a grown-up to a child. In one of his early novels the hero, who was unabatedly like Dos himself, said of his mother that she was the only person who

2. Each parent had one child by an earlier marriage.
3. The first wife, a Catholic and said to be mentally ill, had refused divorce. She died in 1920, but Dos took on the Dos Passos name in 1912.

had ever really had any importance to him, and went on to describe how she, who had "led a dreadfully thwarted life," had given him piano lessons and in effect brought him into the world of art. Yet in the letters that have been passed down, the father figures as the important one. In old age the father was a loner too but not for the son's reasons.

> It was the loneliness of a man who has outlived his generation. More and more he found himself on the unpopular side of political questions. He opposed votes for women and President Wilson's putting through legislation for an eight-hour day. He was suspicious of the direct primary. He made speeches and circulated a pamphlet against the election of United States Senators by popular vote, which he felt would upset the balance of powers set up under the Constitution.

The father may have been a loner when he was young as well, but he was hardly shy and retiring. Dos reported in some amazement that he seemed to *know* everybody, and when he walked from his home on Fifty-ninth Street in New York to his downtown law office he would speak to "cops on the beat, cabdrivers, whitewings and lawclerks." He was also arrogant, boastful, excessively sure of himself, and determined—if erratically—to make young Dos in his image. At least Dos said this of him indirectly in a late book, *Chosen Country,* to which he referred biographer Melvin Landsberg for information about the father saying: "My relations with my father whom I came to admire greatly before he died were much too complicated to go into here [that is, in a letter]. For a *fictional* approximation, see *The Chosen Country,* the Pignatellis." Landsberg notes that the young man of the Pignatelli family had a "horrible" childhood, partly because he was illegitimate and was moved from school to school, and partly because his father pushed him too hard. The mother said to him, "He's such a strong swimmer, Jay, and he wants you to be a strong swimmer too. . . . You've got to learn to keep up with him." The result of his familial predicament was that for life he had a low opinion of his physical self. And he was awkward. He could not dance, or play any sport well. He stuttered when excited, and he was unsure of himself in company. He described himself in *Chosen Country* as "a long-necked pie-faced boy with glasses." The description had merit.

But the father's letters to Dos in the last years are the letters of a man trying hard to be close to his son, even though the son was busy being inadequate. And certainly, as Dos said, the father was a man to admire. He had started with no money, but he had worked up in the world to make money—and to spend it. He sat around reading Milton conspicuously. He wrote a learned book on legal reform, then another on monopolies (in which he saw labor unions as monopolies as much to be feared as corporations), then still another on the wonders of Anglo-Saxon culture—though he was only half Anglo-Saxon himself—in which he proposed an English-speaking union, to ward off the heathen. Shades of Jack London. He loved the water, loved his Virginia estate at Sandy Point, loved his yacht, the *Gaivota,* and loved crows: "He said their caw-caw was really ha-ha. They were laughing at us. He would dance his little dance and pace the deck of the *Gaivota* with his bantam swagger and laugh back at the laughing crows: 'Ha-haha.'"

When Dos in Spain, age twenty-one, received word of his father's death, all he could think of "was the Commodore's voice calling back at the crows on the Sandy Point beach: 'Ha-haha!'" The father had given him, aside from inhibitions and a lingering sense of physical ineptness, an awareness that there was a good deal to laugh at and react to in this world, after the manner of crows. He had also given him—with the mother's help—a lofty upper-class perch from which to laugh, something the father himself hadn't had. And of course by dying when Dos was still young the father had given him in effect an open, empty world, given it to him by simply not being present as antagonist in the familiar father-son entanglements. All through his twenties Dos was "frantic to be gone," but with the father and mother dead there was the difficulty for him that there was little that was local and familial to be gone *from.* Their sudden early absence encouraged his lifelong attentiveness to the problems of the nation, rather than the intimate problems of close lives.

Harvard helped him think big too. Not that he ever let on that he liked Harvard. When he graduated in 1916 he said to a friend that he felt he could now go out in the world and start educating himself, adding, "It's wonderful how much college interferes with education," and all through his later life he took pot shots at Harvard, and at American education in general. English teachers were a "benighted lot" and the college system as a whole was designed to fit students to the American stockbroker mold. Yet Harvard was the place where, partly in rebellion against that institution, and partly because his peers there did for him what the institution did not, he grew into his early high—and sometimes snobbish—idealism. Harvard made him into an odd mix of aesthete and realist, and encouraged him, as he put it later, to keep mounting his "fiery steed and riding off in all directions." The place could not have been all bad, especially since it helped him meet E. E. Cummings who was to be a lifelong friend, Robert Hillyer with whom he collaborated on an early novel, and many others, including Edward Nagel who "introduced us to the world of 'the modern.'" Dos added,

> It was Nagel who infected both Cummings and me with the excitements and the experiments of the school of Paris. In the arts everything was abolished. Everything must be reinvented from scratch. It was in Nagel's room I saw my first copies of BLAST, with Eliot's early poems. Diaghilev's Ballet and the novelties at the Boston opera and the Armory Show did the rest.

It was Nagel also, he might have said, who introduced him seriously to thoughts of political revolution, so that when he was overseas in World War I and writing revolutionary thoughts in his letters and fearing the censors, he would not use the word *revolution* but would instead say that things were "Nageling."

There is a fine collection of such early letters (in print in *The Fourteenth Chronicle*) to a boy four years younger than he, letters in which intellectual vagaries are mixed with adolescent pedantry, telling him what to read and how to live. The boy's name was Rumsey Marvin, and Dos would say to him, "Look here, Rummy, don't you go getting down at the mouth about your poetry," or "Finally, Rummy, man is a *thinking* animal": but in context the lofty instructions were not belittling. Dos got on well with Rummy, and he spent as much time telling him of uncertainties as of certainties, especially the uncertainties of the war. In 1916, for instance, Rummy, who was only sixteen, was thinking about military service, and Dos, whose ideas on that subject were riding off in all directions, wrote him a fine, confused polemic. He said that the lonely life was not enough and that for a person like Rummy who wished for "the extremist sociability" the military service would be great—if only the military service were well run. It "would make young men rub shoulders more, get to know people outside of their class—be actually instead of theoretically democratic." But of course, said Dos, the military service was not well run. It was run by "the insufferable snobbery of army officers," with the result that the happy "picture of a military democracy—poet and peasant, doctor and butcher, arm in arm, sweating together, marching together, heroizing together, to the tune of a patriotic song—sort of fades away." Then there was also the difficulty that "when you have an army you want to use it." What to do? Dos suggested that Rummy and he take a two-day walk together in the Catskills, for which all that would be needed would be "a toothbrush, comb and clean socks and books of verse—of course."

The letters were heavily literary, with Dos recommending that Rummy read Swinburne, Cervantes, Dumas, Tennyson, Kipling, Stevenson, Browning, Housman, Verlaine, Benvenuto Cellini, Keats, Shelley and Hugh Walpole. Nagel had taught him to be modern but he was hardly throwing everything away and starting from scratch. He was full of the Georgians—as in fact D. H. Lawrence was at the time as well—and thought of them as representing the last word in facing up to life and living it to the full. The Georgians were several light years away from the imagists, but that didn't matter, and what Dos liked about them particularly was the *music* of their poetry, which was where they were most old-fashioned. Dos's own verse at the time was occasionally and cautiously "free," with regularity always creeping in. Once he quoted strongly iambic lines by Masefield to Rummy, saying, "Can anything be more rhythmic than this? . . . All the poetry I love best is intensely musical." And one of his own early efforts was so intensely musical that it sounded like Poe's "The Bells":

> Green against a livid sky
> In their square dun-tinted towers
> Hang the bronze bells of Castile.
> In their square light brown towers
> Rising from the furrowed hills,
> Clang the bells of all the churches
> The dust-brown churches of Castile.

In other words poetry was for him at the time, despite his protestations to Rummy that he did not like to talk style, an old-fashioned prosodic enterprise, but about the *subjects* of poetry he could be revolutionary with conviction.

> By all the gods of Flaubert, of Homer, of modern realism and the new
> poetry, I conjure you, Oh Rummy, to take back them words. Prize fights

are every bit as good a subject for poetry as fine ladies and illicit love affairs. What is the *Iliad* but a succession of rather sweaty and infinitely bombastic prize fights? Admitted that excessive and artificial use of "sweat and swear" to make poems seem manly and modern is abominable and heinous and in every way to be brought up before the tribunals of good taste and good sense—still, I insist that every subject under the sun which has anything to do with human beings—man, woman, or child—is susceptible of poetic treatment.

There's an outburst for you.

Naturally he did not always heed his own words against sweat-and-swear literature. A poem of his about night life in Venice ended

> And later
> One goes
> And pukes beautifully beneath the moon,
> Champagne-colored

Beyond sweat-and-swear he was also Prufrockish in sensibility, that is, proud of his own, and confident that his private responses to, say, a landscape would be of universal interest:

> Smoke settling,
> Black, sootladen
> About the roofs of the city
> That jut out of the pool of night
> Into the warm purpurate gloaming . . .

What he did do in his verse at this time that was not narcissistic or verbally exhibitionistic was to work at providing good solid detail. An early effort at describing a medieval Venetian scene was typical. The scene went through several drafts in his diary, and even the first drafts showed his interest in fullness, in getting it all down. Draft one described the "Doges coming down to the sea/To inspect wharves and cargoes." Draft two gave the Doges beady eyes and informed us that the cargoes came from Crete, Mytilene, Cyprus, and Joppa. Draft three added details about the black slaves loading the cargoes. The thing got bigger and bigger.

Ah, but then he decided that it was too big, that the detail was excessive; so in draft four he cut the detail severely and became Prufrock again, commenting inwardly about his own poetic ineptness:

My verse is no upholstered chariot,
Gliding oil-smooth on oiled wheels
No swift and shining limousine
But a pushcart rather . . .

In these early poems, and in his talk about poems, his most common theme was that being literary was not enough. Right there at Harvard he kept swearing off being an aesthete, and though he didn't succeed in not being, his letters, at least to Rummy, showed that he was always reaching out far beyond literature and its issues to big sociocultural matters. For example, he was regularly full of outbursts against conventional assumptions about class differences that he found around him—in his elders, in his classmates, even in Rummy. (He once picked on a thoughtless phrase of Rummy's—"life's meaner things"—as occasion to give a short lecture on "stockbrokers and hypocritical clergymen" who were at least as mean as "women of the street or prizefighters.") And he was also full of an unliterary obsession with the importance of ideas.

He liked ideas, liked to fool around with them, liked them floating in his neighborhood—Shaw's ideas were especially attractive—and in several places in the Rummy letters he described ideas as if they were the exclusive property of the unconventional people—that is the good people—of the world. Conventional people simply didn't think, didn't *have* ideas. To think was to react against conventional thinking.

And so he was himself a great reactor—against muddle-headedness, bureaucracy, tyranny, hypocrisy, those usual evils, plus the evils that the modernists of art and poetry were attacking, the evils of the old, the worn-out. In his reacting he was—though he wouldn't have liked to think so—a rather ordinary young intellectual of his time.

Yet he was, his Harvard friends reported later, not at all an ordinary undergraduate in appearance and demeanor. He had a foreign accent and "continental mannerisms," said one classmate, and according to Cummings he was "about the least American-looking person" imaginable. Also, he was unusual even in his American-ness, having travelled more, lived in more hotel rooms, and seen more kinds of humans than most of his classmates. In his best books later—and especially in *USA*—he drew steadily on the big contrasts of life his childhood travel had brought home to him, the toughness of city life, the homebodiness of Sandy Point, the ordinariness of the high and mighty (in *USA* he reported seeing Teddy Roosevelt ride by alone, like any other rider, on a bay horse), and the constant jostlings of class difference. One touching account was of being on the eastern shore of Maryland—he had sailed there from Sandy Point in the *Gaivota*—where he saw, on a siding in a boxcar, a young man he obviously wished he could be: "He had curly hair and wisps of hay in it and through his open shirt you could see his body was burned brown to the waist. I guess he wasn't much account but he'd bummed all the way from Minnesota he was going south and when I told him about Chesapeake Bay he wasn't surprised but said I guess it's too fur to swim it I'll get a job in a menhaden boat."

There was romance for him—and probably sexual feeling too—in the lives of boys like that, boys somehow free of the system. He mixed such real romance with literary romance, approving both:

> You liked books and Gibbon's Decline and Fall of the Roman Empire and Captain Marryat's novels and wanted to go away and to sea and to foreign cities Carcassone Marrakesh Isfahan and liked things to be beautiful and wished you had the nerve to hug and kiss Martha the colored girl they said was half Indian old Emma's daughter and little red-headed Mary I taught how to swim if only I had the nerve breathless nights when the moon was full but Oh God not lilies.

His view later of his own adolescent life and of the adolescent lives of others was most tender. His young were always hopeful and naive, always suckers but resourceful too, and always gentle-spirited. In many respects Dos became one of the most hopeful writers about *people* that America has produced, but the hope stayed mostly with the young.

Even when the young were stupid he liked them, and he made his own stupidities attractive. His own tended to be those of a conformist, which Dos could see that he had been, and could enjoy having been:

> Afterwards we went to the Brevoort it was much nicer everybody who was anybody was there and there was Emma Goldman eating frankfurters and sauerkraut and everybody looked at Emma Goldman and at everybody else that was anybody and everybody was for peace and the cooperative commonwealth and the Russian Revolution and we talked about red flags and barricades and suitable posts for machine guns.

Obviously it had been stupid but exciting to have been one of the everybody, to have been desperate to get into the war (as he had been) but desperately pacifistic (as he had been). One has to read Dos's endless accounts of World War I with a pleasant feeling for the ambiguities in his own passions as he became involved in the war; for the war conditioned him as no other event in his life did. And his youth at the time was both burden and salvation.

He was a pacifist but he was too near-sighted to be accepted by the army anyway. He looked for an ambulance corps to join, though in addition to his bad eyes he was a terrible driver. He found the Norton-Harjes Ambulance Corps that Cummings and Hillyer had signed with, shipped overseas, and immediately had three weeks of front-line duty at Verdun that he was lucky to survive. Those weeks gave him his first two novels, and they gave him the ineradicable view of the world—to appear in all his novels—that it was a mix of vicious system and hopeful flesh.

These first two novels were *One Man's Initiation* and *Three Soldiers,* and they were brash young things. (His first novel now in general circulation is *Manhattan Transfer,* 1924.) To be precise the first, *One Man's Initiation,* was an outgrowth of an unnamed and unpublished collaborative venture with Hillyer, who was in Ambulance Section Number Sixty with him.[4] With the shells falling around them at Verdun the time seemed a poor one to start a book, but they did. They were on duty for twenty-four hours, then off the same, and when they were off duty they were pleasantly located in the garden of a house that no longer existed, where "beautiful brown and white snails crawled among the twining honeysuckle," helping them to feel literary. Also they were desperate to write *something.* At least Dos was. He said in his diary, just before the collaboration began, "I'm dying to write—but all my methods of doing things in the past merely disgust me now. . . . Horror is so piled on horror that there can be no more—Despair gives place to delirious laughter."

So Hillyer and he started their novel with their hero in childhood (the progression to manhood was to be the narrative background of most of Dos's works), but they had barely written him through prep school when the Verdun offensive was over, they were still alive, and Hillyer was called home for a family emergency. Dos was then trans-

4. Cummings was in a different section, and apparently their paths did not cross at all during the war itself.

ferred from Norton-Harjes to the Red Cross Ambulance Service in Italy. A less persistent scribbler would have given the work up, but he pressed on alone, writing in his diary for instance, for inclusion in the novel, a fatuous address that he imagined Nicholas Murray Butler giving to the students of Columbia University about the "noble men of allied nations" fighting "on land and sea." Soon he was in part three of the novel, and soon part three *was* the novel. But it was not to be completed in Italy. He was suddenly removed from the Red Cross there, under a cloud, for having incautiously written to a Spanish friend,

> It's up to you, who can make revolutions either quietly or violently, who are trying vainly, perhaps, to evolve a purpose for the life of our times, it is up to you to safeguard all the finest human things while the rest of us struggle on brutally and with suicidal madness . . .
>
> Everywhere it seems to me there is nothing, either for the rich or the poor, but slavery; to industry, to money, to the mammon of business, the great God of our times. . . . It seems to me that only in your Spain and in Russia is the conquest not quite complete—it is in part because of that I love Spain so much.
>
> And my own poor country—it seems to me that with the war, with the military service law, liberty is extinguished there for a long time to come, and the day of triumph for plutocracy has arrived.

The letter was read by a censor, just as a letter written by Slater Brown in the Norton-Harjes Corps was read at nearly the same time, causing the incarceration of Brown and E. E. Cummings in "the enormous room" that Dos would later encourage Cummings to write about. Dos was lucky and was soon aboard the steamer *Espagne,* heading home to see if he could join the Army Medical Corps, and writing his novel. He traveled, he later noted with a smirk, first class.

One Man's Initiation was not a novel with a plot like the novels of London and Sinclair. It was the story of the author's life in transparent disguise, but unlike the early part written with Hillyer it at least had a clear focus. The focus was in the title. His one man, Arthur Howe, was initiated into war and death. He was also initiated into the lies surrounding war and death, and the lies were what the book was really about.

First there were the lies about the Germans, about their raping and murdering civilians. Dos handled these with heavy irony, using an idiot speaker: "The curs! The Huns! Let me tell you just one story

. . . I know it'll make your blood boil. It's absolutely authentic, too. I heard it before I left New York from a girl who's really the best friend I have on earth. She got it from a friend of hers who got it directly from a little Belgian girl, poor little thing, who was in the convent at the time. . . ."

Then there were the bigger lies, "the ocean of lies through all the ages" that had made the war possible, lies "industriously pumped out of press and pulpit." Those big lies—about the glory of serving God and Nation—were what maddened Dos most, and he had so much to say about them that he had little space left in the novel for the war he had actually been living.

Then at the end of the novel he ignored noveling completely, providing instead a debate between three suddenly trumped-up French philosophical characters, just as Upton Sinclair had done at the end of *The Jungle*. [5] The characters, all French, were a Catholic, a Socialist, and an anarchist, and Dos put them to work disposing of the world's lies, each in his own way but always abstractly, remotely. The Catholic announced that the wise should "rule and direct the stupid," so that love could replace force. The Socialist wanted organization to begin at the bottom, with the rich being "extinguished". And the anarchist disposed of government entirely in a single page, muttering, "Organization is death. It is disorganization, not organization, that is the aim of life."

Then the three debaters joined with Dos's hero and another American in a toast "To Revolution, to Anarchy, to the Socialist State!" and all would have been fine if Dos had not decided at that point to end the three of them and the novel, with the killing of them all on the spot with a random shell.

He landed in New York with his manuscript, put the finishing touches on it there, and sent it to a publisher. With the book out of his hands he managed to have himself assigned to an army medical unit in Pennsylvania, where he was instantly put on KP and thereby encouraged to think again all the impious thoughts that had brought

5. The parallel to Sinclair's debate (1905) seems too close to be fortuitous. Sinclair had for a cast a Christian Socialist with some specific suggestions for how the meek should inherit the earth, a Socialist politician who was a party hack getting out the vote, and a hard-nosed journalist who kept pointing out how hard it was to effect significant social change. The comparative practicality of Sinclair's debaters is the most striking difference.

him trouble in Italy. Soon he was at work on novel number two, *Three Soldiers*. He shipped out again for Europe with his medical unit the day the war ended, and then at great labor in Paris arranged for his honorary discharge overseas—so that he might discover freedom again.

He took courses at the Sorbonne and lounged about Paris with young American writers and artists like himself.[6] Soon the novel was done and he was back in the States *again*—but not for long. He assured his friends that he had come home "not to stay home . . . but to find means to finance fresh trips." Luckily he was able to sell *Three Soldiers*—the Lord did provide.

Three Soldiers had Dos in it and all over it, but it had others too. It was a big step forward for him in noveling, as well as in becoming a chronicler, a recorder for the tribe. And for the first time his dialogue was credible, the war scenes bloody but convincing. Only the book's ideology was false.

It was false because Dos insistently made high drama out of the mundane, converting a bumbling American military machine with a few callous corporals and chauvinistic lieutenants into a monstrous tyranny. (He would provide more credible tyrannies later.) When he had his hero led off at the end as a deserter he was obviously thinking of what might have happened to himself—but, significantly, didn't— because of his radicalism, and he also wanted something in the novel beyond American rice pudding, something Russian. But he couldn't pull it off; he knew too much experientially by then about American army life to convert it into something that he didn't know, and to impose convincing high tragedy upon it. ("How," Robert Frost asked at about this time, "are we to write the Russian novel in America as long as life goes so unterribly?") After all, he had washed windows in the army in Pennsylvania, and had wandered from desk to desk in the army bureaucracy in Paris without starving or having his thumbs cut off. But with that knowledge he should not have tried what he did try, and particularly should not have dared the finale he concocted. Endings were starting to trouble him, for there, reaching for a Russian

6. His best friends in Paris were three young radicals: Griffin Barry who was "full of the lingo of Mabel Dodge's salon in New York," Bob Minor "whose charcoal cartoons we had all admired in *The Masses*," and Jack Lawson whom Dos thought would be "the greatest playwright ever," and to whom he read parts of *Three Soldiers*.

effect, he had his writer-hero led off by the MPs, and he showed the hero's desk with all of the hero's immortal creations upon it. What happened? A cruel wind came in a neglected window, sweeping the creations away, sheet by sheet. The end of art.

It can be argued that blind-force doctrine, such as that which swept Dos himself away in fancy at the ends of the first two novels, has been the death of ideas in America, the death of faith in the power of ideas to do anything intelligent and humane about human society. Those who have been hopeful about blind force, such as the laissez-faire people, have been *content* with what Dos called "dawg-eat-dawg," and have generally feared ideologues, while those who have been fatalists have shipped out for the islands, as Henry Adams did. But, happy or unhappy, those who have accepted the dominance of blind force have mostly been led, unlike Adams, to put ideas aside as rootedly utopian, leaving us all to heaven and the psychobiographers and the pollsters.

But it can also be argued—and is argued constantly by many of those Dos thought of as liars—that America has a substitute for ideas that is not a blind force, namely the will of the people. The people feel their way to the right, to truth, to justice. They do it at election time, they do it in the Neilsen ratings, they do it without knowing an idea from a handsaw, but they do it; and the results are mostly good beyond their knowing. Theirs is consensus wisdom, a *wisdom* beyond the ideological. What they know they just know, and it is the right that they know.

In *One Man's Initiation* Dos took potshots at the people on odd pages, and showed faith in them on the even. The debate at the end of the novel was preceded by the observation by one of the Frenchmen (an observation with which the Americans present agreed): "Americans never think." Yet minutes later Dos arranged to have another Frenchman praise the "fundamental kindness" and "fraternity" of these thoughtless people. Then a page later another trumped-up Frenchman took the stupidity of these "average working people" as reason to suppose that lies would always triumph. Back and forth. Meanwhile Dos himself was sitting somewhere in the middle, disgusted with his fellow Americans for being "dupes," yet ideologically dependent upon their final good sense to sustain the only kind of socialism he could imagine living with, anarcho-socialism, a socialism of a beautiful withered state in which the dawgs willingly consented *not* to eat the dawgs. In his first two novels he had handled his dilemma clumsily; later he would become more readily cynical; but he never became totally, finally cynical, never gave up thoughts of some happy even though human change:

> O it is so much harder than it has ever been before to lead a good life, to dominate life instead of being driven in the herd. Intellect, vigor have more to struggle against than ever before, except perhaps in the darkest of feudal times, when religion held the world crouched in gibbering fear. This all pervading spirit of commerce—this new religion of steel and stamped paper! O it is time for Roland to blow his horn that the last fight may start.

One of the most instructive early moments of *sturm and drang* for him came in a 1920 letter he wrote to Stewart Mitchell, an old Harvard friend who had just started up a new round of the *Dial*. Dos, in Spain, received the first issue and wrote "Auk" apologetically to say that the magazine was "so flat it might have been the *Atlantic Monthly* for the year 1889." But when he got around to saying *why* the magazine was flat he was incoherent. He said that as a writer he felt obligated to break with all the pasts, yet he feared the narrowness of modernity. He said that as a political animal he knew the *Dial* ought to be in there pitching somehow—but how he couldn't say. He went through the issue in detail, complaining about "those sophomoric dribblings of Edith Wharton and Loeffler and that miserable snobbism of Symons about Thomas Hardy," praising Sandburg and Cummings, and worrying that the magazine seemed to lack direction. Finally he wound up his rhetorical machine and let fly at the magazine's artiness, an artiness he found unhealthy at a moment in history when the question confronting intelligent minds was "whether civilization or barbarism rules our continent and the world." He raved,

> In ten years we may be cavemen snatching the last bit of food from each others mouths amid the stinking ruins of our cities, or we may be slaving—antlike—in some utterly systematized world where the individual will be utterly crushed that the mob (or the princes) may live. Every written word should be thought of as possibly the last that humanity will ever write, every gesture of freedom the last before the shackles close indefinitely. And we who have worshipped freedom and writing as God—shall we be annihilated by destiny filling up the precious printed pages with spacefillers?

Poor Auk, stuck with saving civilization, must have wondered what sort of an issue of the *Dial* would have satisfied Dos, but Dos must have wondered too. *How,* as an artist, did one go about saving civilization? In 1920 the artist's role, as Dos conceived it, was as grand as it had ever been, but how to fill the role was a mystery. The artist couldn't go along with the mob *or* the princes, couldn't take any of the positions in sight, yet he still had civilization on his hands.

Dos was therefore apologetic to Auk for his outburst, and said that he was being "shockingly impudent." He added that his impudence proceeded from being "truly detached from the world at present."

Yes, he was detached, but he was about to become even more detached, and from great remoteness to keep storming barricades. He derived two travel books from his detachment.

He took off. He headed for very foreign parts while at the same time dreaming, like Henry Adams in the South Seas and Jack London aboard *The Snark,* that his travels would bring him great social awareness. For more than a year, a pen in hand and little money in pocket, he became a world-wanderer. He took in Spain with Cummings (going there via the Azores on a tramp steamer) and produced a quick book of essays, *Rosinante to the Road Again,* on the wonders of Spanish culture, the "classic home of the anarchist . . . where people have lived until very recently—and still do—in villages hidden away among the bare ribs of mountains . . . where every region is cut off from every other by high passes [and] where the Iberian race has grown up centerless." Then he boarded the Orient Express, without Cummings, and arrived in Constantinople in time to see Turks massacring Armenians. Then east (working briefly for a do-gooder outfit he detested, Near East Relief) to Georgia, where the Bolsheviks were doing the massacring. Then south to Mount Ararat, under which "half naked children with sagging cheeks and swollen bellies of starvation cower[ed] like hurt animals in doorways and recesses in the walls." This trip was good for a travel book too, called *Orient Express,* and he capped the experience with a journey by camel from Baghdad to Damascus, living among desert people who were like the Spaniards in their fine anarchy and who knew that each man had to stand up "by himself, in the fearful wind, under the enormous sky." Dos made good friends with the leader of the caravan, but when at the end of the journey he shaved off his beard the leader was filled with "incredulous horror," made "a gesture of utter repudiation," and it was time for Dos to head home with his notebooks.

He did get home (briefly, always briefly), and in 1922 he could be found lunching uneasily at the Plaza with a writer with none of his collectivist ambiguities, Scott Fitzgerald, and with Zelda.

He was uneasy with Scott and Zelda, he said much later, because they were "celebrities and they loved it . . . celebrities in the Sunday supplement sense of the word." He added that "the idea of being that kind of celebrity set [his] teeth on edge." *Three Soldiers* had sold well and he hoped to make a living by his writing, but a living for him was not like a living for Scott and Zelda. Dos was riding his ships and camels into a future that did not include lunches at the Plaza, and did not have him meeting *Saturday Evening Post* deadlines or sending cables to Scribners for money, money. In setting up shop as an author Dos was only incidentally concerned with dollars and a literary reputation:

> I had taken a private vow of allegiance to an imaginary humanist republic which to me represented the struggle for life against the backdrag of death and stagnation. Figures like Giordano Bruno, Erasmus, Rabelais, Montaigne presided over my republic of letters. Among its latterday saints I classed Shelley, Stendhal, Flaubert, possibly Walt Whitman and Rimbaud . . . In this contest the number of copies a book sold was neither here nor there. The celebrity racket made no sense at all.

In 1922 he still had one bad egocentric novel left in him, something called *Streets of Night* in which the young hero, fresh out of Harvard, felt "always alone, moral, refined, restrained," but the "humanist republic" in the back of his head was driving him away from that kind of literature. In the next few years he searched for that republic in his travels and, not finding it, constantly set up, against its imagined presence, "the backdrag of death and stagnation" that he saw around him in his own country—when he was in it. He also traveled to two countries of revolution, Mexico and the USSR, and was ambiguously impressed.

When he was traveling, and before he became an activist, he wrote *Manhattan Transfer* (1924), a fine piece of reporting, a big step beyond *Streets of Night,* showing off for the first time his powers of social observation. A Washington Square bus "smelled of gasoline and asphalt, of spearmint and talcum powder and perfume from the couples that jiggled closer and closer together." A restaurant kitchen was filled with "the smell of swill and hot soapsuds," as one of the characters went "twice around with the little mop, dip, rinse and pile in the rack." On gray winter mornings Eleventh Avenue was "full of icy dust, of grinding rattle of wheels and scrape of hoofs on the cobblestones," and the people themselves were gray too, struggling for a dollar or a meal, and reading with heavy irony the slogans of the city of the time, the Gay White Way and "the land of opportunity." Dos did most of his scenes with a broad brush, and he surrounded his hero, Jimmy Herf, who was a hard-up wanderer in the city like himself, with a cross-section of city strugglers, all in trouble somehow with the "backdrag of death and stagnation."

Sinclair Lewis reviewed the book, saying it presented "the panorama, the sense, the smell, the sound, the soul, of New York." And it did. And in doing this it pointed the way—as nothing before it had—to the chronicle genre he was to make his own.

What the novel did not have was a display of commitment. The hero moved unhappily from job to job, and discovered chiefly that society expected him to conform to a set of rules that he could not in good conscience accept. The traveler in Dos was still triumphant over the activist. The traveler in him kept him from thinking of his career as something to settle down and into. All through the early twenties he quested after his elusive republic as if the republic were itself on the move, and the quest did not give him time to feather his nest. All he knew was that wherever the republic was it would have a place for him in it.

Of course no matter where it was, it was also sure to have a little of Greenwich Village in it, with the artistic radicals there joining him "in revolt against Main Street, against the power of money, against Victorian morality."

And no matter where it was, it was sure to have a little of Paris in it too, where modernism by the early twenties was already passé, but where art was the art of all nations and, it seemed to him then, the liveliest force in the world.

And no matter where that good humanist place was it would naturally subordinate the artist's private ambitions to a lovely general social condition, communal but without tyrants and bureaucrats, and without, if the truth were known, restraints of any kind on the artist's private ambitions.

Yes, the humanist republic was fine, but it did need to settle down a bit in one place. For Dos it would never really do so, but at least it *tended* to settle down in New York and environs for a considerable period starting in the mid-twenties. At that time Dos was being as settled as he would ever be, and he was also learning, and practicing, that which goes with settling down: commitment.

While living in New York he worked with the editors of the *New Masses,* and also directed a workers' theater group. He also fought with them, and expressed his collectivist feelings ambiguously. "*We* radicals didn't think alike. Damned if we would [my italics]." Just being with such groups pushed him into more sallies typical in his writings, and that made him an expressionist for a bit, on stage.

He wrote two expressionist plays. He had tried poetry, fiction, travelogues, and cultural essays, but when he rode forth into drama he thought he had really found the proper genre for an artist with a social conscience. He dreamed of a "national theater" that would help with "the welding of our cities into living organisms" out of "the junk heaps of boxed and predatory individuals that they are at present." And when he came to his own plays, *The Garbage Man* (alternate title, *The Moon Is a Gong*) and *Airways, Inc.,* he went at the welding by making the characters little types who could be known, completely known, by their names alone. *The Garbage Man* was the best of the two—which isn't saying much—but its characters, numbering fifty, were typical of both plays, and were all played by just a few actors. They had such names as A Workman, A Man With A Cigar, An Old Man, A Teadrinker. The Garbage Man himself was Death.

Predictably, the play's dialogue was ritualistic, wooden: "You must do what you're told, say what you're told, know what you're told. . . . Every loyal American should be an agent of the Department of Justice." The social criticism was heavy and relentless, describing "tides of people, their minds clicking like adding machines, their fingers itching for the round silver pieces, the crinkly green dollars, walkinglockstep, shackled in Arrow Collar shackles." It was bad, but it was modernist in its way, and au courant. *The Garbage Man* was put on once at Harvard in 1924, then again in New York when Dos had his workers' theater; and though it was bad it pointed to some of the kinds of typicality that he would work with more successfully, in *USA.* Also of course it satisfied his urge to ride off in all directions at once, and be both modernist artistically and activist politically.[7]

7. Upton Sinclair wrote a play, *Singing Jailbirds,* that was produced by Dos's theater group, and it was probably as expressionist and modern as Upton ever managed to be.

Probably it was more fashionable for an intellectual to be radical in the twenties and thirties than it had been in the prewar period that conditioned Jack London and Upton Sinclair, but the social circumstances in both times were superficially similar. The unions were slowly gathering unto themselves strength and competence, but the process was so tedious, and corporate resistance so steady, that the whole conflict—maybe the most important conflict of the age—had the texture of a medieval religious war. Upton and Jack had been born too late to be active in the biggest social crisis of their period, the Haymarket Riot of 1887 with its subsequent trial of seven anarchists, but they were bred up on the tensions of Haymarket (the fears of bomb-throwing aliens) and they had their own causes to be stirred up about—the unemployment marches of 1894, the Paterson textile strike of 1913, the Ludlow massacre of 1915. Dos in turn came of age politically with *his* era's equivalent of Haymarket, which was the Sacco-Vanzetti case; and though by his time the role of anarchists in the union movement must have been negligible, their bogey-man presence was not to be overlooked. Sacco-Vanzetti helped to continue them in that image, and it also helped to keep anarchist dialectic circulating. So did the developing fight between equivalent forces in the USSR. In Dos's maturing radicalism the many different radical options were always confronting him, not letting him be simply a Socialist, like Jack and Upton in their early days. The Socialists themselves in the twenties begin to look namby-pamby to him, and in the early thirties he referred to them once as "near-beer." The Communists meanwhile were beginning to establish the meaning of Stalinism.

The anarchists had earned a public reputation for being the most dangerous of the lot. They were mad aliens with bombs. At the time of Haymarket the mad aliens were German, and happened to edit a German-language newspaper in Chicago that did preach violence just before the actual Haymarket violence occurred. Thirty years later Sacco and Vanzetti were Italian aliens, which was just as bad, and they were discovered to have distributed handbills advocating violence just before the crimes occurred for which they were brought to trial. In both cases the evidence connecting the victims with criminal action was circumstantial and flimsy, but the evidence that they were anarchists was clear. To be a professed anarchist was to be in trouble, at least with the press.

But there was another side to anarchism—and that was the side attractive to intellectuals like Dos—the free-thinker side. Jack and Upton had been able to be free-thinking Socialists within the Socialist party before World War I, and the party had liked them for what they were, mostly, had liked to encourage the kind of high thought that Jack listened to at Oakland meetings, and that Upton tacked onto the end of *The Jungle*. But by the twenties and thirties the tone of radical politics had been altered by the Communists, who were by then on the scene in force, with their imperative for unity. How Jack would have dealt with party-liners if he had lived into the thirties is anybody's guess, but Upton dealt with them by ignoring them. He kept his independence, and preached socialist unity from his solitary, sometimes anarchist woodsy platforms. Then on particular occasions he would rush out of the woods and join picket lines.

As for Dos, he managed to live with the Communists until the mid-thirties, having grown into radicalism in their presence; but he reacted against their conformist prescriptions as early as 1926. In his early pieces for the *New Masses* he wanted everybody marching together, but at the same time he became alarmed when anyone suggested that a writer should be a proselytizer for marching together. And he urged the editors of the *New Masses* to think of the magazine as a "highly flexible receiving station" rather than just a programmer, just a publisher of instructions and prescriptions. It was supposed to "find out what's in the air in the country anyhow."

He personally went out to find out what was in the air, and found Sacco-Vanzetti. The early stages of that case had taken place while he was traveling in Spain and the Near East; he came in late, for the finale, traveling to Boston in 1926 to interview Sacco, and write *Facing the Chair* for the Sacco-Vanzetti Defense Committee just before the two men were executed (in 1927); but when he came in, he came in hard.

Facing the Chair was a polemic, but it was a fine documentary too, a complete history of the case, as well as a summary of its social background, in 120 pages. Dos turned the pamphlet out dutifully, and dutifully picketed the Massachusetts State House. He even had his picture taken being arrested for picketing. (In the picture a policeman is holding him loosely by the upper arm and looking unhappy, but Dos is smiling a well-now-I-have-done-it smile, and striding forward purposefully.) But of course the executions took place anyway, and two martyrs were born, along with at least two new American villains, Judge Thayer of Dedham and President Lowell of Harvard. Dos walked away from the affair thinking that the United States was somewhat worse than the USSR. Nor was he alone in the walking and thinking. Dorothy Parker and Edna St. Vincent Millay walked behind him in the picket line. Upton Sinclair, Maxwell Anderson, William Carlos Williams, and a couple of dozen other prominent writers wrote poems, plays, and novels about it. Every intellectual in the country managed to be stirred, but it was Dos who took the documentary approach.

The fury of Sacco-Vanzetti, and the pressures of the workers' theater, went to Dos's head in the late twenties, and he was sometimes more kind toward the Communists than his anarchism approved. There was always the dream in him—even after Stalin began his liquidations in 1928—that the Soviets would not do what they were doing, and since his activism had become urgent in him anyway, he might have become a truly radical politico in the thirties if he had not continued to be frantic to be gone. As it was he found himself elected, constantly, to committees. He became chairman of the National Committee to Aid Striking Miners Facing Starvation in 1931, treasurer of the Emergency Committee for Southern Political Prisoners in 1930, money-raiser for the Communist-dominated National Student League in 1931. He was always being asked to serve, to act, to write, and these pressures did not encourage the contemplative life. He was not strong on that anyway. He was peripatetic in mind and soul, and all the good characters of his novels turned out that way too, turned out to be confirmed on-the-roaders. As a result he was not, though well read, a constant and addicted reader, one who took his life-cues from books. If the time had been ripe for plunging into Sir Charles Lyell or Herbert Spencer, he would have been dilatory about it, and there is little evidence that he was not dilatory about reading many of the thinkers that the times were ripe for. Even what he said about the biggest figures of his time, Marx and Freud, was referential and could well have been second hand. Science he had no truck with, and social Darwinism was reduced in his mind to dawg-eat-dawg—though he was strong on Veblen. When his wanderings took him from culture to culture he let the new surroundings seep in from his senses, not from libraries. Henry Adams had carted a trunkful of German writings on old cultures up the Nile on his honeymoon, but Dos in the Near East took along only notebooks to write and paint in (he was a good watercolorist), and was embarrassed to be caught carrying even that much excess baggage.

Yet while in Spain with Cummings in 1922 they had read Brooks Adams's *Law of Civilization and Decay* together. (Dos hated it, he said, because "it went against the Walt-Whitman-nardnik optimism I've never quite lived down.") And Dos tried to keep up with current literary excitements like *Ulysses* ("I read the book in one gulp . . . parts I found boring and parts I found magnificent") and he became very strong on Spanish and Russian dramas. Some of the last became his prime ideological sources for a while, evoking from him the most activist, party-line statements about the function of art that he would utter in his life. Comparing the Russian theater with the New York theater—in the *New Republic* in 1930—he said that New Yorkers went to the theater because they wanted to "feel part of the imperialist progression towards more money, more varnish, more ritz, that obsesses all our lives," while Muscovites went to the theater "to feel part of the victorious march through history of the world proletariat." He went on to acknowledge censorship in the Russian theater and other "disadvantages" of its being "so directly under government control," but he insisted that those difficulties didn't "hold a candle to the difficulties under which sincere theater workers in New York operate, struggling in the tangles of the angel-speculator combination." He concluded with the sort of assertion about the benignity of government controls that is conspicuously missing from his later anthologies of his own writings: "The Russian government imposes a certain propaganda or education control . . . but leaves them alone completely as far as style of presentation is concerned. . . . [Like religious painting] the imposing or taking for granted of content has never had a bad effect on any art in the past, and there is no reason it should be bad now."

Even Upton, for all his insistence that art should perform a propaganda function, would never have said such a thing; so it may be fortunate that Dos in these commitment years never stayed in one place long enough to let his theory of commitment actually commit him. He had sneaked away to the Virginia mountains in the middle of the Sacco-Vanzetti uproar (1926), and had been pleased to find that nobody up there had heard of Sacco-Vanzetti. He had also gone off to Mexico at that time, where there were plenty of radicals, and a real revolution, but the radicals (he was pleased to report), were not so much like radicals as wild gunmen in a western movie. And in 1928 he had sailed for the USSR to be indoctrinated, but had livened up the ideology side of the trip by taking a five-day voyage down the Volga on a sternwheeler that kept running aground, and by hiking into the Georgian mountains so far that he met a man who had never even heard of *Moscow*.

He traveled so much that it was a wonder he could keep up with any political commitments, much less write. Coming back from six months in the Soviet Union in 1928 he stayed in New York for only a couple of winter months (but that was long enough to make him think he had "almost lost his mind" working with his theater group) and then shipped off to see Hemingway in the spring in Key West— Key West being, at the time, he was careful to explain, a true island and genuinely remote—and met a Hemingway friend, Katherine Smith, whom he married in August but not before he had nearly finished the first volume of his *USA* trilogy, which he had worked on before and during his Russian trip. After the marriage he and Kay dashed off to Spain and France on their honeymoon.[8] The life did not seem to be that of a dedicated revolutionary.

Still, the travel remained for him a steady ideological source in itself. He believed in it. It was the only alternative to the dull death drag at home with the money people. He was like Jack London (whom he read with pleasure, and also read a children's biography of, while in the USSR) in the sense that he was in his element on the move, like Jack floating down the Des Moines River. His political activism seemed more active to him somehow when he was on the move, and he put his respect for motion right into the obscure title of *USA*'s first book, *42nd Parallel*. The 42nd parallel, he said in a note to the first edition (the note was not reprinted later), is the latitudinal line that storms crossing the nation seem generally to follow eastward. He was suggesting that the country's energy and driving power to combat the settled eastern death drag was in the unsettled West. He saw a freedom of motion and thought in western radicalism—especially in the I.W.W.—that was not evident to him in the established East. Where

8. He wrote Hemingway of his marriage and of the book, mentioning that the book now was about to be a trilogy. Hemingway wrote back congratulating the "citizens" upon the marriage and saying that trilogies were the thing: "Look at the Father Son and Holy Ghost—nothing's gone bigger than that."

had he picked up the notion? Perhaps Jack London had helped. Anyway an easy western radicalism pervaded the first book of the trilogy, but from then on life became harder for his radicals. *USA* was in a sense a history of the good old days of the American radical, the days before World War I. Dos was writing his trilogy in the thirties and was full of the urgencies of that period, but he was being nostalgic at the same time. He was looking back at his past, marking the time when the treadmill took over. Oddly, though the book was praised by the thirties radicals when it appeared, the vision in it of postwar American society was close to that in Eliot's *Waste Land*. And though Dos, unlike Eliot, had set up shop as a radical, he was much less prepared than Eliot to search out solutions to the wasteland. (Eliot at the time leaned steadily to economic and ideological analyses in his magazine, the *Criterion*.) If anything the wasteland of the American thirties was more thoroughly waste for Dos than the World War I wasteland of his first novel in 1919. In that novel he had at least felt that he could allow his characters to have an interesting debate about their future before he blew them up. In *USA* such debates lost stature. They were not so much debates as illustrations of what representative people were thinking and saying. They were barroom talk as the wasteland wasted.

Of course the process of social change had been Henry Adams's obsession too, and by luck or amazing prescience he had settled on a date for the arrival of the wasteland remarkably close to Eliot's and Dos's. He had done so without knowing of World War I, had sat at his desk in the early century and allowed his "law of acceleration" to tell him that the religious phase of man's thinking life had lasted ninety thousand years up to Lord Bacon, that the Baconian phase had lasted three hundred years up to the age of the Dynamo, and that the age of the Dynamo would last only a decade or so, up to perhaps 1920, at which point man would be due for yet another intellectual upheaval, one that would make him even less able to order his affairs, cope rationally with his world. Henry was a convinced things-fall-apart man before it was conventional to be one, and as he transferred his Rube Goldberg scientism to the world of politics and international affairs, he imagined that the chaos of the Dynamo age was only prelude to a time when nobody at all would be in charge but only force, blind force. Perhaps it is lucky that he did not write a novel to document his prophecy. The novels *Democracy* and *Esther,* written twenty years before he concocted his law, were not unremittingly determinist and were probably the better for not being. His later thinking would probably have swept up his characters into the machinery of accelerating mental force, for he became in his old age a true early prophet of all the ills of consensus culture.

Jack and Upton before the war had been earnest students of process too, but they had been optimists assuming that rational, humane governance would replace the Law of Tooth and Claw. Jack's optimism did not last long, but even in his dour moments his interest was not in fated persons but in characters who chose their own destinies, who were special and distinctive, who managed to be themselves beyond all conditioning. And Upton, the permanent optimist, went right through the wasteland without seeing that it was there, went through it with his thin smile firmly set. He had a faith that was a permanent fixture in his mental parlor, a faith in the capacity of those of good will to convert any sandy place into a green and fertile valley by the normal democratic process. Dos in the thirties with his unhappy determinism was closer to conservative Henry than to Jack and Upton. The determinism had been in his own makeup early, and was reinforced by communist thought. Though he was theoretically too libertarian to be a good Communist, he was too much impressed and depressed by the magnitude of the forces of social conditioning around him to be a good anarchist either. *USA* was his study of social process, and the study kept finding that individuals were ground up in the process. As *USA* went on the exploited ones in it began to be exploited by the Communists *too*. Also, the exploited ones began to lose their once salvageable personalities, and become as brutalized as the exploiters. The battleground became not a battleground of the Marxist dialectic, but a battleground like World War I, a battleground where everybody lost except a tiny group of connivers and betrayers, a battleground that was a steady education in the dehumanizing effects of the treadmill.

There was Ben Compton, for example. Ben passed through several stages in becoming a true revolutionary, but when he was past them he was a lost soul.

Or take Richard Savage. Savage went the unrevolutionary way. Savage was modeled after Dos in his youth, attending Harvard, taking in the war via the ambulance corps; but unlike Dos this young aesthete decided to be a success-story American. He *didn't* write treasonous letters for the censors to read—or rather, he wrote one and tore it up—and *didn't* criticize his superiors but buttered them up. As a result he became a big man in public relations, drinking like a fish and hating himself since, in Dos's social spectrum, those who made it to the top became lost souls too.

And in between Ben Compton and Richard Savage there were other lost souls. There was Joe Williams particularly, one of Dos's most pleasant characters, an unpretentious, likeable sailor always frantic to be gone, whom Dos could not spare either, killing him off in a barroom brawl.

To sum up the pervasive mood of the trilogy, Dos tacked on at the end a strange, short passage, called "Vag," in which the vagrant at its center was a hungry hitchhiker who had been beaten down by all the forces of American civilization. ("Went to school, books said opportunity, ads promised speed, own your own home.") As the novel ended, Vag was standing on the edge of the concrete with his thumb up, trying to get "a hundred miles down the road."

The thirties radicals who praised Dos for *USA* were blind to Dos's insistent doubt that society would *make* it a hundred miles down the road. One of the strongest admirers of the book was Granville Hicks, who in the mid-thirties not only described Dos as a writer in the "great tradition," but then went on to write a book about that tradition as he conceived it. It was the book that F. R. Leavis must have been replying to in his own later version of the "great tradition"—both their books had the same title—and it was certainly full of the blindness. Hicks was blind chiefly to the dangers of the Marxist historical process, as that process was being directed and staged by the Communists, the dangers described by thinkers like Dos. Hicks's constant thesis was that the revolutionary movement would open, not close, men's minds. How spacious life and literature would be, when social injustice receded into the past, and humanity, with its eyes at last opened, saw itself in its wholeness. But Dos had come to think otherwise, and *USA*—reaching out for the literary spaciousness that the Communists preached—showed his doubts.

It also showed, and in detail for thirteen hundred pages, our own fearsome national fault, the fault that would make the literary man's job progressively harder as he tried to confront his national image as homeland rather than enemy: the fault of bigness, and the fault of uniformity raging through the bigness, the fault of consensus thinking. Other literary minds of the thirties, and later, would deal with the fault by evasion, but Dos—with his tribal-recorder theory now well in hand—took on the whole national swamp. *USA* was a genuine national event in a country whose literature was still mostly islanded by regions and class, but it did not present a happy picture of the national condition. It was a thirteen-hundred-page demonstration that the nation was not an acceptable wholeness for a free spirit. In effect Dos, moving in from the left, was agreeing with regional conservatives like Allen Tate that the country's imperatives were inhumanly confining and oppressive.

So *USA* was an unpromising picture of the national promise; but it was also a great literary experiment simply because it took on the national organism. After *USA* the issues of our national consensus were largely taken over by social scientists and journalists, and their takeover meant that the complex vision of the nature of nation that Dos had been working on—with a constant tension showing itself between the individual and the consensus—was reduced to a vision of *only* the consensus. Dos had wanted his vision to be a double one, and in some measure he succeeded.

The success has not generally been acknowledged in literary circles. Dos has been taped as an idealist who slowly grew up. And since he became, in the late thirties, one of the prominent party-line backtrackers, the fact of his switch to conservatism has merely buttressed the prevalent theory that ideologues are always immature. Daniel Aaron in *Writers on the Left* fits him to this pattern.

For Aaron, Dos was a good example of a political literary activist who followed the usual activist road. He had "radical adventures" from the days of his youth to the days of his disillusionment, after which he was radical no more, but allowed himself to be "absorbed" by his society, so that he could go on with literature. Well, it is true that the works after *USA* were political poison for any Communist. In *Adventures of a Young Man* (1939) Dos built his story on a Communist betrayal of a sensitive, well-intentioned radical. In *Grand Design* (1949) he made a hero out of a conservative, anti-New-Deal businessman. And in *Chosen Country* (1951) he had his lawyer hero unadventurously choose, after four hundred pages of radical dabbling, the American Way without reservations, praising persons who went about "innocently and cheerfully" making money, finding the country not full of "the deathdrag of death and stagnation" but full of hope and innocence, a country that made him feel "proud and humble when he saw the striped flag fly." Dos had parodied such attitudes, and such language, in early works and in *USA,* and so in a sense Aaron is right; Dos's political shift was classic and definitive, a conversion true to the social agony of the thirties. But in another sense Aaron quite misses the narrowness of the shift which, though away from radicalism and into the heart of the Right, was not away from his "chronicle" procedure and its significance. If anything the chronicling took over from the literature more thoroughly in the late years than the early, and took over when, aging, he indulged in a lot of sloppy, pontifical generalization. *USA* was much the high point for his mode of literary thought, but it was not the end of it. What he abandoned after the Spanish War was his ideal humanist republic, in favor of his father's capitalism.

The Spanish event that ended his always-uneasy tie to the Communists was the execution of a good Communist friend by the Communists—or so Dos always afterward believed—for failing to obey Party instructions. The event was a major cause of the cooling of his friendship with Hemingway (who continued to back the Loyalist cause though he knew of the event), and it appears now as the immediate cause of his political conversion too. From then on Dos had an obsession about betrayal.

Another biographer, John Wrenn, has located the betrayal theme in Dos's "discovery" in the mid-thirties (before Spain) that he and his artist friends had been selling their own country short. In 1936 Dos Passos wrote Scott Fitzgerald that he was "trying to take a course in American history," and suggested, as Wrenn put it, that Scott might also be saved by so doing. Soon he was writing documentaries of American heroes, starting with *The Living Thoughts of Tom Paine,* and moving on to Jefferson, Hamilton, others. For Wrenn this new interest showed that by the mid-thirties Dos was at last "homeward bound" after a life without home or nation, a life of homelessness begun at birth in a Chicago hotel room; showed that by the mid-thirties Dos had begun to believe that his social complaints since college had had the wrong target all along; that he had been betrayed by false hopes. Wrenn did not go so far as to say that Dos came to think of his old expatriate literary friends as the abetting betrayers, but he did say that, in the process of conversion, Dos came to place citizenship above his art. Wrenn described the nature of citizenship in such a way as to make art and citizenship incompatible, saying that Dos became "less concerned to produce lasting works of the imagination-art—and more concerned to devote his efforts to maintaining a civilization in which art is possible"—the opposite of the Aaron point that he switched his politics so that he could stick with his art.

Wrenn tried to demonstrate the shift statistically, observing that before 1938 Dos had written 14 volumes, of which only 2½ had been nonfiction, and between 1938 and 1960 he had written 15 volumes, of which 9 were nonfiction. In other words Dos had switched genres. That was what becoming a citizen meant. For better or worse, being homeward bound entailed giving up, at least partly, art.

The Wrenn point seems as wrong to me as the Aaron point, but Dos must have believed some of it himself. Not that he lashed out at his artist friends for betraying their country. In *The Best Years* he looked back at the trying late thirties with a display of official kindness toward his old friends. Yet he clearly felt alienated, not only from friends but from the literary life itself. Reacting to it he sometimes sounded like a good philistine citizen in Sinclair Lewis's *Main Street*.

But to see beyond the political shift we should remember that he had been leaving that literary life for most of his adulthood, had been leaving it when he complained about the arty crowd at Harvard, had been leaving it when he moved out of the "art-novel" world into the "chronicle." Who is to say whether his chronicles, right up to about 1960, are novels or history? To classify them flatly as fiction or nonfiction is to ignore how hard Dos worked to escape such classification.

The "homeward bound" chronicles were generically as slippery as *USA. Chosen Country,* for example, was fiction, but it was also history. It continued the biographical sketches to be found in *USA,* but merged them *into* the fiction (in *USA* they were separate; they were interludes) by giving the biographies pseudonyms, changing a few dates, and integrating them with the fictional action. Thus Clarence Darrow (1857–1938) became Elisha Croft (1865–1930) so that he could be a fictional participant; his birth (in Farmington, Indiana) and upbringing and early career went unchanged, as did his legal philosophy. And Dos accomplished the same minimal fictionalizing of other persons, notably an American radical named Anna Louise Strong, whom Dos had met in Russia in 1928 and now re-created as Anne Comfort Welsh, a constant and loyal activist. Then there was the Norton of Norton-Harjes, whom Dos re-created as a Boston snob named Eliot Story Bradford. History? Fiction? Dos had always wanted to blur the two, and until his final decline—I can only call it that—into Republican politics and the *National Review* he succeeded; that is, he kept a foot in literature while writing social history.

He did so up through *Midcentury* (1961). After *Midcentury* he let travel books and reminiscences take over his writing life, and he was feted and well paid for them. In 1962, "before an audience of some 18,000 conservatives in Madison Square Garden, he received a second annual award certificate from the Young Americans for Freedom, Inc." In 1964 he attended the Republican National Convention and whooped it up for Goldwater. In 1966 he berated the New Left so heartily in the *National Review* that liberal Edmund Wilson, who had managed to stay friends with him, wrote, "Your pronouncements on current events continue to give me the creeps."

Meanwhile with his wife, Elizabeth, he was visiting Italy, Japan, and several countries in South and Central America, receiving prizes and making speeches notable for a mixture of pleasantness and polemic about his old, familiar subjects, such as the evils of bureaucracy (he had been complaining about them since World War I) and political dogmatism. The pie-faced boy with heavy glasses still had the circular face and the glasses, and he still had his anarchist individualism ready at hand, but now the presence behind the face and the anarchism was one that nobody would find clumsy or inadequate. In the sixties he must have been like his father had been, or like the father that he had chronicled, in that he seemed to know everybody and to be full of assurance about his place in a room or world. The isolated wanderer had turned into a gregarious conversationalist in a crowded cocktail bar, glass in hand, reminiscing over a pleasant din.

Yet the angry late writings that gave Wilson the creeps also show, I think, that the old betrayals, as Dos conceived them, still rankled. And they could not have been simply the betrayals of life with the 'isms. They had to have been betrayals of a personal kind too, self-betrayals. As he said in a speech at Carleton College in 1960 he was indeed a disappointed novelist.[9] I look back to where he began at Harvard—calling American literature rice pudding and casually set-

9. Luddington quotes this from the speech: "Satire is the state of mind of a disappointed novelist. It was in the cards that the writing of a would-be chronicler like myself should become more and more satirical as the years went by."

ting up Dostoyevsky as a model—and I can't help noticing how far he remained from the Dostoyevsky model in his own work. From his childhood in hotel rooms to his final journeys over the world with Elizabeth he remained a literary tourist, not disposed to write about the closenesses yet not able to linger long with organizing an abstraction either. As he said early and late, "Organization is death," and so he was always frantic to be gone from such commitments. The chronicle form he settled on—in order to cope somehow with a whole vast nation—satisfied his ideals for his art but did not meet his expectations for himself as a twenty-four-carat novelist with both depth and range. At the end he was no longer looking a hundred miles down the road with "Vag" but wishing that he could look or had looked—at any rate wishing. At least he should have taken satisfaction—and perhaps he did—in having wished harder and further than most.

SIX

The Secret Wisdom of Allen Tate

In 1959 I was asked to contribute to an issue of the *Sewanee Review* honoring Allen Tate on his sixtieth birthday. I chose to compare his way of thought with that of his favorite intellectual enemy, Henry Adams. He was, as I recall, politely silent at the time.[1]

When, much later, I sent him an early version of the Adams essay

---

1. Allen Tate's "Ode to the Confederate Dead" is the only poem of his discussed here, and it is to be found in most anthologies of modern poetry. His own essay on the poem, "Narcissus as Narcissus," is in several collections of his essays, of which the most comprehensive (containing also his other essays referred to here) is *Essays of Four Decades* (Chicago: Swallow Press, 1968). His two biographies are *Stonewall Jackson, The Good Soldier* (New York: Milton Balch & Co., 1928); and *Jefferson Davis: His Rise and Fall, a Biographical Narrative* (New York: Milton Balch & Co., 1929). Then there is his one novel, *The Fathers* (originally New York: G. P Putnam's Sons, 1939. Reprinted with "Introduction" by Arthur Mizener, London: Penguin, 1960).

There is, I believe, just one full biography, *Allen Tate: A Literary Biography* by James Radcliffe Squires (New York: Pegasus, 1971). Squires also compiled a collection of essays about Tate, together with an immense bibliography, *Allen Tate and his Work: Critical Evaluations* (Minneapolis: University of Minnesota Press, 1972). I should add that a small recent work, not referred to here, is an interesting commentary on Tate's late life, mostly in Nashville and Sewanee, *Allen Tate: A Recollection* by Walter Sullivan (Baton Rouge: Louisiana State University Press, 1988).

The big Agrarian volume of the thirties to which Tate contributed was *I'll Take My Stand: The South and the Agrarian Tradition* by Twelve Southerners. He also contributed to, and helped edit, with Herbert Ager, *Who Owns America? A New Declaration of Independence* (Freeport, New York: Books for Libraries Press, 1936).

H. L. Mencken's *Prejudices, Second Series,* contains "Sahara of the Bozart." Also referred to are *The Letters of Ezra Pound, 1907–1941,* ed. D. D. Paige; *Opinions of Oliver Allston,* by Van Wyck Brooks; and *The Dream of Descartes* by Jacques Maritain. Finally there is *The Southern Mandarins: Letters of Caroline Gordon to Sally Wood* (Baton Rouge: Louisiana State University Press, 1984).

that appears in this book, he wrote back to say that he liked it and that it made him dislike the man more than ever.

Allen's chief complaint about Adams—which is to be found in his essay, "Religion and the Old South"—was that Adams, and possibly all true New Englanders (like myself), thought too much. They were unable to rely on "custom, breeding, ingrained moral decision" at critical moments, and instead had to decide how to act by "a process of moral reasoning." Of course it was a specious bit of such reasoning that got Macbeth to kill off poor old Duncan, but Allen wasn't thinking of Macbeth. He had found the moral-reasoning phrase in correspondence between Thomas Jefferson and John Adams, and had shifted it over to Henry Adams. Henry, he said, carried the Adams reasonableness so far that he was unable to act naturally and instinctively, like a human being. Such is the heresy of New England. (And of most of William Carlos Williams's puritans.)

In 1959 Allen bore up well, being likened to Henry, and he bore up well again in Nashville in 1976 when I visited him. He was miserably bedridden then, and would die in three years, but faced by subjects such as Adams he could still brighten. He oddly brought up my comparing him with Henry himself, and said that years earlier T. S. Eliot had also likened him to Henry. Allen had submitted "Religion and the Old South" to Eliot at the *Criterion* in 1930, and Eliot had turned it down, saying that Allen was just as capable of being abstract as Adams. With such reinforcement I naturally had to go on.

He was a small man with a large head and high brow. He liked liquor (he gave fine parties), women (he married three times), and literary politics (he was never out of them), and each of these passions fueled his eminence in literary places for decades. He was a gossip and a raconteur. He spoke with southern softness but expected to be heard. He matched charm with bite and was always reaching for clever put-downs. He would have been a very good professional man if he had not been too unsettled, too intelligent. As he was what he was he became a poet who wrote unusually few poems, a good deal of criticism, two biographies (failing to write one of Robert E. Lee), and an excellent novel. He also became a prominent spokesman for the southern "position," in the days when there seemed to be one. But even in those days that position, when presented by Allen, generally turned out to be several positions. He liked to quote the truism that the sign of a good mind was its capacity to entertain two conflicting ideas at once.

He was born in Winchester, Kentucky, which his mother had thought a poor idea and had tried to keep secret from him all her life. She led him to suppose that he had been born in the good idea known as Virginia, since, he recalled, "She always bent reality to her wishes." She had wanted her family to be Old Virginia, so she took Allen on a pilgrimage to Jamestown when he was young, to see where his forebears had landed and suffered. But Allen in his memoirs ridiculed her Jamestown dream, saying that though he was sure he was *not* descended from anyone in the Jamestown colony, he imagined that if he had been he would have descended from the gentleman who in the first winter ate the corpse of his wife. Allen's mother lost her struggle to make Allen a "good old boy."

Or perhaps it was the father who lost the struggle for her, not being a good old boy himself. He was a floater, always without money. His parents had land in Kentucky, but his destiny was to sell off that land, piece by piece, for money for his family to live on. He moved from enterprise to enterprise, the family with him, and they all became increasingly withdrawn from the dying culture that Allen would later, ambiguously, defend. Young Allen attended private schools in Nashville and Louisville and public high schools in Ashland (Kentucky), Evansville (Indiana) and Cincinnati. By the time he entered Vanderbilt the family land was "almost gone, except a few slum houses" that his mother owned in Washington.

It was a sad decline for the mother, whose family *had* been, aside from her dream of it, part of the antebellum society in Washington and Virginia. Allen's brother Ben remarked that, having been born with silver spoons in their mouths, they were now expected to eat the spoons.

So low did the family's funds sink that it was brother Ben who put Allen through the last two years at Vanderbilt. Ben made a million by the time he was twenty-five or so Allen, who liked to exaggerate, said. Ben was a fine figure of a capitalist. Ben was in the modern, industrial, national mode that Allen would intermittently rage against later. And Ben, displaced to Civil War days, was also to appear later as the unpredictable hero of Allen's novel, *The Fathers*. That novel proposed that southern traditionalists could never admire the likes of Ben, he being an outsider to their culture, but the novel also displayed the young narrator (Allen transported back to the Civil War) admiring him. And outside the novel, in real Tennessee and elsewhere, Ben repaid the compliment by being Allen's frequent salvation.

Was Allen more of an insider than Ben? In *The Fathers* he appeared as a boy loyal to the Southern cause wondering *why* he admired the likes of Ben. And late in life Allen continued to worry the contradiction, saying that it was the kind of problem that made writers writers. (He liked to quote Yeats on the point: "We make of our quarrels with others rhetoric; of our quarrels with ourselves poetry.") Nor was the contradiction just ideological, since Allen spent much of his life physically in the North as he defended southern traditionalism.

But it was in the South, at Vanderbilt, that the contradiction first blossomed for him—if contradictions can blossom—and it blossomed there also for his peers in the Fugitive group: John Crowe Ransom, Donald Davidson, Robert Penn Warren, Merrill Moore, and others. Their works, correspondence, and the files of their little magazine, the *Fugitive,* are now at rest in an elegant, establishment room of the Vanderbilt library, where scholars can go and wonder why the Fugitives called themselves fugitives in the first place.

The group began, as has been reported many times, as just a literary discussion group that met regularly at the home of one Sidney Hirsch ("a man of vast if somewhat perverse erudition . . . a mystic and I think a Rosicrucian," said Tate) and talked about poems, often their own. They were hard on each other, but that was because they were trying to be analytical, objective, impersonal. To an outsider—that is, an unliterary person—their sessions would have seemed devoted to the trivial. Why, a social activist like Upton Sinclair might have asked, didn't they discuss issues like Truth and Social Justice? But their answer might well have been that they did. They were talking about them in their own way, in terms of language. In Cleanth Brooks's words, they were thinking of language as "the special means by, and through, which man realizes his humanity."

When the talk moved away from specific poems it gravitated to the subject of the modernist impulse in poetry and what the impulse meant. For instance Donald Davidson reported to Allen, when Allen could not attend a meeting, that a fierce visitor from Kenyon College had attacked them for being "sloppy technicians, obscurantists and too modernly modern." Davidson was proud to add that they had dealt the visitor some "good wallops." But they were not in steady accord about being modern. There was the case of T. S. Eliot, for example.

Allen was their Eliot enthusiast, and he brought the Truth about him to them. They were not impressed. He said, "I think for all time— so important is *The Waste Land*—Mr. Eliot has demonstrated the necessity, in special cases, of an aberrant versification." He then characterized its "inexplicable framework" as "inevitable and final." A curious critique indeed. If we say of it that Allen meant that its lack of a clear logical or narrative structure was necessary to fit the wasteland it described,[2] we are still stuck with the oddity of describing the poem's whole relationship to the modern world as a "special case." I assume that this is the way the Fugitives talked with each other over at Sidney Hirsch's, but even so it was not a happy evening. Ransom and Allen disagreed about Eliot. They also disagreed about Baudelaire. Allen translated a Baudelaire poem, "Correspondences," in which Baudelaire gave a little aesthetic lesson in synaesthesia. "Man wanders," the poem said, "in a forest of accords," where "perfumes and colors and sounds correspond." Ransom was not taken in by Allen's enthusiasm about the accords. He was a traditional rationalist, liking his tropes orderly and precise. Allen finally won him over on such matters—and later regretted his impertinence. Allen after all was in the process of becoming a conservative too, and mixing modernism and conservatism was not easy in Nashville (or in London for that matter, where Eliot was trying it). And in the very first issue of their magazine the complications of tying literature to the world appeared. There they couldn't stick to poems but had to attack the southern culture in which they were writing them. "The *Fugitive*," they announced, "flees from nothing faster than the high-caste Brahmins of the old South. Without raising the question of whether the blood in the veins of its editors runs red, they are at any rate not advertising it as blue."

So their first *social* enemy (they would soon have many more) would seem to have been southern bluebloods (like Allen's long-suffering mother perhaps). None of them could afford to be brahmins socially, but they were young intellectuals possessed of the snobbery that young intellectuals are prone to, and they headed out after the

---

2. The critic Yvor Winters indignantly described this aesthetic as the fallacy of imitative form.

part of their own Old South that H. L. Mencken had ridiculed in his essay, "The Sahara of the Bozart." There Mencken quoted two lines from a famously bad poet, J. Gordon Coogler, to demonstrate that southern literature did not really exist: "Alas! for the South! her books have grown fewer— / She never was much given to literature."

Tate admired Mencken at the time—he would change his mind— and could also then agree with Mencken's other complaint, that the South was ideologically a vacuum. "No sane man," Mencken said, "would look for intelligible political ideas, for example, in Delaware, or Arkansas, or Georgia." He then added that Virginia was an even sadder case because, having once "lifted politics to the level of a science and an art," it had now made it "merely a trade, and a very sordid one at that." Donald Davidson was more conservative than Tate, but on the subject of the South's mindlessness he, too, could go along with Mencken. In fact all of the Fugitives had a society, they were discovering, from which to be fugitive. They had merely to look across the street from the university and see why.

The brown Parthenon across the street told them that Nashville society was not all brahmins—far from it—but a mix of brahmins and new industrialists. The Parthenon told them that Nashville became "the Athens of the South" because it imported its culture. The importing had begun with the Wall Street and railroad money of Cornelius Vanderbilt for the university after the Civil War, but the Parthenon was put up two decades later by the Nashville Board of Trade, "to divert the attention of the public" *from* the depression of 1893. It was part of the Nashville Centennial Exposition of that year, but it is still exceedingly there, the only building remaining from the exposition.[3]

Beside it is a statue of its entrepreneur, John W. Thomas, who was also a railroad man but a southerner, and who is described on his statue's plaque as both "an efficient man of affairs" and "a Christian and a gentleman." Right there, surely, is the double or triple meaning for "good old boy."

For the Fugitives the Parthenon was a bad joke. Davidson wrote a poem about it, calling it a monument to wisdom and virtue in a place essentially without either, and saying that it was simply a southern

3. The exposition was a monument to the past in general, with samples of Greek, Roman, Renaissance, Egyptian, Spanish Renaissance and Colonial architecture.

bribe against the South's unilluminated fate. Yes, but what is still impressive about it, to a visitor, is the magnitude and earnestness of the bribe. In the nowhere of an un-Greek park full of sunbathers and cars, it squats like a heavy space ship, bursting with alien energy. There is nothing to equal it in any northern city, yet the energy is neither Greek nor southern.

Henry Adams probably had his own reasons for *not* coming to the Nashville Exposition (he liked expositions humming with modern science), but he did know the southern confusion behind it. He described the confusion—in a passage in *The Education* that Allen particularly disliked—by characterizing a single southern classmate of his at Harvard, Rooney Lee. Rooney was a true Confederate Lee, but he had much in common with John W. Thomas. He was a Christian and a gentleman, would become a man of affairs, and had the habit of command. He was also, Adams said, without brains, that is, the Adams kind of brains that Tate said he disliked: "Strictly, the Southerner (Rooney) had no mind; he had temperament. He was not a scholar; he had no intellectual training; he could not analyze an idea, and he could not even conceive of admitting two; but in life one could get along very well without ideas, if one had the social instinct."

A decade or so after the Fugitive meetings Tate would, as will be seen, argue in favor of such mindlessness—perhaps partly to rebut Henry—but in the Fugitive time, looking across the street, he could be critical of the Parthenon because it too was brainless. It was, and is, a good example of a dead symbol.

So there the Fugitives were in Sidney Hirsch's parlor, accumulating evidence that they were separated from their culture by virtue of their aesthetic (printing poems that the culture couldn't understand in a magazine the culture could hardly be expected to buy) as well as their idealistic sense of what culture *should* be. Sharing these views they settled on the magazine's name. Of the name Allen later wrote, ironically, "A Fugitive was quite simply the poet: the Wanderer, or even the Wandering Jew, the Outcast, the man who carried the secret wisdom around the world. It was a fairly heavy responsibility for us to undertake."

A tantalizing remark. It invites the biographer to plumb legends as well as vital statistics. Thus the legend of Ahasuerus the Wandering Jew can be swerved a bit to fit the occupants of the Hirsch parlor. Though they did not scorn Jesus on his way to Calvary, they did scorn the Nashville brahmins and the Christian gentleman John W. Thomas. And their punishment, which can be labeled a punishment for im-piety—was to wander over the earth indefinitely as social outcasts. (In the legend Ahasuerus was to do so until the Second Coming.) In that predicament they were oddly also destined to be, like Ahasuerus, possessed of the wisdom of the ages. They were positioned to see what the nonwanderers of civilization, the established ones, could not see.

The legend applies particularly well to Allen, since he was the first of the group to wander off—at age twenty-five—to the North. Though he ridiculed the wisdom role as "a fairly heavy responsibil-ity" he had it in his head, and worried it, for the rest of his life. It can be seen particularly in his best-known poem *Ode to the Confederate Dead* (and in his commentary on the poem, *Narcissus as Narcissus*), but is evident in many of his essays also, especially his contribution to the agrarian volume I am coming to, *I'll Take My Stand*. The wander-ing off to New York was just the first leg of a lifelong trip in and out of "exile."

In practical terms he simply traveled to New York to make his way as a writer. He wrote reviews and edited copy for a pulps pub-lisher, and he settled into the projects of his own he hoped would make money—two biographies—and the poems he already knew would not. The New York he confronted was not, he discovered quickly, any more interested in the "secret wisdom" than the South was. It was just the North of commercial publishing, a good place to study the modern wasteland. He settled in. He met and married Car-oline Gordon (who was to be a better novelist, at least commercially, than he), and he corresponded with the Fugitives back home. At one point Davidson wrote him that the magazine was dying but that Ran-som had proposed they start a poetry society in its place. Allen was already full of what the North thought of poetry societies, and he wrote back that the idea struck him with "horror and amusement." Yet he was not good at being a New Yorker or a creature of the com-mercial market. He was broke most of the time and was most suc-cessful financially when he landed a noncommercial Guggenheim Fellowship for a book of poems he had already written. The Gug-genheim money took Caroline (now with an infant daughter) and Allen to Paris where he did have time to write the biographies he had planned. Naturally they were both about the South and the Civil War.

The first biography, of Stonewall Jackson, became what now seems a most naive rendering of the Southern condition, and less like a biography than a first novel. It had all the faults of a first novel except subjectivity. In tone it was often like the pulp stories he had been proofreading, and the pulp stories Upton Sinclair had written as an adolescent. Here is a sample.

> General Bee galloped by, shouting to his men. He rode up to Jackson.
> "General, they are beating us back, they are beating us back."
> Jackson was perfectly calm. He replied,
> "Then, sir, we will give them the bayonet." His thin lips closed in a straight line.

But unlike Upton Sinclair, Allen and other writers of pulps, were at least trying to catch the flavor of a real as opposed to a representative man. Armed with that intent he was also aware, as Upton was not, that characters like Stonewall Jackson were not just heroic but were also, sometimes, stupid and comic. Still, the depths of Jackson's feelings and thoughts were conspicuously absent, and there were long stretches of melodrama, relieved by long stretches of military gamesmanship. (There was some truth to a snide northern criticism of his work—reported by Allen himself—that his "one intransigent desire [was] to have been a Confederate general.")

And let me complain still more. Many passages in the biography were "written down" as if for a popular audience, while others were elevated and abstruse. Allen was putting one foot in the commercial swamp, then pulling it back. He had not decided what kind of a book it was to be.

Clearly he saw its limitations even while he was writing it, since in tackling the companion work, about Jefferson Davis, he provided no melodrama, no grim-lipped dialogue. More important, he tried out with the Davis story the agrarian theme that was soon to be central to the "secret wisdom." Some of that was not secret at all.

In it he described Lincoln as a leader who thought he could achieve national unity but who achieved instead conformity. Lincoln failed because he misunderstood the *North,* underestimated it as an economic and ideological *force* (shades of Henry Adams). He vainly imagined that the North was a benevolent entity that the South could accept while retaining its cultural integrity. He thought that slavery was only in the South, whereas any intelligent Southerner, like Calhoun, knew otherwise, knew that Negro slavery was only one kind of slavery; commerce, industrialism, progress were others. In order to be emphatic on the point Allen did not set Lincoln up against Calhoun but against a Southern fanatic, Robert Barnwell Brent, and let the fanatic be the true prophet.

> The only idea of Lincoln's to be realized was the geographical union, and he is actually the most defeated man in American history. The most completely vindicated is the little known Robert Barnwell Brent, the prophet of secession who, from the dingy office of the Charleston *Mercury,* had thundered forth against half measures in the South for more than twenty years. The South was destroyed, and the American nation became what Brent said it would become. . . . The North was at the time the most advanced modern state, in which government and men, as political entities, were instrumental to (i.e., slaves to) the superior ends of commerce and trade.

So that was the feeling about Northern force that Allen was working up to while writing about the South in New York and Paris. As for Jefferson Davis, Allen thought he was as blind as Lincoln to the North's menace. So was his vice president, Alexander Stephens. They didn't recognize how "implacable" was the power of the North. As a result they imagined compromises; they became statesmen of expedience; they failed to see that whatever consensus might be arrived at with the North would be remote from anything they could accept.

In asserting Davis's flaw, Allen was still ostensibly back in the Civil War—and it was to continue to be his base, his starting point for all cultural discourse—but in his intensities against compromisers like Davis he was now past the war and writing of his own time. For him the North was no longer just the North of McClellan and Grant, nor just the North of Henry Adams either. The North was the whole modern social condition, which he knew and was living in, discovering, for example, in his own field, that "the American public sees the writer as a business man because it cannot see any other kind of man, and respects him according to his income." He was not planning to fight the Civil War again, but he was working up to the modern confrontations.

And the failures of both biographies to achieve significant sales helped him along. He was broke, he was spoiling for *something* to fight for in his exile, and his image of the South was improving. Meanwhile, however, he had been confronting his own being as a force, himself as a poet with the "secret wisdom." It was during this time that he wrote the work for which he is best known, his "Ode to the Confederate Dead."

Perhaps the first thing to note about the poem is that he is himself in it and back in the South in it. Perhaps the second thing to note is that his role in it is that of the Wandering Jew, the observer of generations and, in the poem's instance, of the generation of those who went to their death in the war's cause. The poem has been so battered by criticism that I don't wish to pause long on it, but mainly to suggest that in it the wanderer role has pushed him in upon himself. As Allen noted in his essay, "Narcissus as Narcissus" the poem is "about" solecism, "a philosophical doctrine which says that we create the world in the act of perceiving it." In other words, he was examining the nature of his own wisdom, or as he put it, "reminding himself repeatedly of his subjective prison." Thus the exploits of the Civil War's heroes, thought of in the context of the graveyard with its "uncomfortable angels" rotting "on the slabs," do not exalt, do not inspire. The graves remind him only of how dead the dead are, and therefore bring him a kind of knowledge that is "carried to the heart," a knowledge of the futility of actions such as those of the war's heroes, as well as of the futility of his own contemporary actions. The poem, which was first in the Guggenheim volume of 1928, is thematically the opposite of the aggressive themes to be found in *I'll Take My Stand* (1930), yet it informs the latter constantly. By this time in Allen's life the poet's secret wisdom always had at least two sides to it, or perhaps I should say two visions of the world he is condemned to. In *I'll Take My Stand* that vision is largely of the "other" around him, that which he is in exile from, such as the world described by fanatic Brent. But in the "Ode" the world includes the exile's self as well, the self meditating *upon* itself and then, "like the jaguar leap(ing)/ For his own image in a jungle pool, his victim."

Now what I have read about the wanderer legend tells me that narcissism of this kind was not an element in it. By the nature of his punishment Ahasuerus was fated to remain on earth as the sole living witness to Christ, hence possessed of secret—that is, personal, direct— spiritual knowledge. (Here is the Protestantism embedded in the legend.) But in the scope of the legend that knowledge was of personal salvation, whereas the secret knowledge of Allen's modern wanderer becomes the reverse of that.

The ultimate solution, if it was that, for Allen was conversion to the Rock of Catholicism, hence theoretical abandonment of such unpleasant direct visions; but that solution would come two decades later. In the meantime poor Ahasuerus was stuck with being both an exile in a world he had not made and a self-prisoner. How did he move in his thoughts from such oppressiveness to the aggressiveness of the 1930 agrarian volume?

The long-term answer is that he didn't, that *I'll Take My Stand* was an episode merely, an interlude in his life as exile. But the immediate answer is simpler. He was broke in New York, so he moved back "home."

Allen had remained close to brother Ben, and in 1930 Ben had, despite the new depression, money. Allen did not. So in 1930 Ben gave Allen a hundred acres of good farmland upon which to be a fugitive from the North. It was fifty miles northwest of Nashville, and it had a good farmhouse on it. Allen, Caroline, and child Nancy moved in, christened it "Benfolly," and went about being southern again.

It would be pleasant to believe that having a hundred acres made Allen a sudden farmer, but I am told he turned the farming over to a neighbor, concerning himself as usual with his writing and with entertaining other literary lights. (For an outcast, he was remarkably sociable.) It is therefore less pleasant but more sensible to believe that he dove into agrarianism in a momentary fury with the arrival of a successful literary acquaintance who had just landed a Hollywood contract.

At the time Caroline and Allen were carrying on separate creative lives but enjoying together a large company of mostly urban intellectual friends—rich and poor, northern and southern. So they were thoroughly in touch with the American—that is the New York—publishing scene, though at the same time renewing southern friendships. (Caroline herself was from Todd County, Kentucky.) Caroline is the source of news about the lucky visitor; he is in one of her stories about Benfolly, and he must have been real because she also mentions him in her letters at the time. I'm not sure I believe he had landed the contract for a Civil War *poem* (could it have been Stephen Vincent Benet?), but I have little trouble imagining Allen's annoyance even if the visitor had only sold a novel. Yet Caroline does not have Allen display envy. She pictures the two authors joking about what military campaign Allen was at the moment struggling with, in the process making clear that he was "doing" campaigns because he was at work on what was to be his last effort at the biographical big-time, the biography of Lee he would never finish. Lee was obviously becoming too much, and the visitor's success didn't help. Could not Lee have been becoming *Allen,* seeing all the futility?

Unfinished works are sometimes an author's best education, and my own guess is that Allen's failure with Lee not only drove Allen out of biography and into the agrarian project, but it also became the impetus for the directional change his career took in the thirties, when he put commercial publishing to the side and began to think of himself as a writer only half the time. His other half was to be a Man of Letters, a Poet in Residence, a literary politico. The agrarian project was indeed an interlude.

There were twelve contributors to *I'll Take My Stand,*[4] and all were southerners. Four had been Fugitives (Tate, Ransom, Davidson, Warren). Each essayist had a loosely assigned topic within their common ideological "stand," and at the beginning of the volume was a statement of principles that Allen had much to do with. In general they were now agreed that they had much to worry about other than poems in the parlor.

They had mostly been living sheltered literary or academic lives— Allen was an exception—and questioning literary values around them, but now the depression was upon them, and much wickedness from the North was encouraging political thoughts. Ransom later described the book as just another part of their youthful period, their "last fling," but for most of them it was more than that. Some of them had worked up a rage about the North like that of fanatic Brent, and some of them were moderate in their rage and meditating about southern troubles, but all had a stable full of complaints, and all seemed to be addressing their remarks to northern liberals and radicals, a new twist for them. Allen commented later that Vanderbilt had not subjected him, as an undergraduate, to any "advanced ideas," but at the beginning of the thirties advanced ideas were everywhere—even at Vanderbilt—and the agrarians still didn't like them. There was much new in the universe that they didn't like, as a small sampling of their essays will show.

Ransom declared that the "Southern idea [was] down, the American or progressive idea [was] up." He described progressivism as

4. An alternate title, favored by Allen, was *A Tract Against Communism!*

"boundless aggression" from persons displaying no sense of "our precarious position in the universe," and he proposed, with tremendous caution, that the agrarian, conservative anti-industrial Democrats be looked to for political leadership.

Donald Davidson's subject was art and literature. He announced that the *American* culture had alienated the artistic spirits of the country completely, since the *American* view of art was that "civilized people" were "supposed to have it" and *could* have it if they would simply "buy it, hire it, can it or—most conclusively—manufacture it." And he pictured the "industrialists of art" making their appeal to the lowest common denominator, with such effect that any serious artist's function had become just "resistance to the milieu."

John Gould Fletcher took on education, pitting Jefferson's "selectivity" against Horace Mann's efforts toward a uniform national education that made "the public school product of New York City or Chicago a behaviorist, an experimental scientist in sex and firearms, a militant atheist, a reader of detective fiction, and a good salesman." He added that he had become "suspicious of all schemes that propose to coerce people to their own alleged benefit."

A strong racist, Frank Lawrence Owsley said that slavery had been an imposition upon the South by England and New England, and was not the foundation of southern agrarianism but, in fact, an impediment to it.

Robert Penn Warren took something of the Owsley line but with concern for the Negro predicament, a concern for what was happening to him as a result of transplantation into the industrial world. He declared that "a general and fundamental restoration" (of the Negro to a provincial life and the land) was needed rather than "inter-racial conferences and the devices of organized philanthropy."

And to my taste Andrew Lytle stole the agrarian show by actually sounding like a farmer. He described in pastoral detail a southern farm and the life upon it, but he sprinkled the sentiment with pithy remarks: "As soon as a farmer begins to keep books he'll go broke shore as hell"; "A farm is not a place to grow wealthy, it is a place to grow corn"; and "The Agrarian South should dread Industrialism like a pizen snake." Then there was this lovely comment on the virtues of regionalism:

> There were "hill people" in the 1850s who were mixed in their geography, who thought for example that New York lay to the south of Ten-

nessee. . . . It was the tragedy of these people that they ever learned where New York lay, for such knowledge has taken them from a place where they knew little geography but knew it well, to places where they see much and know nothing.

All the essays, supported by the "Introduction," insisted upon the basic conflict between the industrial and agrarian ways of life. Some of them managed to sound as if another Civil War were near (though it was not clear who was going to fight it). And the sweepingness of their condemnation of the industrialism around them was enough to have been looked upon as gross impiety if they had happened to have an army behind them and Allen as general.

But they had no army, Allen was planning no campaigns, and such readers as they had in the North were merely annoyed or amused. Collectively their aim seemed to be to construct an ideal humanist republic of their own, as a device for scoring a few social points. And Allen in his essay—it was the one Eliot had rejected for the *Criterion*—was particularly anxious to be understood as laboring in the world of political theory rather than practice.

Were they therefore being too general, too abstract? Of course. So Allen characteristically proceeded to be abstract in defense of the concrete. He was not thinking of the concrete as were some of the poets in the North, not thinking of ideas residing in things, not postulating a painter's world. What he meant by the concrete was specificity of action, a particular person doing a particular something in a particular place and time. Over and over he insisted that the provincialism of the South had at least the merit of being rooted in the conduct of real people.

Or real horses. He stationed a sensible southern horse in the essay cropping bluegrass on somebody's front lawn. The horse was not a quadruped or a producer of horsepower, he wrote, but a *whole* horse. He said that the trouble with modern America was that it could, and did, isolate parts of the horse; the modern American mind kept seeing only half-horses. But religion and poetry could not do that.

Then he abandoned the horse image in favor of a disquisition on short and long views of history.

Long views were the equivalent of half-horses. They were reductive views, views like Hegel's and Spengler's (and of course like those of Brooks and Henry Adams). In his long-view way Allen was all for short views: "For the short view, history is the specific account of the doings of specific men who acted their parts in a rich and contemporaneous setting which bewildered them [this was to be the kind of history he would reach for in his novel, *The Fathers*]. . . . The short view holds that the proper series for history to be placed in is the temporary or concrete series."

He then added that the short-view thinker doesn't think about the horse, or about history. He just sees the horse and lives history. In other words he is mindless about them, like Rooney Lee. Very well, and the southern mind (except perhaps for his own mind and the agrarians') had always been like this. In other words he was now agreeing with Henry Adams, but approving.

Trying then to be fair he observed that the northern mind had also been, sometimes, a short-view mind, and therefore worth living with. For instance, Emily Dickinson's ideas "were deeply imbedded in her character, not from the latest tract," with the result that she did not have to debate with herself about them (like the narrator in "Ode to the Confederate Dead"?) but could use them in the best poetic way, that is, thoughtlessly.

The key word in this last remark was "tract." A tract for Allen was somebody's fiat, something to be accepted a priori, and he was convinced the South had been submerged in tracts for too long, in fact right from the beginning, tracts that kept even the South from seeing whole horses. From the beginning it had been given the wrong religion, and was, despite its agrarian character, stuck with it.

The beginning was Jamestown, which he described as "a capitalistic enterprise undertaken by Europeans who were already convinced adherents of large-scale exploitation of nature." Jamestown gave the South a "non-agrarian and trading religion." There was the crux. The South had been fated to be dominated by northern doctrine from the beginning, and this unavoidable fate was what an individual southerner with wit had to exercise his wit to avoid.

The end of the essay contained the paradox explicitly. Having said that the great Southern error in the Civil War had been to imagine that mere political maneuverings would save the South, he then still proposed that the individual modern southerner proceed politically: "The Southerner must use an instrument, which is political, and so unrealistic that he cannot believe in it, to reestablish a private, self-contained and essentially spiritual life." That was the end of the essay, except for this last irresolute fling: "I say that he must do this; but that remains to be seen."

The anthology as a whole was wonderfully spirited in its attack on the industrial, collectivist enemy—though that enemy frequently appeared as big government rather than big business, and in fact the introduction worked hard to identify the two.[5] Even for a liberal who grew up admiring FDR the book is still a delight to read, filled with impieties about our culture readily transferable to the nineties. It was one of the ideological triumphs of the thirties, and it would now be even less welcome.

One other anthology to which Allen contributed in the early thirties needs to be mentioned before moving back to literature, a minor book, perhaps an aberration, but showing how worked-up Allen became briefly—along with everyone else in the depression—about the economic roots of the culture's ills. It was called *Who Owns America?* and its contributors were not all southerners. Allen's contribution was one that he later did not like, "Notes on Liberty and Property." (He did not reprint it with his collected essays in 1948.) The burden of the volume as a whole was, Get rid of monopoly capitalism but keep a modest, regional capitalism, and Allen was more emphatic than anyone else. He insisted, furthermore, that nobody should ever construe their "program" as related to socialism in any form: "The collectivist state is the logical development of giant corporate ownership, and, if it comes, will signal the final triumph of Big Business. 'All the arts,' said Walter Pater, 'strive toward the condition of music.' Corporate structure strives toward the condition of Moscow."

Having established what he didn't want in general, he went on to what he didn't want in particular, and that was the plutocracy running the country at the moment (1936). He quoted a popular economics text to the effect that about two thousand persons were directing over half the country's production, via the big corporations (brother Ben, as a small, regional capitalist, was still removed from such direction),

5. "Even the apologists of industrialism have been obliged to admit that some economic evils follow in the wake of the machines. . . . But the remedies proposed by the apologists are always homeopathic. They expect the evils to disappear when we have bigger and better machines. . . . Sometimes they expect to find super-engineers, in the shape of Boards of Control, who will adapt production to consumption and regulate prices and guarantee business against fluctuations: they are Soviets. With respect to these last it must be insisted that the true Soviets or Communists—if the term may be used here in the European sense—are the industrialists themselves. . . . We therefore look upon the Communist menace as a menace indeed, but not as a Red one."

and he thought it would be pleasant to dispose of the two thousand. The point he wanted to make was also to be James Burnham's point in *The Managerial Revolution* in 1940, that the greedy two thousand were turning America's private ownership economy into a farce by controlling so much more than they really owned:

> A farm is not necessarily property. We want to make it property again by making sure that the farmer has control of what he produces. A small grocery store may represent certain paper property rights, but in view of the six chain stores surrounding it, it doesn't represent the same property rights as it did a hundred years ago. We want the store to be property again. Altogether it does seem a modest wish.

Modest or not, he could hardly have had hopes for a quick turn-around. He seems to have felt that he was on thematic assignment for the book, and had to reinforce its underlying tract even if he were skeptical of it. His participation in the volume was probably the high point of his activism, forms of which he would soon be calling, with contempt, positivism.

His novel, *The Fathers* (1938), was quite another matter, a work of the imagination rather than the will (he liked that Yeatsian distinction), a work in which he didn't have to be a missionary, but could put down his stored-up observations of the North-South, agrarian-industrial, feudal-modern, whole-horse-half-horse conflict without feeling that he had also to propose a big program for the country's future. *The Fathers* was in some respects as ideological as any novel by Upton Sinclair, but it was not directly programmatic. And in not being so it was a fine example of whole-horse doctrine. It was not, though, a popular novel. As Arthur Mizener once noted, it sold "respectably" but probably did so at the time because readers expected it to be another *Gone With The Wind*. In fact, said Mizener, "it was the novel *Gone With The Wind* should have been."

Its most interesting character was George Posey, modeled after Ben. With Posey, Allen was able to do what the programmatic essays had kept him from doing; he was able to display sympathy and understanding for what had been, in the essays, the wrong cause. Posey was a Southerner, but he had too much of the North in him to be a *good* Southerner. (When Allen was asked where he picked up the idea of having Posey sell arms to both sides in the conflict, he said he merely wished to make him representative of the modern capitalist. Posey was like Ben in his nonallegiances, but he was also like Allen, Allen the traveler, urban dweller, and (sociable) loner, cut off ideologically and instinctively from consensus, North or South.)[6] One of the Southerners in the novel who disapproved of Posey described him as alone in the way that a tornado was alone, whose purpose was "to whirl, to brush aside obstacles." That kind of aloneness struck a chord in Allen's narrator.

In my conversations with Allen forty years later I tried to get him to straighten out for me the tangle of his ties to southern gentility, Ben, and the rest, but he didn't wish to untangle. He said he had always felt alienated from the "business civilization" that was Nashville, yet of Ben's role in it he said, "I have no bone to pick with Ben. Ben was merely using civilization to get rich."

With the publication of *The Fathers,* Allen had spent more than fifteen years in the writing *business.* He was forty. He had moved about in the literary circles of New York, Paris, and London. He had also moved about in the genres—in history, biography, literary criticism, and the impolite polite essay. He had a widespread acquaintance now, and he was known as a decorous but polemical, intellectual, unacademic southerner who wore his southernness like a badge. He would never quite stop talking and writing about the Civil War, but it was time to call a truce. So now he shifted his business a little, drifting back to the original, unregional literary concerns of the Fugitives. For writing—the lonely act itself—was his inescapable subject, the way to such grace as there was in the world, North or South. He had found out that there was no money, except tangentially, in poetry, but poetry remained his center even when he was not writing it. Its exile as a genre from Grub Street was a heavy sign for him of the whole modern writing condition. It was therefore a serious—seriously unprofitable—business, and all of his feelings about the surrounding culture appeared in tandem with his thoughts about the genre. A poem was a cerebral event for him and verbally prickly. He didn't give up traditional prosody, but in his hands it was seldom

6. Posey appeared first, in the novel, in a bad mood because he was being subjected to a long, ritualistic day of a Southern funeral. At the end of the novel he was presented as being unable to live with either side in the War. And throughout the book his younger brother, the narrator, admired him greatly, admired his strength in isolation from those who "do nothing but die and marry and think about the honor of Virginia."

melodic, predictable.[7] There were always clashings in the lines; he couldn't condone the easy, the slick. At the very end of his life he turned to writing verses excessively simple, pathetically simple, verses to three children he sired in old age. The switch seems, however, to have been a mark of declining health, not a reaction to having been difficult. Throughout his active years he had persisted in matching his poetry with his prickly aesthetic, and the audience for both was as limited as he seems, defiantly, to have wanted it to be. Yet it is not easy to reconcile his insistence upon a poem's obligations to its creator's complex soul with his own long life as a literary lion happy with acclaim.

The coming of World War II made his contradictions even more conspicuous, but it drove him to some of his best prose. He said later that he had been pushed to write in the "convention" of the attack, but perhaps he should have said "counterattack." Attacks he had been writing in the agrarian period, but the war put him on the defensive. He and his disciples were suddenly discovered to be "irresponsibles." A villain's role proved stimulating to him.

His best opponent was a friend, Archibald MacLeish, and author of a small book actually called *The Irresponsibles.* In 1940 MacLeish was librarian of Congress, having already been an editor of *Fortune,* and having performed as a speechwriter for FDR. At the start of the war he delivered a number of much-publicized attacks on intellectual dissidents, accusing them of failing to stand up and defend the "common culture" of the West against Hitler. It was prime time for such accusations, and MacLeish made them (in prose and verse) in a rhetoric that Allen despised. Thus, *America Was Promises* began with an imperative and exclamation points—"Listen! Brothers! Generations!"—and continued, relentlessly, to order readers about—"Oh believe this!"

Ten years earlier the Agrarians had described their job as that of saving the South *from* the common culture. The war changed things but not wholly. Allen tried to face the fact of Hitler without losing sight of his other cause, but his adjustment was slow, grudging. In

---

7. As a sample, in a poem about the subway in New York he made appropriate subway sounds, trying to convey the wholeness of the subway's presence. It was a "harshly articulate, musical steel shell" being "hurled religiously . . . into the iron forestries of hell."

"The Present Function of Criticism" (1940) he said that while he might be happy to die for his country he was not happy to be told—as Mac-Leish was telling him—that he should write *poems* in its defense. He also complained about "positivists" in general, MacLeish being just one example of the breed. He described them as follows:

> Let us put three persons together who soon discover that they do not agree. No matter; they quickly find a procedure, a program, an objective. So they do agree there is something to be *done,* though they may not be certain why they are doing it and they may not be interested in the results, the meaning of which is not very important. This state of mind is positivism. It assumes that the communication of ideas toward the formulation of truths is irrelevant to action; the program is an end in itself.

By implication he was then proposing—and it was a bad time to do it—that he himself continue at the labor of truth, or of making poetic wholes, despite the war urgencies. Faced with positivist pressures to act rather than to know, he became stubborn. In the same essay he mentioned totalitarianism as the force he was being asked to be programmatic about, and said that the totalitarianism he feared was in his own country, taking aim at the "national socialism" of FDR: "The first ominous signs of this change are before us. The tradition of free ideas is as dead in the United States as it is in Germany." FDR was not really his target though; he was after monopoly capitalism and a great deal else in the country, especially in education: "We are entering a period in which we shall pay dearly for having turned our public education over to the professional 'educationists' and the sociologists. These men have taught the present generation that the least thing about man is his intelligence, if he have it at all; the greatest thing his adjustment to Society."

Most of the people who seriously annoyed him were not sociologists or educationists but literary people like MacLeish. Still, anyone in the social sciences was always fair game for him since he saw, as a common theme running through enemy ranks, efforts to adjust *him.* He kept trying to distinguish between his being adjusted to the war— he could go along with that adjustment—and being adjusted to flim-flam. But it was wartime. He was fighting a losing battle.

Besides MacLeish there were, among literary opponents, Van Wyck Brooks and Sidney Hook. Brooks was not a friend of Allen's, as MacLeish was, but Allen liked to mention MacLeish and Brooks together as a terrible duo standing menacingly, in magazines of large circulation, for the "common culture." In Brooks's view there was a "primary literature" that all sensible people—Allen was not one—could always recognize *as* primary, and then there was "coterie literature." Coterie literature was everything bad, and had begun in modern times with negativism, feudalism, antiprogressivism, and the general cultural secessionism of Joyce, Proust, Eliot, Stein, Pound, and the like. Brooks shared with MacLeish a heavy rhetorical manner, though he did not use it in verse: "Were these writers really a vanguard, or were they not retrograde? Did they not represent a 'cultural lag?' Were they not a 'dead hand,' the dead hand of the fin de siecle, which had prolonged its grasp for forty years?"

With such sweepingly unquestioning questions flowing from his pen Brooks had little time to devote to southerners, but he was at least able to note that they had "swarmed all over the field of American letters," and they were deeply responsible for the New Criticism. Sidney Hook was not intentionally less offensive—he entitled an angry letter to the *Southern Review,* "The Late Mr. Tate"—but he couldn't manage Brooks's decibels, contenting himself with saying that Allen had bad intellectual manners and knew no philosophy. Hook was a defeated man of another order than the Fugitives, a defeated Marxist, and so he found the southern position historically *and* ideologically improbable. And Allen's reputation at this time became, suddenly, very big. Not only was he under attack and fighting back, but he had just landed an historic post at Princeton, poet in residence, historic because being a poet in residence, then, in America, was like being a Martian on campus (hence tenure did not go along with it). This new academic connection made him, on the spot, a defender of scholars, of poets, and of their common privilege not to be adjusted. He proved to be a good defender,[8] though not a good public speaker. He could attractively mix polemical intemperance with civilized intellectual sociability, could batter away at the enemy and then sit down with

---

8. Allen even tried his hand at a kind of public satiric verse he was not good at, mentioning MacLeish, Brooks, and others by name in it. It was in a form too rigid for satire: "Once more the country calls / Froom sleep, as from doom, / Each citizen to take / His modest state / Where the sky falls / With a Pacific boom" presumably these lines, from "To the young pro-Consuls," were intended as a parody of the MacLeish lines (from "America Was Promises") quoted above.

him for a drink. His attacks on MacLeish seem merely to have endeared him to MacLeish, for MacLeish was a civilized polemicist too, and it was not long before Allen was a MacLeish-appointed poetry consultant at the Library of Congress.

Allen immediately put his stamp on the job—a new one as Allen went about defining it, playing the role of impietist so well that library officials saw that the position needed to be supported from private rather than public funds. Soon he was instrumental also—see below—in bringing the Bollingen Award for poetry into the library's orbit. For many years he mixed academic and editorial jobs in whole-horse fashion. He was briefly an editor at Henry Holt & Company, then the editor of the *Sewanee Review* (where he quickly moved that genteel organ over into the New Criticism), then professor of English at the University of Minnesota, where tenure at last awaited.

Henry Adams and John Dos Passos had said it was impossible to get an education at Harvard. Upton Sinclair had said that the trustees of big American universities were in the pocket of J. P. Morgan. William Carlos Williams had been convinced that American colleges were puritan strongholds keeping the imagination of America in chains. And his friend Pound had written the Alumni Office of the University of Pennsylvania to say that the University had no respect at all for anybody with talent. The listing could go on. Up to Allen's time the American literary community had not been happy with academia, but while Allen was not particularly happy with it either, he discovered that he could live with it, live rather well. And reform it too. From the time of his Princeton appointment (1939) to his retirement at Minnesota in the seventies he was an antiestablishment force of such consequence in these and other establishments that he began to resemble establishment. He became a high official in the American Academy of Arts and Letters. He hosted the best literary parties in the country[9] and attracted some of the country's best-known poets to events in Minneapolis. He also influenced the publications of the University of Minnesota Press and the character of the university's English graduate program, giving both of them instruction in whole-

9. His second wife, Isabella Gardner, was an important figure here. Following Allen's divorce from Caroline in 1959, Isabella and Allen married and lived in a comfortable house in the Mount Curve section of Minneapolis, and entertained guests such as Frost, Auden, Lowell, and Eliot.

horse doctrine. And as if these cultural labors were not enough, he, following in Eliot's footsteps, moved in on religion.

At the time of World War II, during his wrestlings with the intellectual's responsibility for national welfare, Allen began to think of becoming a Catholic. He formally converted in 1950, having persuaded Caroline also to do so by giving her, as he put it, "the books." One of the books was Jacques Maritain's *The Dream of Descartes*.

Allen had met Maritain while at Princeton, where Maritain translated Allen's "Ode to the Confederate Dead" into French, and reinforced Allen's whole-horse doctrine with his accounts of the health of Catholic doctrine. In his Descartes essay Maritain explained at length how Cartesian dogma had given man a philosophic basis for becoming "the master and possessor of nature," but at the same time it had given him the tragic opportunity to divorce himself *from* nature, to chop up horses. Man in the Cartesian system neither spoke to nature, nor was spoken to; instead he lived above and out of nature in a universe that was, to him, dumb.

Maritain added that man also had become dumb, in the sense of being unable to speak to himself *of* himself, since his mental apparatus had been programmed by Cartesianism to work separately from his emotional-spiritual nature (Allen's old complaint about Henry Adams). Maritain may or may not have given Allen personally a greater capacity to speak with nature, but his influence can be clearly seen in Allen's subsequent writings about the manner in which modern men were speaking amongst themselves, that is, as positivists. With Maritain behind him Allen went after positivism hard, describing it as not only the narrow and pernicious doctrine of pragmatic Americans trying to be effective doers, but also as the chief mark of the modern scientific mind, a mind with blinders on. In 1951 he made his case against the obvious science targets of the time, the atomic bomb people, doing so in yet another reply to MacLeish, in which he began by picking on Einstein. The essay was called, "To Whom Is the Poet Responsible?"

> Mr. Einstein not long ago warned us that we now have the power to destroy ourselves. There was in his statement no reference to his own great and perhaps crucial share in the scientific progress which had made the holocaust possible. If it occurs, will Mr. Einstein be partly to blame, provided there is anyone left to blame him? Will God hold him responsible?

After Einstein, Allen went on to the president of Harvard, Dr. Conant, who had watched with Vannevar Bush the first Los Alamos explosion and had been reported to have jumped about and shouted with delight. "Nobody then or since," wrote Allen, "has said that Mr. Conant's emotions, whatever they may have been on that occasion, were irresponsible."

The scientists' dubious claim to "responsibility" had been a subject of interest to the Fugitives for a long time. Andrew Lytle had, for instance, taken out after the British scientist J. B. S. Haldane in the thirties for prophesying that ancient-life on the farm would no longer be practicable, after the scientists had "rubbed their bottle a few more times." Lytle enjoyed the metaphor, saying, "The trouble is that already science has rubbed the bottle too many times. Forgetting in its nasty greed to put the stopper in, it has let the genius out."

As for Allen, having begun by attacking Einstein and Conant, he then characteristically moved on to other fields—especially to the liberal politicians around him, whom he found quite untouched by "responsibility"—and then returned to MacLeish's attack on poets. He now changed the essay's title's question to "For What Is the Poet Responsible?" The answer: "He is responsible for the virtue proper to him as a poet, for his special arête; for the mastery of a disciplined language which will not shun the full report of the reality conveyed to him by his awareness: He must hold, in Yeats's great phrase, 'reality and justice in a single thought.'" The thrust of that remark may be obscured by the words in it about language, for with those words the remark can be read as a defense of a *narrow* view of poetry, conjuring up images of poetic technicians. But the key phrase of the remark is in his demand that the poet not shun the "full report" of the reality of which he is aware. In effect Allen was saying that the poets had been accused of being irresponsible for performing what they conceived to *be* their responsibilities.

He ended the essay protesting that the trouble did not lie, as MacLeish had charged, with the poets and their "report," but with the readers of the poets, or rather the nonreaders, those who simply could or would not take in what the poets were reporting. The problem? "We have seen," he said, "a powerful attempt in our time to purify ourselves of the knowledge of evil in man. Poetry is one of the sources of that knowledge." He then gave, as an interesting example of the purification process, Winston Churchill's public quoting of Arthur

Hugh Clough—the poet of "Say not the struggle naught availeth"—when he would have been more responsible "had he quoted the second part of Eliot's *The Waste Land.*" The second part of *The Waste Land* has God speaking to man, and proposing to show him "fear in a handful of dust."

Combating MacLeish and the positivists, Allen was on strong ground, especially when the war urgencies came to an end. (His complaints against science, specialization, conformity, and so on also seem appropriate now). But he was in a soft marsh in the matter of the Bollingen Award to Pound in 1949. As is well known, Pound, living in Italy in the thirties, decided to be a crusader, but a crusader for the causes of the Axis. His approval of national socialism, as he saw it in Italy, did not, in his mind, make him an unpatriotic American, since he believed America to be in the toils of a great vice, usury, which fascism's approach to banking and credit would help eliminate. For years before World War II he backed an eccentric British economist, Major C. H. Douglas, whose scheme for "social credit" was aimed at eliminating private bankers' control over interest rates (presumably he would also have opposed the current Federal Reserve strategies); and the Douglas scheme was close enough to Mussolini's and Hitler's closed economies to get him into trouble, but not great trouble, until about 1935. It was then that his reformist obsession began to mount, and he wrote William Carlos Williams, "In yewth we cd set in the daisy fields but at fifty we got to take the white man's / I mean we have got to work ON the bastuds who are actually making the laws and deciding what is to be done NOW, this week."

One of the results of his new compulsion was that he made a running commentary on the evils of usury an integral part of his poetry. Up to 1931 his *Cantos* had been, as Allen noted in a review at the time, largely good poetic conversation, covering many subjects casually while remaining poems formally. Allen could not have said the same about the *Cantos* that followed, beginning with number 31. Canto 31 was extremely dogmatic, for Pound was now working on the "bastuds" full time, and from Canto 31 up through another fifty cantos—perhaps ten years' worth—the same urgency was visible,[10] with the poetry sometimes sounding like a chronicle of the cultural

10. Eliot printed some of these and some of his more moderate prose in the *Criterion.*

evils of usury down through the ages (à la Brooks Adams). In them Pound could be said to have become a responsible poet in the way that MacLeish had proposed, except that in his allegiance to social credit he kept being responsible to the enemy's cause. The result was that by 1939 he could be found propagandizing—by all the means at his disposal including Rome Radio—the virtues of Mussolini's Italy, the folly of America's engaging in a war with Italy, and the need for America's leaders to recognize that usury had taken their country over. (What would he think now?) He was convinced that he was a patriot as he preached, but after war was actually declared, *he* was declared to be a traitor, so that following the war he was brought home for trial. The trial did not take place. He was placed in St. Elizabeth's Hospital in Washington instead, and was there when awarded the Bollingen Prize for his *Pisan Cantos.*

Later Allen asserted that as far as the profession of poetry was concerned there was little to choose between MacLeish's preachings and Pound's; the preachings were wrong in both cases because they took the poets away from their responsibilities to their "special arête." In 1950 Allen wrote,

> What I cannot easily forgive him was his thumping any tub at all—unless, as a private citizen, dissociated from the poet, at some modest level, such as giving his life for his country, where whatever he did would be as inconspicuous as his ejaculatory political philosophy demanded that it be. But on Rome Radio he appeared as professor Ezra Pound, the Great American poet. Much the same can be said of Mr. MacLeish himself. It is irrelevant that I find his political principles (I distinguish the principles from his views), in so far as I understand them, more congenial than Mr. Pound's. The immediate views of these poets seem to me equally hortatory, quasi-lyrical and ill-grounded. We might imagine for them a pleasant voyage in one of Percy Shelley's toy boats in Hyde park. If society indicated and condemned poets for the mixture and misuse of two great modes of action, poetry and politics, we might have to indict Pound a second time . . . and we should in fairness have to provide an adjoining cell for Mr. MacLeish.

These remarks were perhaps consistent with Allen's earlier insistence that *he* would be ready to die for his country before he would be ready to write poems in its defense, but it was not consistent with his vote in the award of the Bollingen Prize. There he took the position that Pound had successfully separated the poetry from his activism, or in other words, that the poetry stood on its own as poetry, as a responsible manifestation of his "special arête." (In Nashville in 1978 he told me that the rationale was poor, but the committee "had to think of something."[11]) So when the award went to Pound, and the fur flew, Allen found himself arguing for the separation of poetry and politics in relation to a book by Pound that did not well represent what he thought Pound—the good Pound, the Pound that he admired in 1931—stood for. The argument heated up, in the pages of the *Partisan Review,* to a point at which Allen declared to one of his opponents that they had best settle their difference on the field of honor.

It is a bizarre process to watch in America, the gathering and dissipating of cultural force. One cannot really explain how the Fugitives, Agrarians, and New Critics, topped off by a bit of social credit and a couple of religious conversions, managed to combine to give the English departments of America a new configuration, but that they did. For perhaps three decades they gave the departments the configuration of the "full report." Up and down the land English teachers struggled endlessly to prime their students to the difference between a poem's statement and its totality. In doing so they were harkening to the Tate message that one must distinguish between a work of literature and a tract. But they were harkening to the earlier version of full report explored in Sidney Hirsch's parlor, sidestepping the Agrarians and the political overtones of Allen's later remarks, such as the one about Churchill reading the wrong poets.

Their sidestepping is important, especially in connection with Allen's view of a poet's responsibilities. From his first reading of *The Waste Land* Allen had been a dutiful follower of Eliot in literature, politics, and religion. He had tried to sell Ransom on *The Waste Land* in 1923; he had sold Eliot on the merits of Agrarianism in the thirties (Eliot had spoken well of it in the *Criterion* then, and may have agreed to deliver his "heretical" lectures at the University of Virginia because of his friendship with Allen.[12]) And Allen had emulated Eliot's con-

---

11. Allen also said that Eliot stood with Karl Shapiro—despite Shapiro's denial—in voting against the award to Pound. Shapiro's account is that he was the only dissenter to the award on the committee and that as a Jew he felt he had no choice. In essays written following the award (in *In Defense of Ignorance*), he had good words for Pound, whom he called a scapegoat, but bad words for Eliot.

12. The lectures were published in *After Strange Gods: A Primer of Modern Heresy.*

version to Anglicanism by turning Catholic in 1950. So it is not surprising that Allen's and Eliot's views of a poet's responsibilities should have been similar. They were both, roughly, whole-horse thinkers, and they were both in favor of social and spiritual doctrines not controlled by money or momentary, collective, democratic "perceptions." Both were committed to an ideological poetry that English departments late in the century managed to abandon.

The best way to describe that commitment may be to say that they thought good poetry to be political but always more than political. Good poetry explored doctrine—and favored or rejected doctrine—but it did not simply sell doctrine.

A natural corollary to their belief was that poetry that did not explore doctrine was deficient. The corollary was necessary for both of them. A full report was a cultural as well as a private report. As for Eliot, when his long editorship of the *Criterion* ended in 1939 he declared the enterprise a failure—this in the last issue—because it had not done enough for the "situation of enforced insularity" that all European writers were confronting. More and more, he said, he found he was editing a magazine whose literary "framework" would not stretch beyond the literary. He was especially disappointed at his editorial failures in economics (having been a banker and knowing much more about finance than his regular contributor Pound), and he complained of the narrowness of the economic thinking around him, "technical economics," he called it, which tended "to divide rather than unite." He praised the *New English Weekly,* to which Pound with his social credit was also a regular contributor, for setting economics "in a wider context of social values," and he found the *Criterion's* isolation from such matters indicative of its (and literature's) state.

These were his "Last Words" in the magazine, and they closed with a remark on which he would elaborate in *Notes Towards The Definition of Culture* (a remark to be damned as elitish by Williams and others). For some time, he said, "the continuity of culture may have to be maintained by a very small number of people indeed."

Allen must have agreed with all of these last words. For both of them the split between their spacious doctrines and the world's unreadiness for them was insoluble, and fifteen years after the war the split was climactically evident in the lecture given by Eliot (introduced by Allen, who arranged the affair) in Minneapolis, before fifteen thousand people, in a basketball arena.[13] It was a dull lecture and seemed duller in the arena, a setting more appropriate for a Churchill. The setting pointed up the fallacy of trying to bring full-report doctrine to the masses at all. There was little cheering in the arena that night. As for Allen, he never of course enjoyed anything approaching Eliot's mysterious popularity.

While Eliot was in Minneapolis he and Allen went to church together—to Eliot's church, since Eliot was the guest. Allen reported that he, Catholic Allen, performed the high Episcopal ritual with such gusto that Eliot inquired, "Aren't you being too much of a latitudinarian?" Allen didn't report his reply, thinking he didn't need to. In a democratic culture neither of them would ever have been described, except jokingly, as latitudinarian. Neither was capable of easy trade-offs, or of giving in to the big battalions of the "common culture." Allen's failure began with his difficult verse (MacLeish's campaign for a poetry of "public speech" went right past him), and while Eliot was much more flexible in adapting to speech patterns (he could be a real ham while imitating cockney), neither of them would ever be in the "mainstream" mode praised by Van Wyck Brooks. They were elitists even as they tried to be spacious, and Allen particularly kept being confronted, as he aged, with his insularity.

His reputation declined. The poetry growing up around him became alien to him, and a kind he could not respect. In turn the new poets could not respect *his* poetry. He had good luck in making friends with Williams, whom the new poets did respect, but Williams remained leery of Allen's intellectualism (he nervously boned up on prosody in a textbook before serving on a panel with Allen), and Allen was leery of Williams's yawp (he once described Williams as, like Rooney Lee, possessed of "no mind"). Also he found some of Williams's younger backers, like Charles Olson and Allen Ginsberg, much less congenial than Williams himself. He had no time for Olson's "uneducated literary thought," and he described Ginsberg as a poet of "hortatory homosexuality," with hostile emphasis on "hortatory."

In 1977 he was dying and knew it. He lay with an oxygen machine

---

13. Biographer Squire's account: "The sudoriferous vistas of the gymnasium were disguised by potted palms, gigantic philodendrums and ferns tiered against one end of the arena. Through this tropical fauna Tate and Eliot emerged as though they had just been swinging cutlasses together in the hot jungle."

by his side in a small room at home, frightened by the shortness of his breath and deeply depressed, but still much occupied by his old literary political battles. He was sourer than he had ever been, and was severe about friends and heroes as well as enemies and villains. But even the severities could be amusing, and they were expressed, as always, in soft, cultured, southern tones. Gertrude Stein "said she was a favorite pupil of William James, but she never read anything but the Northwest Mounted Police." "Hemingway was a bastard," but that was all right because "he liked poets; they were not in competition with him."[14] Robert Lowell was ignorant. Thomas Jefferson was a fraud. Edmund Wilson "didn't do anything well." John Berryman was "mad all the time." Karl Shapiro was a liar. Wallace Stevens was "not a man of good will." Red Warren was "too rhetorical" and "got his signals from the wrong people" (Emerson and Whitman). And Ford Madox Ford was a *lovely* liar: "If he met somebody from Poland he would say, 'Oh yes, I have a second cousin there.'"

As for MacLeish, MacLeish thought that "if we hadn't had Marcel Proust we wouldn't have had World War II."

Even at the end Allen remained convinced that the southern way of life—the way that never was but might have been—was a worthy model. Of what did the model consist? Of "creative provincialism," that is, a regionalism modified and deepened by an awareness of the world beyond the province, awareness that one simply did not find, he said acidly, in places like Sewanee.

For at the end he could be sour even about Sewanee (home of the University of the South and the *Sewanee Review*) though it must have been the most importantly agrarian, regional, provincial place of his experience, and is the place where he is buried. In his final gloom it emerged as a natural place for him to fix on, in order to be reminded of how much he liked big towns.

14. Williams's widow had a different, though related report of Hemingway's competitiveness. She described a tennis match between Williams and Hemingway in Paris, saying that Hemingway tired of the match when he found he couldn't win it. "He quit or Bill would have beaten him."

APPENDIX

Three Nineteenth-Century Naturalists

In the nineteenth century there were many kinds of naturalists, all students of natural history, but they were not all scientists in the modern sense. Theologians, poets, and historians shared the title. Charles Darwin was a naturalist, but so were dozens of weekend butterfly collectors. (Darwin started as one of those.) Natural history was a lovely history-philosophy-science-art, a fine nineteenth-century hybrid, and it was destined to both blossom greatly and decline greatly in that century.[1]

The important museums of natural history in Europe and America were founded in the last half of that century, and most still flourish. Yet in turn-of-the-century encyclopedias natural history was often not even given an entry of its own. Why did one have to look under "Pliny the Elder" or some other ancient heading to find in-passing remarks about a term that at the same time was chiseled in granite above museum doors?

A clue suggesting an answer has been planted in the contemporary *Columbia Encyclopedia,* which has no entry for natural history but blithely assumes its existence under its entry for the Museum of

1. Charles Darwin's *Voyage of the Beagle* (1831) and subsequent *Autobiography,* ed. Sir Francis Darwin (New York: Schuman, 1950); Henry David Thoreau's *Journal,* ed. Bradford Torrey, and Francis Allen (New York: Dover, 1962); and *Maine Woods,* ed. Joseph Moldenhauer (Princeton, N. J.: Princeton University Press, 1972); and Gerard Manley Hopkins, *A Hopkins Reader,* ed. John Pick (Garden City, N. Y.: Image Books, 1966) are the big items. Add, if you find it, Alexander Humboldt's *Personal Narrative of Travels to the Equinoctial Regions of America.* The voyage itself began in 1799, and I used a now-lost early translation of the account. As for his monster *Kosmos,* that appeared in 1860. The poem referred to by Erasmus Darwin, *Botanic Garden,* appeared in 1798.

Natural History in New York. There the clue tells us that the museum "maintains exhibitions in all branches of natural history, including anthropology and ecology." The amateur detective looking at that statement would not be doing his job if he were satisfied with deducing that the author of the account was declaring anthropology and ecology to be late comers to the "discipline." No, he should also ask who was the likely author. My own answer is that obviously a museum personage wrote it. And my further deduction is that museum entries are written by museum people, but encyclopedias are edited by encyclopedia people. It seems clear that encyclopedia people of the twentieth century have not thought the umbrella subject "natural history" to be a true scientific discipline but only an aged trunk out of which the "branches" of true science grow. So the museum people write museum pieces for them declaring it to be a science, but the encyclopedists, together with the scientists who write the pieces about the branches, constitute a heavy weight of scientific opinion rejecting the old integrative trunk *as* science.

A few years ago I saw the rejection proceedings at work while I was teaching at a small college in the Midwest. There a biologist colleague continually expressed a low opinion of a naturalist colleague who worked in the next office. The naturalist was an ornithologist primarily, though I don't think he ever called himself that. He was a naturalist of the nineteenth-century kind. He liked *National Geographic,* he liked the whole wide world of a natural history museum, and, happening to be especially deep in birds, he liked Audubon and Walt Disney (for whom he worked for a while, taking penguin pictures on ice floes). He liked real birds, painted birds, photographed birds, and stuffed birds, especially stuffed birds. The stuffed birds were all over his office and in the halls. Worse, they were up and down the stairway that the scornful biologist had to use, dozens of owls, herons, blue jays, robins, finches, and the like, with their glass eyes staring out of glass cases. The biologist hated those birds; he couldn't imagine what they were doing in a hall of *science.* He was extremely happy when certain precocious students—could he have hired them?— took the birds from their cases one night and planted them in odd niches all over campus—in classrooms, in the chapel pulpit, beside the swimming pool. The collection was never fully reassembled, and it was not only ornithology that suffered. Natural history did too, being defended at that college, as I recall, by no scientist other than the bird man. The bird man's many talents were not respected there. He was what the biologist called an appreciator of nature. The biologist despised appreciators.

I am neither a museum man nor a scientist. Even in the nineteenth century I would not have called myself a naturalist. I am struck, though, by the odd cultural process that produced the biologist's disapproval of the bird man, particularly since the bird man was the kind of naturalist who, in the nineteenth century, often passed as a literary man. For not only did the fragmentation of the sciences begin there. So too did the two-culture split between science and the humanities, especially literature.

The fragmentation and this split are now excessively familiar to us. And the decline of integrative natural history as an intellectual subject is a kind of forerunner of all that. Before the age of Darwin, museums of natural history were, more properly, museums of natural phenomena. With varying degrees of dignity they were freak shows, shows of natural oddities from all over. The Darwinian thrust did not at first eliminate the freaks, but it diminished them by explaining them. Its very success—manifest in the heyday of the museums—eventually produced many opponents other than religious fundamentalists and appreciative bird watchers. The whole separatist drift of modern literature was helped along by writers' reactions to excessively orderly scientism. The two-culture split was part of that drift, a product of general discontent with an oppressive unity that was hard to escape. In order to look at the beginnings of discontent with the new orderers, let me describe briefly three naturalist personalities—Darwin himself, Thoreau, and Gerard Manley Hopkins—of the nineteenth century. The three are not only interesting in themselves, but they also well display the breadth of the naturalist spectrum as modernity began. Their journals and notebooks are my focal point.

Charles Darwin, the greatest and most clearly modern naturalist of the century, should of course lead off, yet a way of understanding Charles is to look first at his grandfather Erasmus, who wrote an epic poem in couplets about plants. He prefaced the epic with a remark that must stand as one of the earliest expressions of the two-culture motif:

> The general design of the following sheets is to enlist Imagination under the banner of Science, and to lead her votaries from the looser analogies,

which dress out the imagery of poetry, to the stricter ones, which form the ratiocination of philosophy.

Then in eight heavy cantos, supplemented by elaborate footnotes and appendices, as well as carefully drawn illustrations of flowers and plants (mixed with nymphs under trees), Erasmus tried to set the poetry part of his labors on the right track by avoiding the "loose analogies" and showing his talent as a straight scientific thinker. He was tireless in his doubleness. He solemnly indited lines like the following, and then turned around and de-poetized them:

> Now snowdrops cold, and blue-eyed harebells blend
> Their tender tears, as o'er the stream they bend;
> The love-sick Violet, and the primrose pale,
> Bow their sweet heads, and whisper to the gale;
> With secret sighs the Virgin Lily droops,
> And jealous cowslips hang their tawny cups.

John Ruskin came along later to label such attributions to Nature instances of the "poetic fallacy," but they were not fallacies to the Romantic poets and their readers. Though Erasmus's couplets became unfashionable, his procedures for synthesizing the forces underlying all life forms continued to be taken seriously—until Victorian Scientism set in. An industrious modern scholar, Desmond King-Hele, has demonstrated at length that Blake, Wordsworth, Coleridge, Shelley, Keats, and a package of lesser artistic figures were constantly borrowing his notions. Erasmus was modest and played down his originality, saying in a footnote, for instance, that he derived his theme of "vegetable love" from the botanist Linnaeus who had "demonstrated that all flowers contain families of males or females, or both." But Erasmus had added human connections, and they were important, as Blake could see when he wrote his *Book of Thel* and personified, in word and etching, the loves of the flowers with the above passage in mind.[2] Charles Darwin later complained of his grandfather that he

2. Here is King-Hele's commentary on the Blake tie, in *Erasmus Darwin and the Romantic Poets* (London: Macmillan, 1986). "Shorn of all symbolism, the story of Blake's poem is easily told. For 125 lines the enigmatic Thel, initially a shepherdess (but also called a virgin and 'a shining woman') holds conversations with a cloud, a worm and the matron Clasy. The first and most obvious parallel is that Blake personifies flowers; what is more, the lily is among the first group of flowers mentioned by Darwin—'With Secret sighs the Virgin Lily droops'. . . . The second parallel springs

had an "overpowering tendency to theorize and generalize," but Charles, *like* Ruskin, preferred to keep poetry separate in his mind from science. (He stole evolution from him but not verses!)

Charles may have pushed the separateness because he distrusted himself as a poet. At one point in his autobiography he said he had been poorly endowed with "poetic fancy." At another he confessed that in school he was incompetent at "verse-making." And writing in old age he complained that he had "wholly lost, to his great regret, pleasure from poetry of any kind, including Shakespeare." Obviously he thought of the poetic process as a distinct, separate process, and the separateness made him uneasy. He felt the same way about aesthetic processes in general, and he had to push a little button in himself to get that part of his mind going.

He wrote that he began his life as a naturalist when he began collecting things. First he collected "shells, seals, franks, coins and minerals," and he did so with a passion that was "clearly innate, as none of my sisters or brother ever had this taste." Soon he was on to beetles and learning to be systematic. His first appearance in print was in an insect book. In commenting on that later he hurried to announce himself as a non-poet: "No poet ever felt more delight at seeing his first poem published than I did at seeing in Stephen's *Illustrations of British Insects* the magic words, 'captured by C. Darwin, Esq.'"

His education in the collecting process seems to have given him what he came to prize most, his inductive powers. He said that he began collecting as a sportsman might, partly for the joy of finding a specimen nobody else in the neighborhood had found, and partly to develop his skills in hunting and shooting. Slowly, he added, "the pleasure of observing and reasoning [became] a much higher one than that of skill and sport," leading him at last to be—in a telling statement—civilized: "The primeval instincts of the barbarian slowly yielded to the acquired tastes of the civilized man."

His acquisition of civilization, so defined, seems to have meant the simultaneous abandonment, for him, of the delights—should we call them barbaric?—of poetry and religion. At any rate his great learning period was his five-year voyage on the *H. M. S. Beagle,* and

---

from Blake's similar cast of characters . . . and their similar treatment, Blake has chosen to operate in the botanical world of the gentle, the weak and the delicate, as defined by Darwin."

the journal that he kept then may be taken as a prime manifestation of the civilizing process as he conceived it. An American nineteenth-century naturalist, Asa Gray, described the process as a movement from a "curious pursuit . . . to that of a true science, engaging the reason in the search for causes." Thus was much of the past of natural science rendered "curious."

Darwin's journal is a miscellany, as journals are meant to be, but its miscellaneousness may be said to represent not unfairly the state of natural history—its barbarism, its curiousness—before the civilized orderings took it over. In the first place the journal is a travel story, with problems irrelevant to natural history, like seasickness, muddying the science. (In *Origin of Species* Darwin omitted such personal details.) In the second place it is the story of a naturalist who has not yet decided what he is looking for. It is therefore the seminal place in his writings for us to see his lingering barbarisms—as a hunter, as an appreciator of aesthetic delights, as a conventional thinker. It is also the place, I think, to see *how* conventional his thinking could be. Here was one of the world's great ideological radicals-to-be, out on the seven seas as a daring explorer of the unknown, yet he would prudishly discover that sailors drank too much in port, that the natives were slovenly but that "a few of the principal chiefs had decent suits of English clothes," and that English administrators did not tie up port proceedings with red tape as did the Spanish. His conventionality also extended to his aesthetic for taking in nature's wonders, an aesthetic largely borrowed from the German naturalist Alexander von Humboldt. The great Humboldt had been part way on the same route that the *Beagle* took to South America, and he was very strong on the sublimity of tropical colors. Trying to catch the rhetorical manner of Humboldt, Darwin wrote that even Humboldt, "with his dark blue skies and the rare union of poetry with science," had fallen "far short of the truth"; and at another point, "Already I can understand Humboldt's enthusiasm about the tropical nights; the sky is so clear and lofty, and the stars innumerable shine so bright, that like little moons, they cast their glitter on the waves."

He had his eye, however, on his main naturalist functions at all times, and he would often interestingly mix tourist concerns with his notes on the causes of natural events. In the rare case below he is simultaneously explaining the source of light in a night-time seascape, and reaching out, like Humboldt, for a heady aesthetic comparison.

The night was pitch dark, with a fresh breeze. The sea from its extreme luninousness presented a wonderful and most beautiful appearance; every part of the water which by day is seen as foam, flowed with a pale light. The vessel drove before her bow two billows of liquid phosphorus, and in her wake was a milky train. As far as the eye reached the crest of every wave was bright; and from the reflected light, the sky just above the horizon was not so utterly dark as the rest of the Heavens. It was impossible to behold this plain of matter, as if it were being melted and consumed by heat, without being reminded of Milton's description of the regions of Chaos and Anarchy.

Before the voyage Charles had considered becoming a clergyman, and a phrenologist had declared that he had a "bump of Reverence developed enough for ten priests"; but the *Beagle* voyage changed his thinking processes so much that on his return his ironic father observed that the shape of his head was "quite altered." If anything he had, after the voyage, a bump of relevance instead.

But the relevance bump still had conventional reverence in it too, puritan reverence for hard work and not wasting time and energy. From the beginning of the voyage he preached solid work habits.

It is difficult to mark out any plan, and without method on shipboard I am sure little will be done. The principal objects are, 1st, collecting, observing & reading in all branches of natural history that I can possibly manage. Observations in Meteorology, French and Spanish, Mathematics, and a little Classics, perhaps not more than the Greek Testament on Sundays, I hope generally to have some English book in hand for my amusement, exclusive of the above-mentioned branches. If I have not energy enough to make myself steadily industrious during the voyage, how great an uncommon opportunity for improving myself I shall throw away.

Nor would his attachment to a puritan, or Victorian, work ethic ever leave him. Early in life he wrote that before taking a long voyage "it is necessary to look forward to a harvest, however distant, when some fruit will be reaped." Late in life he said much the same in a fatherly letter to his son Horace, pointing out that success was most likely to come to those who search for meaning in everything that occurs. He might have added that the meaning-searchers of whom he could approve also developed ways of rejecting what did *not* contribute to meaning; for of course Darwinian meaning, once he became "civilized," was always directed, fitting-the-system meaning. For him no naturalist worth his salt went about collecting specimens merely for their oddity, rarity, or beauty. A specimen was collected so that it could be explicated—that was its Darwinian destiny.

I am reminded of a remark once made in my presence to an astronomer by the American painter Morris Graves. The astronomer, Graves, and I were at the Goddard Space Center looking at a small, round, sleek space capsule on exhibition, and the astronomer spent some time describing the great efficiency of the device, everything in its place, everything functional, before asking Graves what he as an artist would like to *add* to the capsule if given a chance. Graves said, very quickly, he would put a small amethyst on the end of one of the capsule's antennae. "For heavens sakes, why?" "Because it would have *no* function."

The astronomer gaped a bit. Would not have Darwin? Would not that amethyst have been barbaric? By the end of the *Beagle* voyage Darwin's dutiful collecting and observing had begun to reward him with a vision of how everything meshed in a great organic scheme, a life order. So it was then that his functionalist drive was at last able to assert itself effectively. The enormity of his subsequent labors remains one of the world's wonders—and no one should deny that those labors were not merely ratiocinative but also labors of the imagination, labors perhaps of a poet as well as a rigorous observer—but what is important here is that his great scientific works, in displaying his functionalism, simply did not display their dependence upon his voyage *experience*. The experience was found to be merely curious, matter for his journal only. "Civilized" modern scientism had triumphed, asserting its exclusions, and natural history as a subject had been redefined to leave out moments such as those when Charles was gaping, speechless, at a sunrise and groping for a line from Humboldt or Milton.

But the other two naturalists to be described here did not accept the Darwinian exclusions. They were like Morris Graves; they wanted barbaric amethysts.

All the nineteenth-century transcendentalists were addicted to loose analogies. They were so persistent in pushing curious connections that one can suspect them of deliberately reacting against much "civilized" thinking around them, thinking, that is, like Darwin's. And on top of their taste for analogies they were much taken by a related intellectual barbarism, popular in the nineteenth century and best represented in Laurence Sterne's great novel *Tristram Shandy*, that of making a good thing of digressions or as Tristram himself put it, making the digressions "progressive too,—and at the same time."

Certainly for Henry David Thoreau the Shandy principle of assuming that everything was relevant was serious business. So was the exploring of analogies no matter how loose. And for Thoreau the business was best practiced at home rather than at the ends of the earth. The first and most obvious difference between Thoreau's twenty-year journal and Darwin's journal aboard the *Beagle* is that Thoreau, when he wrote his, was mostly not going anywhere beyond the edges of town. To say that he traveled a great deal in and around Concord is a bright thought but misleading. He was not an explorer of exotic natural phenomena even near at home, but of the familiar, especially the familiar life of the naturalist himself. His most exotic trip as a naturalist may have been his trip to Minnesota when he was terminally ill, too ill to write up his observations. Before that there had been trips to Maine, Cape Cod, and Montreal, Canada, plus occasional civilized sallies, which made him unhappy, to Boston and New York. Obviously such small journeyings made different demands upon his mind than observing giant lizards on the Galapagos Islands. At the time of the very first entry in Thoreau's journal, made in Concord, he was not in motion either physically or spiritually. He reported that Emerson had asked him if he kept a journal, and he added that the question had provoked him to start one. Something might happen *then*.

What might he have been if he had been a true roamer? Thoreau in Tahiti or Madagascar? Perhaps he would have remained the thinker that we know, and planted his beans amid palms, but nothing seems less likely. His naturalist secret was to stay at home with the mundane and look at it. Near the great African elephant in the entrance hall of the Smithsonian Museum of Natural History should perhaps stand a wax Thoreau in woodland garb, looking forever at a wax frog. On a plaque beneath the statue might be printed his definitive statement on the dangers of the naturalist trade: "It is not worthwhile to go round the world to count the cats in Zanzibar." Obviously he had notions of relevance too, but they were cat notions of close-to-home relevance.

Of course he did not, like Darwin, come from a rich, distinguished, influential family capable of launching him toward expensive explorations. He was a poor boy at Harvard, and almost didn't go there at all. After college he moved into the poorest of occupations, teaching school, but soon quit that, becoming then a handyman, a babysitter, and a helper in his own family's small, erratic pencil business. To his hardworking neighbors he appeared as a man without a mission in life—unless not having a mission is itself a mission—and Darwin would probably have been as critical of him as his neighbors were for his idleness. From very early he was suspect. The president of Harvard doubted his "disposition to exert himself"; one of his classmates found his hand "moist and indifferent," and others commented critically upon his absence from college social rites. Also, at his graduation, he made his first public show of disapproving the American money tree and the kind of puritan relevance it stood for: "Let men make riches the means and not the end of existence, and we shall hear no more of the commercial spirit. The sea will not stagnate, the earth will be as green as ever, and the air as pure."

But most of all he was an intellectual idler, which was not what the world of natural history was looking for in the 1830s. Natural history was becoming big business then, worldwide business, the amassing of specimens and data from all over, but perversely Thoreau liked to go out into the local woods and look at a local tree. Late in life he would display interest in methodical and sophisticated scientific procedures—and be envious of a neighbor's telescope—but on the whole he took on the world with minimal equipment and a ne'er-do-well's sense of the unimportance of the programmatic.

So he "journaled" rather aimlessly for twenty years. He wrote steadily—his biographer Walter Harding estimates that the journals contain a million words—but he was not busy like Darwin at achieving some particular intellectual harvest as he did so. As a naturalist he was a diffident explorer for scientific meaning, being more concerned—as he kept saying—with the meaning of *life,* especially his own. That subjective objective occupied him in all his writings, sometimes to the near exclusion of daily naturalist observations. When he troubled to count the stripes on a tulip it was apt to be prelude to the drawing of a loose analogy:

> The prospect is limited to Nobscot and Acoursnack. The trees stand with boughs downcast like pilgrims beaten by a storm, and the whole landscape wears a sombre aspect. So when thick vapors cloud the soul, it strives in vain to escape from its humble working-day valley, and pierce the dense fog which shuts out from view the blue peaks in its horizon, but must be content to scan its near and homely hills.

Such thinking led directly to *Walden,* and in fact in his first year at Walden Pond his journal was part of the first draft of *Walden.* Much had to be added later, and much would be cut, but the core was there, and it was not at all an observational core like the *Beagle* journal. From beginning to end Thoreau moved from observation to ideas with unscientific haste. At the pond Thoreau was a writer before he was a naturalist, and he knew it.

Oddly it was in the years after his first draft of *Walden* that his naturalist energies began to show in his journal. It was then that he turned to conscientious accounts of bird, plant, and animal sightings. He also followed in detail the progress of seasons, recording spring and fall dates for a number of years for the appearance and disappearance of creatures and vegetation, and providing data on weather changes. Occasionally he picked out a particular organism—say a baby turtle—and followed its development for a few weeks. This last procedure sometimes led to the kind of sustained conclusions that Darwin said the scientist must always be reaching for, but the procedure was not Thoreau's strength or primary interest. *Just* to observe was even occasionally sufficient for him in his recorder moods, as if he had in the back of his mind (rather dreamily) the assembling of a vast descriptive index of natural shapes, sounds, and colorations. Perhaps he was feeling dry in these recorder periods and waiting for something to happen, waiting for the equivalent of a Galapagos eccentricity to leap from the pond. But that waiting was what Darwin said the naturalist should not indulge in. Merely to wait was to be intellectually lazy, a waster of time.

I noted earlier that Darwin as a young man sometimes had trouble doing the naturalist's job as thoroughly as he came to think necessary. Like most tourists he was distracted, and pleasantly so, by grand but somehow irrelevant sights on the tour, especially esthetic sights like sunrises and sunsets. Perhaps because he feared he was wasting time he sometimes seemed slightly embarrassed by such sights, like Mark Twain (Twain ridiculed the sunset-rhetoric trade at length in *Innocents Abroad*), but until he settled down to serious science he did try to contend with them. I hate to burden the reader with a single irrelevant sunrise or sunset, but the subject is in the way and needs to be dealt with. Is a sunset irrelevant to a naturalist?—Let me begin to answer the question with, first, a Thoreauvian sunset.

Thoreau is canoeing with his friend Channing, and sees the sunset scene doubled in the water. He worries briefly about what color the sky and water are, vacillating between brown and dunnish. He then notices darker colors contrasting with the dominant color, and pushes his organ pedals slightly—no great crescendo—to announce that the lower half, the water half, of the scene is "of the deepest tint," where every beauty "is more than ever insisted on." He adds—it being the seventh of September—that "this seems to be the first autumnal sunset" and then diverts us to another sunset watcher, "a stray white cat" on shore, telling us that "this is her hour."

The end? Not at all. The occasion provokes an additional and clinching paragraph about the benignity of such a natural scene of spiritual peace, including a sentence expressing envy for the Indians who in their canoes partake of "so many similar evenings." Obviously Thoreau's preliminary attention to the details of the sunset has all the time been aimed beyond the details themselves to this general life-observation. The generalization is in effect what the sunset has been for.

Now Darwin. Let us inspect a sun*rise* this time, a sunrise behind the volcanic mountain, Teneriff, on one of the Canary Islands. Darwin characterizes the mountain as a "massive pyramid" and announces that its snowy peak appeared before him "in all its grandeur." He adds that its "rugged form" stood in relief against the sky, or was "veiled by white fleecy clouds," all rendering "the scene most beautiful and varied." He ends morosely, thinking of his *mal de mer;* he says that such moments "repay the tedious suffering of sickness."

What is the difference between Darwin's reaction and Thoreau's? Chiefly, I think, it is in Darwin's being content to appreciate-observe *merely,* to announce the beauty of the scene and move away from it, acknowledging it as a digression, not seeing it as a business occasion. Unlike Thoreau he manages to *escape,* if briefly, his lifelong search for a harvest of meaning.

And commonly in such situations he even signalled the reader that he was escaping. For instance he would say that he was at a *loss* to tell anyone how "sufficiently to admire" a scene, or he would defer to another's words: "It is an inexpressible delight to me to behold those constellations (south of the Equator), the first sight of which Humboldt described with such enthusiasm."

Ah, but at the mention of Humboldt I find that I have to insert a Shandyan digression; for it appears that everyone in the nineteenth century, including Darwin and Thoreau, read the great Humboldt, author of dozens of books, explorer of the whole natural universe. Humboldt was ubiquitous and knew everything. Also, unlike Darwin, he felt that he could *describe* everything, and he was persuaded that one of the naturalist's jobs was "to bear witness for the greatness of creation" by "thoughts clothed in exalted forms of speech." In bearing witness he influenced even John Ruskin, England's most exalted nineteenth-century rhetorician. We cannot escape Humboldt any more than we can escape sunrises. So here is a Humboldt sunrise, behind the very same mountain, Teneriffe.

Humboldt is *on* the mountain at sunrise (Darwin and company were unable to go ashore because of a quarantine), and he has just emerged from an ice cave where he spent the night to find that he and his companions are above the clouds and witnessing what modern weathermen call an inversion point:

> A layer of white and fleecy clouds [did Darwin steal his white fleecy clouds from here?] concealed from us the sight of the ocean, and the lower region of the island. This layer did not appear to be above 800 stories high; the clouds were so uniformly spread, and kept so perfect a level that they were the appearance of a vast plain covered with snow. The colossal pyramid [for Darwin it was a massive pyramid] of the peak, the volcanic summits of Lancerota, of Foraventura, and the Isle of Palma, were like rocks amidst this vast sea of vapours, and their black tints were in fine contrast with the whiteness of the clouds.

What strikes me about the passage is that although Humboldt the painter of the sublime is here with his tints, contrast and similes, Humboldt the naturalist is here too. His description of the inversion is precise, and easy for anyone of the air age not only to imagine but see. The simile, "like rocks amidst this vast sea of vapours," is hardly a loose simile, in fact it is hardly a simile at all, since the rocks are rocks and the vapours are a vapour-sea. Erasmus Darwin would have been proud of him.

Humboldt then proceeds for three more pages—he was never at a loss for words—to describe the sunrise in meticulous scientific detail, detail that includes measurements of how long the sun took to rise, speculation that a flattening of the sun's shape must have been caused by the vapours, and observations of a great many other matters that need no attention here. The point is that he did his sunrise up with Humboldtian thoroughness, employing his naturalist and aesthetic sensors simultaneously.

Humboldt was surely the greatest intellectual synthesist of the nineteenth century. Forty years younger than Erasmus Darwin he partook of the climate of the earlier culture, but superimposed upon it the new scientism. Like Erasmus Darwin he aspired to be a natural *philosopher*—the premodern's dream of synthesis—by working toward the formulation of "general ideas on the causes of phenomena and their mutual connection" by inductive procedures *plus* the harnessing of all human knowledge old and new. Thus to formulate his "general ideas" properly he thought it necessary first to undertake a physical description of the whole globe. (Later he enlarged that intent to include the Cosmos, and wrote a three volume work, *Kosmos.*) His physical descriptions included geography, geology, oceanography, botany, zoology, comparative anatomy, meteorology, political science, anthropology, history (mostly of ancient cultures), astronomy, and a good deal else, with asides on trigonometry, navigation, medicine, and—an essential ingredient—views of the "grand scenes." In his way the great Humboldt had as expansive a view of relevance as did Tristram Shandy.

Neither Charles Darwin nor Thoreau ever turned out works of the integrative magnitude of Humboldt's *Personal Narrative of a Journey to the Equinoctial Regions of the New Continent,* or of his *Kosmos;* that is, they never managed to put all their intellectual wheels in motion at once. Yet I think we may forgive them for not being what Humboldt was, especially since the great Humboldt, together with his too-great syntheses, is now in eclipse, while Darwin and Thoreau remain luminous despite their human limits.

Are there any nineteenth-century thinkers still among us *more* luminous than Darwin and Thoreau? I think not. Darwin was able to isolate and concentrate his industry in such a way as to produce an incredible monograph, incredible in both scope and directness. Thoreau in his turn was able to isolate and concentrate upon—what?

What *was* the specialty that leaves him among us today as a preeminent naturalist thinker? Loosely he may of course be cubbyholed as a transcendentalist, but to say that doesn't help much. Thoreau was not Emerson or Carlyle, though much indebted to those men. Thoreau learned from Emerson the trick of merging natural law with human and moral law—and from Emerson and Carlyle the art of the loose analogy—but unlike Emerson and Carlyle he was in fact a genuine naturalist of his time and age; he put in his time as observer and recorder, and that occupation kept him safe from some of the fatuities of what Henry Adams called the Concord Church. Also he made something solid—as I think the other transcendentalists did not—of the transcendental transaction between self and nature, doing so by insisting on his private experience as the prime data-source.

Emerson never learned how to be private. Thoreau taught America about it.

His sunset passage above is characteristic, presenting us with the Indian, hopefully himself, paddling in silence and solitude into a lifetime of sunsets. Neither the other transcendentalists nor Humboldt would have been happy to identify sublimity with isolated private passion, and they would have shared with Darwin doubts about finding the grand plan for the universe within the private life. Thoreau was continually guilty of such a finding, and therefore guilty, in Humboldt's phrase, of "imperfect inductions." (Henry James put it a different way, calling Thoreau an unblushing egotist.) Anyway as a naturalist he was steadily committed to using his observations of the natural world for his own grand plan. As has been noted of him many times he was not a company man.

> "I do not wish to be regarded as a member of any incorporated society which I have not joined"—"Sometimes the best way to serve one's country is by opposing it"—"As a snowdrift is formed where there is a lull in the wind, so, one would say, where there is a lull of truth an institution springs up"—"I have, as it were, my own sun and moon and stars"—"I will breathe after my own fashion."

I could make dozens of additions to these Thoreauisms, and add to them his quarrels with tax collectors and editors and even friends, together with his obvious sexual isolation, add them as evidence of his constitutional incapacity to free himself from the intellectual loneliness that breeds "imperfect inductions;" yet for all that he was—or so it now seems—a kind of naturalist who could make something of "natural history" that Darwin and his kind might think barbaric and irrelevant, but that would survive their complaints. *What* he made of them was his specialty. He was a specialist of private human conduct, and used his naturalist observations as a base to build his own laws for that sphere.

Compared to Darwin and Thoreau, Gerard Manley Hopkins is an obscure figure, a Victorian Jesuit whose accomplishments, a few small intense poems, sit oddly at the beginning of most big modern poetry anthologies, though he died in 1883. As a naturalist his fame is limited to those literary circles where his journals are thought to illuminate his aesthetic, and if he is to be looked at as a naturalist at all—the thought might have surprised him—the justification is to be found in his minute journal descriptions of natural objects, organisms and scenes (yes, including sunsets, dozens of them). He seems not to have been interested in, or influenced by, Darwin, though he lived late enough, as Thoreau did not, to walk about England when Darwin was setting that country on its ear. He seems not to have been touched by Thoreau either, but only by, among Americans, Walt Whitman, whose egotism and vulgarity frightened him. Intellectually he was one of the most curious mixes of ancient and modern that the nineteenth century produced—curious, Darwin would have thought, in the wrong sense—and yet if looked at sympathetically his works do illuminate the world of natural history as well as poetry.

His journals are remarkable miscellanies, not only for their display of his powers of perception, but also for the casual, brilliant exploration of the sources, no less, of beauty. His mind was perhaps investigatory first and theoretic second, yet the theoretic was strong in him too, and led him to order his observations with great rigor. Nobody ever saw the stripes on a tulip more sharply than he, but he was not out for tulip stripes only.

Oddly he did not begin with tulips, or other natural things. In the mid–1860s when he was at Oxford—and when he began keeping journals—his first interest was philology. He was a naturalist of words then, chasing them backwards and sideways. Then he moved on to the minutiae of old buildings, especially medieval church windows, and accompanied his descriptive accounts with intricate line drawings. In this Oxford period his journal entries were random jottings of daily matters like class schedules, lists of books to read, and occasional figures of speech he thought might come in handy, such as, "the fields of heaven . . . white-diapered with stars." He was not above an occasional bawdiness, and he fooled tirelessly with the way a line of verse should be phrased, but in this period he mentioned nature hardly at all. From the written evidence he does not appear to have had a plan, a goal, an imagined destination for his recording energies until about 1866, two years before he became a Catholic. At that point he abruptly began describing bird-flight characteristics and the characteristics of trees, plants, clouds, natural objects, describing them with a glimmer of purpose that would soon become his theory of inscape.

I should avoid, however, asserting that "characteristics" were what he was after. In all his descriptions he was reaching for the natural thing itself, its peculiar, individual properties, rather than the characteristic in the sense of the representative; he was searching out one-and-onlyness, viz: "drops of rain hanging on rails etc seen with only the lower rim lighted like nails (of fingers)."

Also at this time he was generalizing wildly, but not in the journals. He was generalizing in school essays, about Plato, and Beauty, and the future of metaphysics, meanwhile trafficking in minutiae in the journals. As he said of himself in one of his essays, he was at heart "a fingering slave who would peep and botanize on my mother's grave."

A fingering slave. A slave, then, to fingers that must touch? draw? indite? The phrase is ambiguous. Late in life he remarked to a friend that his early ambition had been to be a painter, and perhaps it was as a painter mostly that he felt himself to be a fingerer. I suspect though that he was also referring to the fingering process that his senses went through prior to the act of painting. Especially he fingered a thing with his eyes, to know it.

And he was visually acute, especially with skyscapes. He could not leave a cloud alone; he had to look at it analytically, shredding it, contrasting it with the land underneath, and constantly coloring it. He found that it was pale pink against egg blue or sleepy blue (without liquidity). Or it was pearl gray against soft blue. Or it was sad gray with dirty darker patterning. Day after day he recorded such observations, and once, for a long stretch of journal entries, he became a sort of meteorologist of cloud-color shifts, recording them staccato-fashion as one might record weather data about temperature or precipitation.

Then he moved from skyscapes to mountainscapes. In 1868 he traveled to Switzerland, and his observations of the mountains and glaciers came out like this (a description of the base of the Grindewald glacier): "a foot, a broad limb opening out and reaching the plain, shaped like the fan-fin of a dolphin or a great bivalve shell turned on its face, the flutings in either case being suggested by the crevasses and the ribs by the risings between them, these being swerved and inscaped strictly by the motion of the mass." And here was a waterfall: "The whole cascade is inscaped in fretted falling vandykes in each of which the frets or points . . . keep shooting in races to the bottom."

This last image—of fretted falling vandykes (water falling in the shape of a series of pointed beards) is a good place to reach for his meaning for "inscape." The word is meant to suggest the interior or inside essence of a landscape (seascape, skyscape), but that essence is not conceived as inside in the way that molecules and atoms are the hidden components of matter. Inscape is not hidden but perfectly visible to anyone who knows how to see it. It is a spiritual essence, but it is also aesthetic, formal, structural, in that it consists of the relationships between all the components of that which is observed: colors, textures, shapes, masses. Those components are always in tension, balanced against one another (he called the tension "instress"). As in a painting they may be thought of as diverse forces working toward the singular unity of that painting only, forces that are infinitely abundant in the natural world around us, always seeking new combinations, new unities. Yes, each sunset is *different*. So, again to sunsets. Here, I promise, is the last one:

> At sunset, which was in a grey bank with moist cold dabs and racks, the whole round of a skyline had level clouds naturally lead-colour but the upper parts ruddled, some more, some less, rosy, Spits or beams braided or built in with slanting pellet flakes made their way. Through such clouds anvilshaped pink ones and up-blown fleece-of-wood flat-topped dangerous-looking pieces.

That is a most Hopkinsy sunset, and it seems to be not a moral sunset preaching a lesson to a canoeing Indian, nor a sublime sunset leaving the beholder speechless, and certainly not a sunset that the naturalist feels he must explain scientifically. No, it is an aesthetic sunset, carefully analyzed and explicated to point up all its tricksy visual components and their relationships, and to indicate, by that expository process, its uniqueness. For, according to Hopkins gospel, inscape is nonrepeating; hence the next sunset will need to be analyzed and explicated too. It will not fit in the same museum case.

Hopkins began his meditations about, and observations of, inscape before his conversion to Catholicism, and if he had never become a Catholic we would still be left, I think, with an interesting aesthetic theory, a theory undertaking to explain an extraordinary fact about art, all art, the fact that though it is classifiable by period, genre and so on, each work of art is a new start, a phenomenon, a nonrepeater, a thing by itself. His conversion to Rome did not change the essentials of the theory, and was in fact very easy for him to accommodate to ideologically. The ease of the shift may be illustrated by what he did with an isolated aesthetic observation, in his journal, of a sky color— "the blue was charged with simple instress"—when he wound himself up to the first quatrain of what is probably his greatest poem, "God's Grandeur," a sun*rise* sonnet!

> The world is charged with the grandeur of God,
>   It will flame out, like shining from shook foil.
>   It gathers to a greatness, like the ooze of oil
> Crushed. Why do men then now not reck his rod?

In other words he had the aesthetic theory first, and in isolation from the theological imperative, and when the imperative added itself he still had the theory, but had it now together with an explanation of the source of the infinite variety that the theory delineated, and that he celebrated. What his conversion changed, then, was not the theory but his attitude toward himself as practitioner of the theory, that is, as poet. As he dutifully recorded in his journal he found it hard, in his years as a Jesuit, to justify the egotism of composing isolate, individualistic, inscaped works in the way that poets do; and he did not even send his poems out for publication (except in one abortive instance, when he was rejected). He also destroyed manuscripts on two or three occasions, but seems to have been careful to save the good ones. Yet he did not miss the irony—in fact he wrote about it indirectly in such poems as "The Windhover"—that the submission of his own unique essence to the depersonalizing Jesuit discipline was a fact in constant tension with his faith in a God *of* the unique.

Part of the greatness of Darwin's evolutionary theory is that it allows for infinite variety within its schemata; so one could say that Darwin and Hopkins shared a common respect for the reality of individuality. Yet the difference between them remains crucial. Darwin marshalled all his evidence, no matter how diverse, to the sustaining of unalterable law, while Hopkins did everything in his power—except when doing penance for his doing—to *un*marshall such evidence, to marshall it instead for a private law of constantly energized diversity.

Yes, a private law. Inscape is private in the sense that one has to train one's *self* to the perception of it—the perception is part of what is seen—whereas nobody has to go into training to be in the evolutionary chain. Hopkins was perfectly aware of this esoteric side to his theory, feeling sorry that the "beauty of inscape was unknown and buried away from simple people," when "how near at hand it was if they had eyes to see it." But how sorry he was we cannot know. We only know that his own poems, themselves examples of poetic inscape, are mostly not for "simple people." They even confused his academic friend Robert Bridges.

But they are good poems. No matter what the simple people may think, Hopkins was a fine poet, surely a better poet than a naturalist. Yet the naturalist in him obviously triggered the poet in him, and the naturalist in him was an odd searcher for the marvelous rather than the orderly. Darwin would surely have thought him a queer duck as naturalist as well as poet, yet as queer-duck poet he was one of the important figures in the historic process of our culture becoming two cultures. Inadvertantly—for he was not antiscience—he helped divide the literary shop from the science shop, and thus he remains one of our most prized early modernists.

Index

DATE DUE